KEEPING THE IMMIGRANT BARGAIN

KEEPING THE IMMIGRANT BARGAIN

THE COSTS AND REWARDS OF SUCCESS IN AMERICA

Vivian Louie

Russell Sage Foundation • New York

The Russell Sage Foundation

The Russell Sage Foundation, one of the oldest of America's general purpose foundations, was established in 1907 by Mrs. Margaret Olivia Sage for "the improvement of social and living conditions in the United States." The Foundation seeks to fulfill this mandate by fostering the development and dissemination of knowledge about the country's political, social, and economic problems. While the Foundation endeavors to assure the accuracy and objectivity of each book it publishes, the conclusions and interpretations in Russell Sage Foundation publications are those of the authors and not of the Foundation, its Trustees, or its staff. Publication by Russell Sage, therefore, does not imply Foundation endorsement.

Library of Congress Cataloging-in-Publication Data

Louie, Vivian S.
Keeping the immigrant bargain : the costs and rewards of success in America / Vivian Louie.
p. cm.
Includes bibliographical references and index.
ISBN 978-0-87154-564-0 (pbk. : alk. paper) — ISBN 978-1-61044-779-9 (ebook)
1. Immigrants—United States—History. 2. Assimilation (Sociology)—United States—History. 3. American Dream. I. Title.
JV6450.L68 2012
305.9'069120973—dc23 2011053538

The paper used in this publication meets the minimum requirements of American National Standard for Information Sciences-Permanence of Paper for Printed Library Materials. ANSI Z39.48-1992.

Text design by Suzanne Nichols.

RUSSELL SAGE FOUNDATION
112 East 64th Street, New York, New York 10065
10 9 8 7 6 5 4 3 2 1

Contents

About the Author

Vivian Louie is associate professor in the Harvard Graduate School of Education.

Acknowledgments

THIS BOOK would not have been possible without the far-reaching generosity, insights, and warmth shared by the second-generation adults and their families, and the Latino communities in which many were embedded. Due to reasons of confidentiality, I cannot thank each respondent personally here. I can express my gratitude to the many individuals and organizations that afforded me crucial pathways to the people who graciously participated. This is at best a partial list, and I apologize for any omissions: Digna M. Mejia Abreu, Samuel Acevedo, Patricia Alvarez, Silvio Almazar, Laura Arenas, Edwin Argueta, Mary Ellen Ashley, Eileen Berger, Hector Bina, Mireya Pérez Bustillo, Ginetta E.B. Candelario, Richard Cassetta, Loida Chi, Silvia Covelli, Tricia Craig, Father Diego, Cristina Escobar, Luis Falcon, Sylvia Gonzales, Claudia Guzman, Ramona Hernandez, Deborah Hirsch, Kathy Jo, Jean-Dany Joachim, Philip Kasinitz, John Kelly, Catalina Leserna, Alejandra Lombardo, Bridget Terry Long, Israel Lopez, Nancy Lopez, Betsy Mariere, Paul Martin, Carlos Matos, Pedro Noguera, Laurie Occhipinti, Gary Orfield, Miriam Ortiz, Gilberto Osario, Estela Perez, Marla Perez, Claudia Pineda, Elena Quiroz, Hilda Ramirez, Sara Rimer, Sandra Rivera, Lorna Rivera, Katharine K. Rodger, Cindy Rodriguez, William Rodriguez, Sylvia Saavedra-Keber, Jorge Santiago, John Sepulveda, Beatriz Sierra, Ned Strong, Carola Suarez-Orozco, Marcelo Suarez-Orozco, Rosa Talero, Miren Uriarte, Miguel Vargas, Jaime Velasquez, Isabel Villar, and Dave Zagunis. I am also indebted to the generous assistance of the Colombian Consulate in Boston, particularly the then Colombian Consul, Juan Ramon Villa and Vice Consul Rosa Amalia Zuluaga. I benefited from the scholarly input of many as we discussed the ideas motivating this study and its analyses: Tamara Buckley, Kay Deaux, Josh DeWind, Erica Foldy, Luis Guarnizo, Jose Itzigsohn, Ruben Rumbaut, Mary Roldan, Arturo Sanchez, Tim Smeeding, Robert Smith, Gillian Stevens, William Trent, and Hiro Yoshikawa.

Cambridge College, Newbury College, Northeastern University, and Northern Essex Community College kindly granted me access to recruit from their student and/or alumni populations. The following organizations gave me insights into the Dominican and Colombian communities of greater Boston and greater New York, or possible leads to explore: Amigos School, La Alianza Hispana, Bajucol, Chelsea Human Services Collaborative, Colombian Colloquium / Harvard–MIT Colombian Society, Concilio Hispano, Congressional Hispanic Caucus Institute, Dominican Studies Institute at CUNY, East Boston Ecumenical Community Council, East Boston Social Centers Inc., El Centro Hispano, Gaston Institute at the University of Massachussetts (Boston), Graduate/Professional Hermana of Sigma Lambda Upsilon/Señoritas Latinas Unidas Sorority, Inc., Higher Education Resource Center in Roxbury and Lawrence, National Society of Hispanic MBAs (Boston Chapter), Society of Hispanic Engineers, and Society of Latin American Alumni.

Several institutions provided invaluable support for the research and writing of this book. I started this project as a Harvard Fellow on Race, Culture, and Education at the Harvard Graduate School of Education. I would like to thank the many leaders with whom I have worked there: John Willett, Judith Singer, Robert Selman, Robert Peterkin, Ellen Condliffe-Lagemann, Kathleen McCartney, Richard Murnane, Robert Schwartz, Catherine Snow, and Hiro Yoshikawa. HGSE's Faculty Research and Innovation Fund, a postdoctoral fellowship from the Social Science Research Council, and a research grant from the David Rockefeller Center for Latin American Studies at Harvard University provided much-needed additional support. I had the opportunity to start writing this book as a visiting scholar at the Russell Sage Foundation after Deborah Davis thoughtfully suggested that I apply.

I simply had a wondrous year at the Russell Sage Foundation. Under Eric Wanner's leadership the Foundation, with its stellar and always warm staff, provided a marvelous context in which to think and write. Pat Woodford, Alexsa Rosa, Galo Falchettore, Vidya Sampath, and John Lee all were crucial sources of support. I am grateful for the discerning comments of the RSF community, especially Eric Wanner, Robert Solow, Joe Tobin, and Aixa Cintron-Velez, in response to my presentation of what would become chapters 2 and 3 of this book. Robert C. Smith, a fellow member of my RSF class, would go on to review the book, offering so many insightful comments with just the right combination of wisdom, wit, and encouragement, for all of which I am grateful. Two anonymous reviewers of the book provided ample intellectual and writerly guidance. I am very grateful to Suzanne Nichols, director of RSF publications, who gracefully shepherded the publication process, and to the expert editing of Cindy Buck and April Rondeau.

No visit to New York City ever seems complete without connecting with the immigration tribe there. Philip Kasinitz is a dear and longtime friend from whom I gained valuable insights about the craft of thinking, writing, and publishing through conversations and his thoughtful comments on an earlier draft of this manuscript, but was never persuaded to be too solemn about any of it—laughter was a must. Carola and Marcelo Suarez-Orozco's elegant home was the site of many lunches and dinners, guidance, and immense good cheer. As busy as the two are, they always had time to listen and offer welcome advice, including on earlier drafts of this manuscript, and I appreciate their friendship. Margaret Chin and Fabienne Doucet always made time to hear about the book and to just see how I was doing. Susan Turner Meiklejohn, whom I also met at RSF, has been an intellectual and emotional mainstay throughout the journey of this book, a source of light and care, not to mention fine dining. Finally, Herbert Gans never lost sight that I was writing this manuscript, even when I sometimes wondered if I had. Our dialogues about mobility and assimilation, where the immigration research has gone and should go, routinely reenergized and reminded me of why I wanted to write this book in the first place.

I have had the amazing good fortune to learn from several leading minds at Harvard University, benefiting from their wisdom and generosity of spirit. They have modeled how to do good work, how to contribute to and challenge the public discourse, and how to be a good person. Heartfelt thanks to Sara Lawrence-Lightfoot, Howard Gardner, Mary Waters, and William Julius Wilson.

I drew from the excellent research and/or transcription expertise of Eileen Berg, Sheila Casey, Silvia Covelli, Eduardo Mosqueda, Rosa Neidl-Cornejo, Maria Orozco, Claudia Pineda, Yeon-Jeong Son, Ana Tavares, Taylor Ware, Karren Wood, and Maggie Yuan. All the wonderful students I have taught, advised, and worked with have pushed my thinking in key ways; I have learned from the important work they themselves have done and are doing in research, practice, and policy. Special thanks to Phitsamay Uy, Kelly Larrow, Sofia Bahena, North Cooc, and Rusty Carlock. I have relied on the warmth and consideration of colleagues, including John Diamond, Lisa Fischer, Wendy Luttrell, and Mark Warren. Anne Blevins rarely asked how the book was going but provided much-needed friendship and assistance that kept me going.

The analyses presented in this book were deepened by the comments I received during presentations at Harvard Migration and Immigrant Incorporation Workshop, Achieving Equality Seminar at the Harvard Graduate School of Education, Latino/a Cultural Center at Northeastern University, Social Science Research Council Conference on Crossing Borders/Constructing Boundaries, Colombian Migration Conference: Connecting Academia and the Community, Conference of the Caribbean Scholars Association of New York, Wellesley College (Sociology), Institute for Globalization and Education in Metropolitan Settings Seminar Series (IGEMS) at New York University, Phillips Academy (Andover),

Visiting Scholars Seminar Series at the Russell Sage Foundation, Working Group on Latin American Migration at Teacher's College & New York University, Center on Family Demography and Public Policy at the School of Social Work at Columbia University, Peopling of New York CUNY Honors College at Hunter College, Colombian Migration Conference: Transnational, Political, and Cultural Perspectives, New York Immigration Series at CUNY Graduate Center, Boston University (Clinical Psychology), College Now, and Pomona College (Sociology).

Friends offered a keen sense of humor about life and lots of heart. Thanks to Kate Bielayze, Silvia Covelli, Regina Deil-Amen, Stephanie DeLuca, Jennifer Holdaway, Denise Lau, Peggy Levitt, Jamie Lew, Bridget Terry Long, Mabel Lam, Jeanne Ng, Mica Pollock, Li Stevens, and Joanne van der Woude. I go way back with Anita Cal, Jennifer Mathis, Charlotte Murphy, and Arthur Park, and they constantly cheered me on and kept the faith.

I have been a member of several organizations that showed me what a spirit of collaboration and civic engagement can accomplish: Gund Kwok, an Asian women's Lion and Dragon dance troupe founded and led by the Rev. Cheng Imm Tan; the Boston Chinatown Neighborhood Center, a community organization that provides resources and support to children, youth, and immigrant families, led by Elaine Ng; and the Jasmine Giving Circle (Boston), which works towards the well-being of women and girls of Asian descent in Massachusetts, chaired by Mabel Lam.

Lastly, I benefited from bastions of family love to help me have the mental and physical energy to research and write and to have welcome distractions (the latter is not hard in our big extended family). Much gratitude to my mother, Daniel Yee, Stephen Louie, Chester Lee, Diana Lee, Melinda Chin and Danny, Nancy, and David for listening and encouraging me, especially when I needed it most. I have come to a renewed appreciation of the arduous bargains that our great-grandparents, grandparents, and/or parents must have made in their own journeys and our obligations, as the generations after them, to do our part in creating the common good.

This book is done—many thanks to all who have had the far more difficult task of living the themes recounted here, and to all for reading.

Chapter 1

Introduction

THIS BOOK recounts the journeys to college of young people living in America. By itself, this story would not be remarkable—except that it is a story of the children of Latino immigrants, a group whose educational success is nearly invisible in popular accounts and not often studied in academic ones. How do children who are typically not expected to achieve very much end up doing so well? This book helps us answer this important question and sheds light on how we can increase the odds of immigrant educational success. Before we can understand these children's journeys to college, however, we first need to consider the journeys their parents have made to and in America.

This prologue might seem familiar, harkening back, as it does, to the oft-told tale of immigrants coming to the United States full of hope and a strong work ethic that fueled their dramatic success. Immigrants and their descendants are typically compared in this way to native-born minority groups, notably African Americans and Puerto Ricans, and held up as exemplars of the motivation needed to overcome obstacles to success. That said, variability in ethnic origins (read: ethnic cultures) is typically cited as a reason why certain immigrant groups have done better or risen faster than others. These two counternarratives—the immigrant analogy and the ethnic culture analogy—have both played out in understandings of Latino outcomes in the United States. By virtue of being immigrants, Latinos are seen as having greater drive and a more positive orientation than African Americans (and thus doing better), but because they are Latino immigrants, they are also seen as having much less drive and a less positive orientation than Asians (and thus not faring as well).

Keeping the Immigrant Bargain tells a different, more complex story by bringing into the picture the often invisible aspects of the immigrant journey, framed in both optimism and pessimism. The parents' immigrant incorporation is bifurcated: they have immigrant optimism about their mobility, regardless of their actual economic gains or losses, and believe in the American Dream, but they also have immigrant pessimism about their assimilation. The journey is not just about the immigrants themselves and the resources they bring or do not bring, but also about American natives and institutions and the ways in which they welcome or reject the integration of newcomers (Eckstein 2006). This perspective helps us understand how different immigrants who come to the United States for the same reason—to make better lives for themselves and for their children—can have dramatically different experiences after arrival. Their experience is as much about the role of institutions in immigrant incorporation as it is about their own desire and capacity to be incorporated.

The story of second-generation success told in this book has two parts. The first gives an account of the interactions between families and institutions that shape the opportunities that families provide to their children for schooling, as well as the constraints on what they can provide. The other equally important part of the story takes place in the children's own interactions with powerful institutional and other nonfamily supports as they seek the guidance they need to succeed in school; information about this guidance and support is often unknown to their parents. This second part of the story challenges our understandings of why immigrants have surpassed some African Americans, who have been here longer, and why certain immigrant groups succeed much more quickly than others.

By focusing on how the institutions of mainstream society, such as the economy and education, simultaneously open up and constrain mobility opportunities for immigrants and their children, and on how immigrant families respond, this book moves us away from approaches centered on immigrants' national origins or on panethnicity. While these two approaches are undeniably important, explanations of mobility and assimilation based on them have tended to marginalize the social processes and social contexts that influence differences in outcomes (Stepick and Dutton-Stepick 2010). Explanations like the immigrant and ethnic analogies often privilege group-based optimism and motivation without adequately examining where these attitudes come from, how they are maintained or dampened, and the extent to which they matter in outcomes. For these reasons, the immigrant and ethnic analogies are provocative, but ultimately incomplete, explanations.

I argue that the key to success, especially for the mostly working-class children we interviewed, was not just that they had hope, motivation, or a work ethic. What it took for them to succeed was strong family care *combined* with powerful institutional and other nonfamily supports. In making this argument, I draw on a three-and-a-half-year survey and interview study of 113 members of Dominican and Colombian families. They included 37 immigrant parents and 76 members of the "1.5 generation"—immigrants who had arrived here by the age of twelve—and the second generation (born in the United States); these young people had transitioned to more than twenty colleges in the northeastern United States, of different types and prestige levels. [1] Let us hear from some of them.

Andrea had just graduated from Cornell University when we met in her Washington Heights neighborhood in upper Manhattan.[2] It was the summer of 2002, and she noted that the once mostly Dominican community had changed some. The drug trade that had been a big issue in the 1980s was largely contained, and more whites were moving into the community, as we saw in the Starbucks where we had coffee. The local Dominicans whom Andrea knew, however, were still factory workers, teachers, and cab drivers. Her own mother was a school bus matron who had raised three children on her own, with no financial support from their father. "Education was the only inheritance she could give us because she didn't have any money," Andrea told me, with a laugh. She went to Cornell on full scholarship; even so, the family had to work hard to pay for the extras, like books and the $80 round-trip bus tickets between Ithaca and New York City. Nevertheless, the importance of education in Andrea's family was never in doubt. "I think, for my family," said Andrea, "in general, success is getting through college. Because, I mean, it kind of opens the door for you to the American Dream. For my mom, who didn't finish college here, it's having her kids go to college."

Andrea's mother, who later met with Ana, an interviewer for the project, said that she had gotten as far as the equivalent of eighth grade in Santiago, Dominican Republic. In the United States, she worked full time during the daytime and took evening classes to earn her general equivalency diploma (GED). But after only two months at a local private college, she had not been able to continue her schooling. She wanted more for her children. So she routinely went to her children's parent-teacher conferences and found out about free classes to prepare Andrea for the entrance examination to the city's much-sought-after specialized high schools. (Andrea would earn a berth at the selective Brooklyn Technical High School.) Andrea had a terrific learning experience at Brooklyn Technical, thanks mainly to the "very highly qualified teachers," with whom she had a good relationship. "They were good teachers, and I might sound like I'm bragging, but I was a good student also. So, I think that combination of both made things turn out pretty well." And even though Andrea's mother did not always understand what her daughter was saying about school, she made sure she listened. Andrea's mother recalled, "We always talked about why a school was a good option or not. She always said that she wanted to attend an Ivy League school, and then I asked why, and she replied saying that those were the best schools in the U.S. So if that was her choice, I would support her all the time."

Billy was born in the United States but grew up both here and in the Dominican Republic. Until he was seven, he lived with his family in Lawrence, Massachusetts, before moving back to Santo Domingo for several years. By the winter of 2004, when Billy spoke with Silvia for the project, he had been back in Lawrence for seven years, along with his mother and brother. To him, life was definitely better in Santo Domingo. Unlike Andrea's mother, who had made a few gains with migration, his family's standard of living had declined dramatically with the move back to the United States. His parents had co-managed a binational check-cashing business in Santo Domingo, which had his father shuttling back and forth between Lawrence and the island. There they had lived in one of the neighborhood's bigger houses and had a basketball court and a maid, and the residents held monthly outdoor meetings to plan activities for the children. Billy had gone to one of the capital's best private schools.

It was a shock to move back to the Broadway Street area of Lawrence, which he described as "low-class" and plagued by a dangerous drug trade. Back in Lawrence there was also a shift in how his parents helped him with schoolwork. In Santo Domingo they had given "100 percent help," but in the United States his mother did not know enough English to understand what he was doing in school. Billy was fortunate because his high school teachers noticed him and steered him toward honors and Advanced Placement (AP) classes. He said, "Teachers were always there to tell me, you know, to vouch for me." Although he had positive things to say about the local public high school, Silvia and I knew that the school had lost its accreditation, owing to academic problems, during his time there. After graduating, he enrolled in the local community college because it was cheaper, and he paid his tuition with earnings from a full-time job as a Verizon Wireless technician. Although Billy's pattern was to go to school for a while and then drop out, only to start again later, he remained hopeful about transitioning to a four-year college.

The educational success of Billy's older sister and brother—both graduates of four-year colleges in the United States—brightened an otherwise bittersweet migration journey for his parents. Each of his parents had only a year or less of postsecondary schooling, but that level of education had still been enough for them to have a relatively good life back home. Billy's mother noted, "You know, we didn't come here for the necessity, we had an apartment over there, it was small, but we were making all the payments, since my husband had a decent job at that time. The reason why we came here is because I guess we wanted to reach higher in life, we wanted more." For a while, those hopes were realized as the success of their binational business allowed them a life of greater comfort back home, while still having stakes in the United States; then they ran afoul of the Internal Revenue Service. Billy's mother returned to the United States to manage the aftermath, while her husband returned to the Dominican Republic. She became a licensed home day-care provider, and after her charges went home she cleaned a local cafeteria in the evenings from 6:00 to 9:45 PM. The family had moved to a somewhat better-off part of town, but she was still always fearful of being robbed. Overall, life in the United States had been quite a fall for the parents. And his mother was worried about Billy because, after three years, he still had no degree.

In May 2005, Herman picked me up at the Lowell, Massachusetts, commuter rail station in his cousin's baby blue Toyota Celica, whose faulty transmission caused it to buckle when in reverse. He joked about it as we drove past his old kindergarten, the supermarket where he had been a part-time produce clerk between the ages of sixteen and twenty-five, and Bally's Gym, where he had worked for six months while completing his bachelor's degree. In the McDonald's, the customers were white (excepting us), and the staff behind the counter was Latino and Asian.

Herman had grown up in the city's public housing projects, and his parents still had an apartment there. Even more so than Billy, Herman believed that he was entirely on his own with school, but he also said that he had made peace with his immigrant parents' limited role. "My parents, they only went to school 'til seventh grade. They weren't the type of parents who enforced, like, if you don't finish your homework, you're not going to go out. They didn't really voice it." Unable to afford the Catholic school system, his parents sent Herman to the local elementary school. In the second grade, Herman was one of the first students to leave bilingual education and join a completely English-speaking class. His second-grade teacher helped with this "nerve-wracking" transition, and he described her as a "good teacher." She was an Argentine native who later taught at the local arts magnet middle school (which he also attended), and "she was stern," Herman said. "So, she got my respect." At Lowell High School, Herman said, he was an "average student" who never got into trouble and always went to class. It was enough to graduate and to go on to Middlesex Community College, which his guidance counselors advised him to do because he had low SAT scores. Even though Herman said his parents did not take on a strong role, they did clearly express the expectation that he would go on to college. With the advice and encouragement of a close older friend who had graduated from the University of Massachusetts–Lowell and was a medical technician, Herman completed an associate's degree, even though it took him four years, and then earned a bachelor's degree himself from UMass–Lowell.

Herman's parents, retired factory workers, confirmed their eldest son's account when they later met with Claudia, another interviewer for the project. Although they had completed only two years of secondary school back in Medellin, Colombia, they believed that there were greater opportunities for schooling in the United States; students here, they observed, could receive good attention from teachers and also financial aid. Herman's father noted, "The one who doesn't want to study here is ignorant. It's completely ignorant in every sense."

His parents believed that their four children never needed much guidance with schooling, at least not from them. Said Herman's father: "They didn't complain about anything. They were never lost. We never told him anything." Added his mother: "They did it themselves. After they entered elementary school, we didn't have to do anything. I am sure that someone helped him." Echoed his father: "They found their way by themselves." In truth, only half the children had completely found their way. Herman's older sister had an associate's degree and was working, but his younger brother and sister had both dropped out of state universities and were trying to figure out what to do next.

All the children interviewed for this book had kept the "immigrant bargain," a term coined by Robert C. Smith (2006) to capture the hope of immigrant families that their children would do well in school and succeed, a feat that would make up for the parents' sacrifices with migration. Many of the children we interviewed were in their early to mid-twenties, so they, along with their parents, were looking back on the immigrant and school journeys. Although the parents were doing better than average for foreign-born Dominicans and Colombians—for instance, in home ownership and, in some cases, occupational status—migration had been accompanied by hardship. The children's schooling success—not all had finished college, but those who had not certainly expected to—validated their parents' decision to migrate and undertake their difficult journeys. As we have just seen, some of those journeys were tougher than others. While Andrea's mother and Herman's parents had benefited some, Billy's family had suffered painful economic losses. Similarly, more than 60 percent of the children's parents had made only modest economic gains, had replicated their low status in the United States, or had seen their status and standard of living decline after continuing to work jobs of lower prestige long after the initial years of settlement. Certainly, the parents welcomed higher wages, new freedoms, and political and economic stability, but the net gains of the immigrant journey, both material and symbolic, were decidedly uneven according to the calculus of the families. Regardless of how the parents had fared in income and job status, all of them had to negotiate certain long-term challenges: the need to become at least proficient in the English language, a goal not easily met; the need to learn and manage unfamiliar American cultural and social norms; and discrimination against immigrants and nonwhites in general.

The children had to win the immigrant bargain because keeping that bargain was by no means easy for them. Their parents had fared better than the average foreign-born Dominican or Colombian, but many of the children still faced daunting obstacles known to derail success. More than two-thirds had grown up in urban neighborhoods that were largely ethnic or panethnic and often working-class or poor. More than one-third had spent some part of their childhood in a female-headed household, and these are typically associated with lower incomes and lower levels of maternal education. Just under one-third (twenty-four respondents) had gone to neighborhood public urban schools, where blacks and Hispanics made up 50 to 80 percent or more of the student body. Students at such minority-majority schools tend to be poor and low income, and these schools usually have fewer institutional resources than average and less than optimal learning conditions (Noguera 2003; Lopez 2004; Orfield and Lee 2006).

In this book, I show how such challenges were especially pronounced among the Dominican families. The Colombian and Dominican families were both mostly working-class. Yet because the Dominicans lived in different residential locations—locations determined, as others have found, by their darker skin color—they faced a much tougher journey to success (Newman 1999; Waters, Mollenkopf, and Kasinitz 1999). A bit more than half of the Colombian children—but only a few of the Dominicans—had grown up in predominantly white, middle-class areas, with the safe streets and good schools that we have come to expect from such areas. In contrast, the Dominicans' neighborhood experiences were consistent with the rising residential segregation of Latinos in high-poverty areas, a trend similar to the intense geographic isolation of poor African Americans in urban neighborhoods characterized by concentrated social problems (Wilson 1980, 1987; Massey and Denton 1993; Massey 2007; Dobbie and Fryer 2009). Dominicans were more likely to grow up in poorer and socially disorganized neighborhoods with dilapidated housing, violent crime, and segregated and low-performing schools (Brooks-Gunn et al. 1993; Duncan and Brooks-Gunn 1997; Kasinitz et al. 2008). One-quarter of the Dominican children reported that violence had occurred in the K-12 schools they attended and that they had witnessed or been the victim of nonfamily violence. Winning the immigrant bargain was tougher for the Dominican children because not only did they have to make it out of these neighborhoods and schooling contexts, but their success was especially contingent on the backing of institutional actors and other powerful nonfamily members.

My prior research with working-class Chinese, who also transitioned to college, reveals what academically successful working-class Dominicans, Colombians, and Chinese all have in common. To begin with, the notion that Latinos and Chinese have anything in common is already noteworthy, since Chinese immigrants, along with other Asian American immigrants, have been held up as the quintessential educational success stories. Supposedly, Asian cultures drive educational success in ways that Latinos cultures do not. My comparison reveals more nuanced mechanisms of success. Second-generation Chinese children benefit from their parents' embeddedness in immigrant communities and their access to flows of transnational capital and social ties to middle-class kin and friends. These resources and social ties are crucial to their working-class parents' access to information about good public schools—information that the Dominicans and Colombians do not have.

This book identifies the powerful ways in which the parents' immigrant status, social class, and ethnicity (especially as related to skin color) influenced the children's life experiences. Growing up in an immigrant family was a shared experience for all our interviewees, but it was lived differently across social class. Simply put, children whose parents replicated their high status with migration or came from dramatically upwardly mobile, middle-class families lived in better-off areas, had more family resources for schooling, and went to better precollegiate schools. The story, however, is not just about social class: some downwardly mobile, working-class parents were able to get useful information from non-ethnic individuals (for example, non-Dominican or non-Colombian) and use it to help their children get into better schools or after-school programs. There was also a clear ethnic gap within the working class—the Dominicans had a more arduous journey to success. In some respects, the class-based experiences of the Colombians and Dominicans evoked similarities to the experiences of their native black and white counterparts, as detailed in the existing research. Yet being the child of parents who were struggling to learn English and figure out where they belonged in America brought distinct constraints.

This argument is based on an analysis of how the respondents interpreted and experienced several core aspects of American life, namely who can become American and what this process involves; what children and their families can expect of the children's schools, and vice versa; and finally, how education is experienced as a channel of upward mobility. Each of these aspects is a key lever of the book. In the first half, I show that the incorporation of the immigrant parents influenced how they were able to assist their children economically, culturally, and practically with schooling. In the second half, I show that the children understood and experienced schooling, assimilation, and mobility in ways specific to being members of the 1.5 and second generations.[3] I show that the children became academic success stories in light of their parents' incorporation into the United States and that the family was only part of the reason for their success. Also contributing to their success were adults outside the family who mentored the children in how to succeed in school, especially adults in institutional settings.

Why This Story Is Important

This immigrant story is compelling for several reasons. In the United States today, about one in five children age eighteen or younger are the U.S.- or foreign-born children of immigrants, and by 2015 they are likely to make up 30 percent of the nation's prekindergarten to grade 12 student population (Fix and Passell 2003). Based on numbers alone, the schooling success of the children of immigrants has become a crucial national goal. This goal echoes the historical importance of earlier waves of European immigrants and their descendants to America's industrialization and its development into an economic powerhouse. The rising importance of a college education, however, is new. A college education has value not only for an individual's lifetime earnings and status but, when aggregated, to the nation's economic well-being. In a rapidly globalizing world, a highly skilled and educated workforce has become integral to how well a nation fares in the world economy (Grissmer 2005).

Nor are the stakes entirely economic. Just as in the past, the ways in which immigrants and their children are embedded into the nation's cultural and social fabric speak to the question of what it means to be an American (Portes and Rumbaut 2001; Suárez-Orozco and Suárez-Orozco 2001; Suárez-Orozco, Suárez-Orozco, and Todorova 2008; Kasinitz et al. 2008). Today the terrain is arguably even more complex. With the resumption of large-scale migratory flows since the 1960s, the complexities of American demographics have intensified: the United States is now home to individuals "from, literally, every civilization and of every nationality, and speaking almost every language" (Prewitt 2001, 3). It remains to be seen whether and how such demographic diversity will redefine conceptions of American national identity.

Given that Latinos make up the most populous stream of post-1965 immigrants, and the nation's largest minority group, it is especially important to understand their integration.[4] According to the U.S. Census 2000, 52 percent of the foreign-born population in the United States was from Latin America, and Latinos made up 14.5 percent of the nation's population. The term "Latino" is constructed as a panethnic category that encompasses individuals of diverse nativity statuses, national origins, ethnic and social class backgrounds, and racial classifications. Despite this diversity, "Latinos" have often been viewed as one group and as not suited to mobility and assimilation thanks to their group origins. In contrast to the successful incorporation of earlier waves of European immigrants in the nineteenth and early twentieth centuries, Latinos are thus thought by some to have a grim prognosis for schooling and assimilation: it is argued that they settle in ethnic enclaves, communicate in Spanish, and generally are unwilling to assimilate. They do not do well in school supposedly because they do not value schooling. While much of the adverse attention has focused on Mexican Americans, the nation's largest immigrant group (Huntington 2004), Latinos of diverse national origins have been universally enveloped in this narrative of threat and negative exceptionalism (Fukuyama 1994; Espenshade and Belanger 1997; Rumbaut 1997; Cornelius 2002).

The bidirectionality of social processes helps explain Mexican American outcomes. In other words, the larger society has great power to make a group's incorporation difficult or easy—for instance, through the opportunities its economy offers to immigrants and the relative openness of the social structure to newcomers (Portes and Rumbaut 1990, 2001; Eckstein 2006; Suárez-Orozco, Suárez-Orozco, and Todorova 2008; Telles and Ortiz 2008; Massey and Sanchez R. 2010; Jiménez 2011). Drawing on a unique data set spanning four generations of Mexican Americans, Edward Telles and Vilma Ortiz (2008) recently showed that, while Mexican Americans have made progress, they continue to trail native white Americans in educational and economic status.[5] The findings of this and other studies, according to the authors, suggest that longtime Mexican Americans are a racialized minority group, particularly in schooling. From a young age, Mexican Americans disproportionately attend poorly financed public schools with less experienced teachers who have low expectations of them. Even when they attend integrated schools, they continue to be tracked into less demanding courses.

Since the so-called new Latinos, including Colombians, Dominicans, Guatemalans, and Salvadorans, have arrived in large numbers only in the post–civil rights era, their experiences are likely to be somewhat different from those of Mexican Americans, who as a group have been here longer (Pachon and DeSipio 1998). This book focuses on Dominicans and Colombians, who make up the fifth- and seventh-largest Latino subgroups, respectively (Fry and Hakimzadeh 2006). There are 1.3 million Hispanics of Dominican origin and 882,000 of Colombian origin in the United States (Pew Hispanic Center 2010a, 2010b). A comparison of Dominicans and Colombians allows us to explore possible differences along the lines of region of origin (the Caribbean versus South America), skin color, parental educational background and financial resources, and family composition, which we know to be important to immigrant incorporation and second-generation outcomes. Furthermore, while there are important differences between the two populations, there is also diversity within each along these indicators (Guarnizo, Sanchez, and Roach 1999; Itzigsohn and Giorguli-Saucedo 2002).

Keeping the Immigrant Bargain has two goals. The first is to explain the schooling success among 1.5- and second-generation Dominicans and Colombians in light of the immigrant journey, especially the interactions between newcomer families and institutions. The second is to draw on the findings to suggest lines of further research and to contribute to public policy recommendations. This is the first contemporaneous study to address such issues from the perspectives of the adult children and their mothers and fathers. Immigration and education are quintessentially family affairs, and yet we seldom hear from both parents and children; rather, the voices of one generation are typically emphasized. This book provides a much-needed comparison of how children and parents alike understand the immigrant journey around education, mobility, and assimilation and what they believe to be possible for themselves and for each other (Waters 2008).[6]

From Whence We Came

Because so much of how we think about immigration, mobility, and assimilation is shaped by the American past, we need to consider that history, especially as it informs public policy and scholarly debates. The emphasis on the ability of immigrant groups to be incorporated rather than the role of institutions in their incorporation dates back to the initial great flows of immigration. From the midnineteenth century until 1924—a period of large-scale immigration in response to the nation's rapid industrialization—it was widely questioned whether immigrants and their children could be absorbed into American life (Hartmann 1948).[7] It seemed unlikely that the immigrants, natives of southern, central, and eastern Europe and of peasant background, would successfully make the transition: many lacked facility with English and were illiterate in their own language, and virtually all subscribed to then-foreign religions, namely Catholicism and Judaism (Gold 2009). It was argued that immigrants did not wish to, or were unable to, assimilate (Walker 1896; Fairchild 1911).

The evidence, however, suggests that there were strong institutional barriers to assimilation. In 1911 the U.S. Immigration Commission published a multivolume study that revealed the relative scarcity of English-language classes for adult immigrants (U.S. Congress 1911).[8] Immigrants faced other challenges, including workdays of twelve or more hours—typically in the mine, factory, or sweatshop—and their tendency to live in urban ethnic communities where English was not necessary to everyday life. It was not surprising, then, that few knew how to write or effectively speak English or had any knowledge of American history and American political institutions.

The role of education in the lives of the children of immigrants shows how an institution can strongly facilitate incorporation. The common school, the precursor to and then the popular name for the American public school, became the site for the Americanization of the children of immigrants from 1900 to 1920 (Graham 2005). The goal of teaching American cultural practices to immigrant children took place in schools that marked a social boundary between children and their immigrant parents, who were quite often seen as suspect (Reisner 1930; Cremin 1951; Weisz 1976; California Tomorrow 1990; Bryk, Lee, and Holland 1993). In the popular American imagination, this project was dramatically successful—the children of immigrants eventually achieved upward mobility and assimilated into the mainstream white, Anglo-Saxon American fold. It was the realization of the American Dream as experienced by the children of European immigrants. Scholars of that era played a part in creating that narrative. As Herbert Gans (2007, 152) tells us, the rise of immigration research in the United States came at a time of "nearly universal upward mobility" among European immigrants, who had arrived with so little that they "could only move up" and who were at the same time assimilating.

This story did have an empirical basis, but the reasons for these trajectories, and the shapes they took, proved much more complex than previously theorized (Lieberson 1980; Alba 1990; Waters 1990; Ignatiev 1995; Brodkin 1998). It typically took three or four generations for these ethnic groups to join the American mainstream, measured in years of schooling and occupations (Foner 2006). So it was the grandchildren and great-grandchildren of the European immigrants who made the leap into the middle class and professional jobs, an intergenerational journey in which both the original migrants and their children encountered significant exclusionary barriers (Alba and Nee 2003). The now-classic paradigm of assimilation and upward mobility—for example, joining the native white middle class—is a historical artifact born of numerous social transformations that gradually opened institutional doors to the descendants of immigrants. These included a decades-long incubatory period between the cessation of large-scale immigration and its resumption in 1970, and even more pivotal was the unparalleled post–World War II economic prosperity enjoyed by the United States. In keeping with the adage that "a rising tide lifts all boats," Richard Alba (2009) argues that the descendants of once-vilified European immigrants benefited from the willingness of native whites to include them in the expanding opportunity structure. Skin color was certainly noteworthy, since blacks were largely shut out of this process of boundary blurring. We should also note that the American cultural mainstream did not remain static; rather, it was transformed by immigration as cultural practices formerly deemed foreign and exotic were gradually incorporated (Alba and Nee 2003). Despite the documented role of institutions, the popular narrative of the historical immigrant story virtually ignores the institutional dimension and maintains that the Europeans and their descendants did what they had to do to move up and become American.

The question of immigrant success and its mechanisms has reemerged in the wake of the post-1965 newcomer flows into a dramatically different American context. Certainly, the newcomers have institutional advantages that were unavailable to their European predecessors. Within the framework of national social subsidy programs, a result of New Deal reforms and the War on Poverty, and legally sanctioned equality of opportunity, a fruit of the civil rights movement, immigrants and their children have access to myriad social insurance policies such as unemployment benefits, housing regulations, and fair labor practices. Although the presence of foreign cultures in the United States is back in the forefront as a contentious issue, today's newcomers, who mainly come from Latin America, the Caribbean, and Asia, benefit from the greater tolerance of ethnic, racial, and religious diversity that resulted from the civil rights movement (Jaret 1999; Levitt 2001). Of course, we should not paint too rosy a picture. A clear signal of anti-immigrant times was the passage of the 1996 Personal Responsibility and Work Opportunity Reconciliation Act (PRWORA). Under this welfare reform legislation, immigrants who had legally entered the United States after August 22, 1996, were barred from receiving federal assistance based on income guidelines, such as Temporary Assistance for Needy Families (TANF), Medicaid, Supplemental Security Income (SSI), and food stamps, for five years after entry (Massey and Sanchez R. 2010). The events of September 11, 2001, and the global economic crisis that started in 2008 intensified an already distinctly chilly climate toward newcomers (Schumacher-Matos 2011).

Immigrants without legal status, however, are a big exception, since many of these institutional benefits are not available to them. Although Asians were a special case, American numerical limits to immigration became decidedly more pronounced only from the 1920s onward.[9] This phenomenon has given rise to the concept of the "illegal alien," or what Mae Ngai (2004, 4) describes as "a social reality but a legal impossibility—a subject without rights and excluded from citizenship." Although undocumented immigrants come from diverse sending nations, limitations placed on immigration from the Western Hemisphere, especially from Mexico, starting in the 1970s have lent this population a particularly Latino cast (Hing 2004; Massey and Sanchez R. 2010). The journeys of immigrants without legal status are decidedly bleaker from entry to settlement (Mahler 1995; Massey, Durand, and Malone 2002) for both the first and 1.5 generations as they face exploitation and legal barriers while protected by few legal rights (Menjívar 2008). The undocumented status of parents has consequences for the developmental contexts and learning of their American-born children during early childhood. The parents' anxiety about their status combines with their harsh working conditions, low wages, and lower access to child-centered day care to become a contributing factor in their children's lower cognitive skills (Yoshikawa 2011).

For all immigrants, institutional shifts have also dramatically increased the stakes of intergenerational mobility. In the wake of post-1960s economic and educational transformations, the shift from a manufacturing to a service economy in the United States accorded higher returns to postsecondary education (Wilson 1999). The children of poor and working-class families now have only a single generation to join the college educated, as compared to the incremental educational trajectory followed by the descendants of earlier immigrants (Portes and Rumbaut 2001). To clear this hurdle, many immigrant children go to an American public school in a K-12 system that was once a key lever for upward mobility but has since deteriorated in some parts of the nation, particularly in the cities. Still seeking solutions to the long-standing black-white achievement gap, the United States finds itself also confronting an achievement gap relative to other nations whose systems of education are outperforming ours. There is clearly a need to maintain rigorous academic standards appropriate for a globalizing world, but relatively little agreement on what needs to be fixed and how.[10]

Nor is getting to college an easy process. College enrollments have risen dramatically, along with the number of postsecondary institutions, but there remain key blockages at critical junctures. The college universe has become more byzantine as the prestige gap has grown between two-year community colleges and four-year schools, between private and public four-year institutions, and among four-year schools (Gelber 2007; Long 2007). Undocumented immigrant adolescents face even greater challenges (Abrego and Gonzales 2010). Although the Supreme Court decision Plyler v. Doe (1982) mandates that public elementary and high schools educate children regardless of documentation status, there are no provisions for higher education. Undocumented students are not eligible for federal financial aid, and they qualify for in-state tuition in only some states (Perez 2009; Flores 2010).

Where Are We Headed?

How can we explain the incorporation of the new second-generation individuals in light of their particular group characteristics and these macro institutional shifts? In 1992 Herbert Gans speculated that the non-white children of post-1965 immigrants would have different outcomes from the classic paradigm of assimilation and upward mobility. He theorized that some, especially the darker phenotypic youth—whose parents arrive with fewer resources and settle near or in native minority communities—might decline the low-paying, low-skilled jobs of their parents. But without the necessary educational advantages, and in the face of racial discrimination, these immigrant children could conceivably join the downwardly mobile.

Using Gans's speculation as a touchstone, segmented assimilation theory offered three possibly prescriptive and causal pathways for the post-1965 second generation, with divergent outlooks on schooling and socioeconomic outcomes (Portes and Zhou 1993; Portes and Rumbaut 2001). Two groups are able to achieve upward mobility: those children who assimilate into the white middle class, as per straight-line or classic assimilation, and those children who are able to draw upon cohesive ethnic communities and develop strong ethnic attachments along with positive outlooks on schooling. The latter may assimilate later into the white middle class. A third group of children who encounter discrimination and settle near native-born minority groups in struggling city neighborhoods have decidedly different outcomes. They tend to adopt their native minority peers' negative outlooks on schooling, do not do well in school, and eventually join the ranks of the urban, native minority poor.

This book, with its focus on social processes, both builds on and pushes beyond segmented assimilation theory, especially its emphasis on the positive influence of cohesive coethnic communities and the negative effect of fragmented native minority neighborhoods. It is the pivotal interplay between institutions and immigrant families and the availability of nonfamily assistance that emerge as key sites of analysis. This approach sheds light on how success happens among those children of Latino immigrants who seem positioned to fail, if only because they come from working-class families, grew up in segregated neighborhoods without much solidarity, and attended de facto segregated schools. These children benefited especially from civil rights–era institutions and policies for fostering diversity programs. Non-ethnic individuals helped both families and children map out the American educational system and offered ways for the children to succeed within it.

In addition, native minority cultures of upward mobility provided some children with the tools to succeed (Neckerman, Carter, and Lee 1999; Carter 2005; Kasinitz et al. 2008; Smith 2008, forthcoming [a]). In contrast to segmented assimilation theory, which is silent about upwardly mobile, urban native minorities, we found that these minorities serve as key connections for some 1.5- and second-generation Dominicans and Colombians. These respondents believed that they shared common goals with the native minority strivers and occupied common ground with them in being racialized as nonwhite and often lower income. They turned to the native minority strivers as touchstones of useful knowledge and for their familiarity with negotiating a sense of marginalization and belief that nonwhites had to do more than whites to be successful. Rather than hew to a single identity, as proposed by segmented assimilation theory, the children we interviewed drew seamlessly on multiple identities, both ethnic and non-ethnic (Smith 2008). On a related note, the children deployed multiple frames of reference, including American and transnational ones, as they made sense of their own outcomes in the United States.

In sum, to increase success, we need to have a better understanding of *how* schooling success happens, especially among groups that conventional wisdom holds to be the least likely to achieve it (Gándara 1995; de los Reyes, Nieto, and Diez 2008). There are plenty of educational volumes on failure or pathology, a number of them about Latinos (Lawrence-Lightfoot 1983; Lawrence-Lightfoot and Davis 1997). We need to step up our efforts to identify areas of advancement and favorable prognoses and align them with studies of risk and resilience to develop more targeted policy interventions (Crosnoe 2005, 583). This book is a contribution to that line of inquiry. Immigrant children's journey to college is a function not simply of the immigrant family, the surrounding community, and macro institutional dynamics but also of the crucial interactions *between* the family and institutions, along with nonfamily individuals who are in a position to offer valuable knowledge and support. This book offers lessons derived from these findings that will help us do a better job of integrating immigrant newcomers, improve our schools, and better serve the children at risk of not succeeding in them.

The Study

The children were interviewed from December 2001 to July 2005, and a subsample of their immigrant parents were interviewed from July 2003 to July 2005. I conducted sixty-four of the children's interviews, and the rest were completed by two research assistants, Claudia Pineda, then a doctoral student, and Silvia Covelli. Both Ms. Covelli and Dr. Pineda are natives of Colombia who came as adults to the United States, and both had done extensive research with Dominican immigrant families in the greater Boston area for the Longitudinal Immigrant Student Adaptation Project, a study led by Carola and Marcelo Suárez-Orozco.[11] The children first filled out a demographic survey asking about such things as K-12 schooling history, various family characteristics, and linguistic patterns, and then they were interviewed in English about their views on and experiences with neighborhood context, K-12 schooling, college, the family immigrant journey, family child-rearing practices, children's identities, success, and discrimination. Dr. Pineda and Ms. Covelli, along with Ana Tavares, a second-generation Dominican American, were all fully bilingual in Spanish and English and interviewed thirty-six of the immigrant parents in Spanish; I also interviewed one parent in English. The parents spoke of their migration to and settlement in the United States, their family histories, the meanings they attached to education, and their knowledge of the American schooling system. They also talked about the identities that their children were adopting and how they self-identified. These data complement the second generation's perspectives and reveal the relative differences or similarities in how immigrant parents and their children understood the immigrant journey.

This kind of in-depth qualitative research approach may have a small, nonrandom sample that limits generalizability, but it is well suited to shedding light on the complex underpinnings of the social processes and social contexts that motivated this study. In-depth qualitative research allows us to understand the meaning of events, concepts, situations, and behaviors to the respondents; to analyze the contradictions in their interpretations; and to describe and explain relationships. In the process, we gain a much-needed understanding of how broader social forces shape the social situations of individuals, or lived experience. We are able to illuminate the specific mechanisms of a social phenomenon—in this case, how the children became academic winners (Smalls 2009). Finally, our insights allow us both to refine existing theories and to develop valuable tools to build new theories through further qualitative research along with larger, representative survey studies (McDermott 2006).

About three-quarters of the children we interviewed had grown up in the greater Boston area or New York City, both regions with substantial Colombian and Dominican migration (Marcelli and Granberry 2006).[12] As table 1.1 indicates, more than four-fifths of the children were between the ages of eighteen and twenty-six, and 60 percent were born in the United States, more so for the Dominicans. The foreign-born arrived during early and middle childhood, clustered more toward the earlier years. Men made up 42 percent of the overall sample. The majority were enrolled in or had graduated from a four-year college at the time of the interview, and 20 percent had attended or were enrolled in a community college or had completed at most a two-year degree. I employed varied methods to diversify the children's sample along multiple lines and produce samples of individuals who were not known to one another. For a more detailed discussion of the methods employed and sample characteristics, please consult the appendix.

To understand the family backgrounds of the children we interviewed, it is helpful first to have a better sense of how distinct migration

Table 1.1 Characteristics of Children of Immigrant Families

	Colombian	Dominican	Total
Male	16	16	32
Age range			
Under eighteen	1	0	1
Eighteen to twenty-two	24	24	48
Twenty-three to twenty-six	7	10	17
Twenty-seven to thirty	4	3	7
Thirty-one to thirty-three	1	1	2
Over forty-one	0	1	1
Generation			
1.5	18	12	30
Second generation	19	27	46
1.5 age at arrival			
Zero to five	3	5	8
Six to ten	12	7	19
Eleven to twelve	3	0	3
N	37	39	76

Source: Author's compilation based on data from the Dominican and Colombian Immigrant Family Study (2009).

patterns have created Dominican and Colombian populations in the United States that have quite different social and demographic characteristics. Dominican immigration has for the most part followed the more traditional economic model. Early waves of migrants were middle-class Dominicans fleeing political instability in the wake of the assassination of dictator Rafael Trujillo and the invasion of the U.S. Marines in 1965. A more socioeconomically diverse group of immigrants started to leave the island during the 1970s, pushed out by the Dominican Republic's severe economic problems in the form of high foreign debt and high oil prices (Torres-Saillant and Hernández 1998; Hernández 2002). From the 1980s onward, the nation's economic picture continued to deteriorate, with estimates that the actual per capita income in 1992 was below what it had been in the early 1970s (Pessar and Graham 2001). The result was increased migration to the United States as an overwhelming number of unskilled workers were joined by a stream of their better skilled counterparts, who were pushed out as well by a decline in good jobs and the plummeting value of the nation's currency (Torres-Saillant and Hernández 1998).

By comparison, Colombian immigration to the United States, more deeply intertwined with political unrest, violence, and declining economic conditions, has seen a more pronounced stream of highly skilled and better-off migrants seeking to escape this combination of factors

(Guarnizo and Diaz 1999). There have been three waves of Colombian immigration to the United States: the first came in the wake of La Violencia, the civil war that dominated the 1950s (Roldan 2002), the effects of which continued to be felt until the late 1970s. The first wave included immigrants of all social class backgrounds in Colombia, although most were from the lower and lower-middle class strata. The second wave, which occurred from the late 1970s through the mid-1990s, continued to be characterized by a socioeconomically diverse stream of migrants, with a rise in those from the middle and upper strata. What distinguished the second wave was the drug war between Colombian drug cartels and the United States; everyday violence such as extortion and kidnapping became more common. Confidence in the nation's institutions waned (Safford and Palacios 2002). Although Colombia's economy was actually doing relatively well, particularly compared to other Latin American nations (Bushnell 1993), the nation's instability drove the flow of migrants.[13] We are currently in the midst of the third wave of immigration, which continues to be diverse but has also brought a marked rise in well-to-do professionals seeking to flee an increasingly complex web of violence, which has become less prevalent in recent years but remains strong (Collier and Gamarra 2001, 3–4).[14] Given their varied motivations for migrating, it is not surprising that Colombians in the United States are more likely to have higher incomes than Dominicans do, to have more education, and to own their homes (U.S. Census Bureau 2000).

The children we spoke with came from family backgrounds consistent with these histories and demographics. The Dominicans were thus more likely to report that their parents migrated to the United States to seek better economic opportunities. Two-thirds of the Dominican children's survey responses framed the immigrant journey along these lines, while fewer than half of the Colombians' responses did.[15] The Colombian children's families were generally doing better. Although more than half of the children in both groups reported growing up with one or two risk factors identified as barriers to college (Schneider and Stevenson 1999; Swail, Cabrera, and Lee 2004),[16] the Colombians nonetheless had more material advantages: their parents were more likely to own their home, and the children were about twice as likely as the Dominicans to have grown up without any form of public assistance.[17] The Dominicans had mostly grown up in urban neighborhoods, where Latinos were a substantial presence or the majority, often with Puerto Rican neighbors and sometimes among African Americans (Newman 1999; Waters, Mollenkopf, and Kasinitz 1999). Their accounts speak to the poverty that accompanied the residential segregation of Latinos during the 1980s and 1990s (Massey 2007).[18] By contrast, fewer than half of the Colombian respondents grew up in mostly urban ethnic or panethnic communities, and the neighborhoods of those who did grow up in such communities not only tended to be different from where the Dominicans lived but also seemed to have fewer issues with poverty and crime. The remainder of the Colombians grew up in mostly white middle-class areas, and some joined an immigrant stream to the nation's suburbs (Jones-Correa 2008). Although I do not have more extensive geographically based information, this contrast between the Dominican and Colombian families is consistent with the findings of Philip Kasinitz and his coauthors in their Immigrant Second Generation in Metropolitan New York Study (ISGMNY). Compared to their South American counterparts, the median Dominican second-generation respondents lived in areas with more social disorganization (Kasinitz et al. 2008).[19]

There was one important difference between national data and the families of my respondents—the latter were better off than the average foreign-born Dominican or Colombian. As the appendix shows, the educational level of the Colombian and Dominican mothers and the rates of family home ownership were higher in my sample, and some of the parents were found in more skilled occupations. Another indicator of the relative advantage of the families in my sample had to do with how far all children in the United States, not just the ones we interviewed, had gone with schooling. Only two Dominican respondents reported having a sibling (a brother) who had dropped out of high school. Most of the children we interviewed reported that their siblings had at least completed high school or a GED. The variation among the respondents' siblings came with the transition to college—namely, who went to college, what kind of college they attended, and who graduated. Finally, although we did not ask questions about documentation status, it was clear that the parents were overwhelmingly documented immigrants, a status that was a great advantage in finding better jobs, receiving financial aid for their children's schooling, and probably just feeling optimistic as a family about life in the United States.[20] As noted earlier, the prospects for undocumented immigrants here have grown increasingly grim.

There are a few additional caveats worth noting. First, the parents were not newcomers to the United States—they had been here long enough to have experienced and come to understand economic and social mobility. We had information on length of residence for about four-fifths of the parents; of these, only 13 percent had been in the United States for fifteen years or less, with nearly half having been here sixteen to thirty years and the remainder longer than that.[21] Second, given how well some of the Colombian parents had done, the transition to college of some of the children only reproduced their family's high status, especially pre-migration, in what we would call a process of social reproduction rather than upward mobility (Feliciano 2008; Zhou and Lee 2007; Rumbaut 2008).[22] Third, the children were distinctive for having made the transition to postsecondary schools.[23] By way of comparison, in the ISGMNY Dominicans were struggling the most out of the second-generation groups, with 16 percent not finishing high school. About three-fifths of both Dominicans and Colombians in that study had completed high school without going on to earn a bachelor's degree. Fourth, the majority of the children were also attending four-year and higher-prestige institutions,[24] in sharp contrast to the overrepresentation of the nation's Latinos in two-year colleges and less selective and public four-year institutions (Swail, Cabrera, and Lee 2004).[25] The children's college selectivity profile was also quite different from the ISGMNY samples, among whom only 4 percent of the South Americans and Dominicans attended a top-tier public or private college.[26] The appendix provides a full listing of the schools attended and a more detailed picture of the selectivity of the children's four-year colleges, along with ethnic differences in attendance, at least some a function of sampling.

In sum, the children we interviewed tended to come from families who were documented, had been here a long while, and were doing better than their conationals on average, and the children themselves were doing well educationally. *Keeping the Immigrant Bargain* was so named to invoke the idea that not only had the children honored the bargain with their immigrant parents, but in the process the immigrant families had in some measure kept their end of the bargain with their new country. In short, the next generation had assimilated linguistically and was poised for some degree of individual mobility through schooling. These families shared an abiding faith in the ideals enshrined in the American Dream. What helped the immigrants and their children to win these bargains, and what made the process difficult? What can we learn from their experiences? And what are the implications for the America that we will all inherit? The rest of this book looks at these questions.

The Plan of the Book

Chapter 2 begins with a look at the immigrant families' shared belief in the American Dream in the context of their varied mobility paths. So begins the immigrant bargain: regardless of the degree of success they attached to their own journey, the parents invested their hopes in their children, as the next generation was seen as not being subject to the same kinds of language and cultural barriers and related adjustments. A dual frame of reference is crucial to showing how mobility was experienced economically and interpreted in non-economic terms. Chapter 3 discusses the concept of social exclusion in the assimilation processes of the immigrant parents. If immigrant optimism emerged from the promise and rewards of the American opportunity structure and the political freedoms and stability here, immigrant pessimism—or a shared immigrant identity—was reactive, based on the lack of acceptance from native Americans. Even very upwardly mobile immigrant parents, who were working in non-ethnic institutions and living in non-ethnic neighborhoods, did not feel themselves to be assimilated. Chapter 4 situates the parents' involvement with their children's schooling in the context of these mobility and assimilation patterns. Because parents and schools were out of sync about their expectations for parental involvement, partly owing to the parents' sense of social exclusion, the children ended up feeling themselves to be on their own in school. Overall, chapters 2 through 4 show how the immigrant journey of the parents, in both its downside and its upside, gave way to the family immigrant bargain. But it was also the challenge of the immigrant journey that could make it difficult for the children to meet their parents' expectations.

Chapter 5 looks at how the children drew on nonfamily supports, especially mentors, to win the immigrant bargain. Who gave the children —and sometimes the parents—the information they needed to know about the American system of education and how to succeed? Chapter 6 builds from one assumption of the immigrant bargain—namely, that with the credentials of higher education the children will experience upward mobility. This analysis looks at how we can understand the seemingly paradoxical ways in which the children made sense of this proposition in the wider context of their views on and experiences with college. Chapter 7 shows that, in contrast to the social exclusion experienced by their parents, the children believed themselves to be very much included in America. For them, being American had to do with abstract egalitarian principles; thus, anyone could be American, including those who had grown up in ethnic home cultures. Overall, the children's identities were multiple and coexisted—they saw themselves as ethnic, Latino, pan-minority, and American.

Chapter 8 concludes with a look at both the past and the future. I argue that this story of immigrant optimism about their mobility and freedom here coexisting with pessimism about whether America will accept them as truly American is distinctive to the contemporary era. This is very different from the greater pessimism and alienation of the European immigrants, who arrived in the nineteenth and early twentieth centuries. The chapter closes with a discussion of the implications for further research, policy, and practice with respect to first and second generations of immigrants—namely, how to better integrate immigrants and how to better educate the children of immigrants.

Chapter 2

In Two Worlds: The Immigrant American Dream

> No one can say, "I am staying in D.R. [the Dominican Republic]," because things over there are really bad. I would like to go there for some time and then come back.
>
> —Mercedes, fifty-one-year-old Dominican mother

> Here with money you can belong anywhere. In Bucaramanga, if an ordinary Joe wanted to join the Commerce Club, we wouldn't let him in. I miss those things from Colombia. But at the same time, I see this is the country of opportunities. It's better here. If you work, you can earn a living. In Colombia, somebody from the lower class cannot make a decent living.
>
> —Paola, forty-eight-year-old Colombian mother

THE IMMIGRANT bargain begins with the parents' journey and the degree to which they succeed (or not) in the United States. How do the parents actually experience social and economic mobility, and how do they understand it? A dual frame of reference is crucial to both processes. In contrast to the dramatic upward mobility typically associated with the immigrant American Dream, the accounts of the parents in this study were far more complex. More than half of the parents had enjoyed upward mobility, but by no means to the same degree. Others only replicated the status they had had before migrating, and some were even doing worse. Yet, regardless of their economic gains or losses, and often more than their circumstances would seem to warrant, the parents expressed a surprising optimism about their lives here. To understand the apparent paradox of immigrant optimism about mobility, we need to know more than just their actual mobility paths. We need to know how the parents deployed a dual frame of reference—the United States and the home country—to situate both the long-term rewards and the long-term costs of their postmigration lives.[1] Mobility is lived not just in economic terms (for example, in terms of wages and social class) but also in the non-economic domain having to do with overall perceptions about the mobility, national security, and freedoms

Table 2.1 Social Class Backgrounds of Immigrant Parents, Overall Sample

	Colombians	Dominicans	Total
Middle-class	12	8	20
Working-class	25	31	56
Total	37	39	76

Source: Author's compilation based on data from the Dominican and Colombian Immigrant Family Study (2009).

available in the United States. For the Colombians, who had lived with systemic violence in their home country, the issue of security was especially important.

Let us first define the actual mobility paths. An immigrant who was a *dramatic riser* met at least two conditions of upward economic mobility, as measured by education, occupation, and wealth in the United States: having some additional schooling (beyond studying English as a second language), having held or holding an occupation higher in prestige than the job(s) held in the home country, and/or owning a home. Dramatic risers were living the classic immigrant version of the American Dream. A *limited riser* was an immigrant who met only one of the conditions of upward economic mobility and thus had not experienced as much mobility. *Replicators* reproduced their status in their country of origin, whether relatively high or low. Someone who was a *high replicator* thus differed from a dramatic riser in having had a high-prestige job and home in the country of origin. Similarly, the key distinction between a *low replicator* and a limited riser, even though their lives were quite similar, was that the former had not done any better with migration in education, occupational prestige, and home ownership.

Upward mobility, however, is not the same as social class background. As table 2.1 shows, only twenty families—eight Dominicans and twelve Colombians—had middle-class backgrounds in the United States.[2] I define middle-class families as those in which at least one parent works in a job that entails a lot of managerial authority or competencies typically associated with a college education (Lareau and Weininger 2008, 122). The middle-class parents in our study were teachers, social workers, engineers, and computer programmers. Working-class families are those in which neither parent has a middle-class job and at least one parent's job has no managerial responsibilities or does not require college-level skills (Lareau and Weininger 2008, 122). Our working-class parents included factory and maintenance workers along with office assistants.

High replicators and some of the dramatically upwardly mobile join the growing numbers of foreign-born middle-class households in the United States, a pattern partially fueled by a unique feature of contemporary flows—the entry of substantial numbers of highly educated and skilled immigrants (Morawska 1990; Portes and Rumbaut 1990, 2001; Kasinitz et al. 2008). In 2004, 27 percent of immigrants had either a bachelor's or advanced degree (Haskins 2007). In 2000, as defined by income, one-fifth of all foreign-born households, both those headed by first-generation immigrants and those headed by immigrants who arrived as children, were middle-class, making up about 8.6 percent of the nation's overall middle-class population (Clark 2003).[3]

Upward mobility and status reproduction, however, did not tell the whole story for the families in this study: overall, 26 percent (twenty children) reported having at least one parent who underwent a decline in occupational status. The occupationally downwardly mobile mothers typically did factory or housekeeping work in the United States; some had been secretaries in either the Dominican Republic or Colombia, and most had received some postsecondary vocational training. The fathers tended to have higher levels of education and to come from more varied occupational backgrounds in their native countries, but they also tended to be clustered in manual labor jobs in maintenance in the United States. These parents joined yet another pattern of contemporary immigration—occupational downgrading (Foner 2000; Akresh 2006). So even though a contemporary immigrant might earn higher wages in the United States—especially given its wage differential with less industrialized nations (Grasmuck and Pessar 1991; Haskins 2007; Sawhill 2007; Dreby 2010)—and experience upward economic mobility here, he or she might work a lower-status occupation (downward economic mobility) and belong to a lower class here (downward social mobility) relative to the home country (Gans 2007, 2009).[4]

As table 2.2 shows, roughly equivalent proportions of the 1.5- and second-generation Dominicans and Colombians in this study grew up in families that had seen either dramatic upward or downward mobility in the United States. There were also ethnic differences consistent with what we know from census data and the ISGMNY findings. The Colombian parents were more likely to be the high replicators, reproducing the high status they had enjoyed prior to migration, albeit after obtaining more postsecondary schooling here. The Dominicans, meanwhile, were more likely to come from families that had seen limited mobility or were replicating a low status here. We also have to keep in mind the caveat that the parents of the children in this study were actually doing better than the average Dominican or Colombian in the United States (see the appendix). The interviews provide a fuller account of experiencing these different types of mobility.

Table 2.2 Mobility Paths of Immigrant Parents, Overall Sample

	Colombians	Dominicans	Total
Dramatic risers	12	12	24
Replicators			
High	5	1	6
Low	2	5	7
Limited risers	7	12	19
Downwardly mobile	11	9	20
Total	37	39	76

Source: Author's compilation based on data from the Dominican and Colombian Immigrant Family Study (2009).
Note: In one case, the Colombian parents were young 1.5ers themselves, so I employed the grandparents as the template for mobility and classified them as limited risers; the grandparents bought a home in the United States but otherwise did not get more education or jobs of equivalent or higher prestige than they had in Colombia.

Living Mobility

Dramatic Risers

In Alfonso's family, the journey of his parents and grandparents to the United States, propelled as it was by the civil war in the Dominican Republic during the mid-1960s, was framed as one of unqualified upward economic and social mobility. The older generations had fled their homes in one of Santo Domingo's shantytowns, first for Flatbush in Brooklyn, New York, and then for Lawrence, Massachusetts. They left to escape not only the poor economic conditions in a country where social class, itself embedded with political influence, was believed to be highly determinative of life chances, but also the political instability and violence as dueling factions battled for control following the assassination of Rafael Trujillo, who served as president and de facto dictator of the nation from 1930 to 1961 (Torres-Saillant and Hernández 1998). As Alfonso said, his parents rarely spoke of their lives back in the Dominican Republic, and when they did, they spoke only of the deprivation and fear.

> And of course, you know, education was incredibly difficult from what they said. With the civil war going on, they couldn't even make it to school, so it was a miracle that they got out. What I remember the most is when they would say, you know, "We used to walk outside our house and there would be dead bodies in the street from the civil war."

In the United States, despite the challenges—his grandmother suffered nerve injuries after years of working in unbearably hot clothing factories—the political peace and economic opportunity were seen as well worth any hardships. And for his parents, who both completed high school and postsecondary education here, there was no looking back. His father, who earned a bachelor's degree from a state college, was principal of a vocational high school for a decade before moving into real estate development. Following his parents' divorce, his mother, a graduate of community college and a legal secretary, moved Alfonso and his younger sister to a public housing project in the Cambridgeport neighborhood of Cambridge, Massachusetts. The housing project was among the city's oldest, and by the time the family moved in it had become less socioeconomically and racially diverse and more black, Latino, and poor; the area itself was by then understood to be a tough neighborhood (Hernandez 2006). However, because the children spent weekends with their father in the home he owned north of Boston and attended a private elementary school, they were sheltered from any potentially disruptive influences in their mother's neighborhood. All of this was seen as a dramatic improvement over the lives that any of them could have had in the Dominican Republic. Alfonso had a deep affection for the island after two visits and a college semester spent studying there, but even he had to agree.

> Over there, everything's so different. You know, the power goes out every few hours, not stable electricity. And you can just see the poverty. You know, there's no middle class. Coming from a place [the United States] where you can survive, and, you know, you see a middle class, at least. Over there, you see very incredible poverty. . . . You know, there are so many opportunities here that just aren't available in those countries in Latin America.

It was the upward mobility that they had experienced in the United States that allowed Alfonso's parents to engage with the Dominican Republic from a much more privileged position than they had previously known. On one level, they derived much satisfaction from how far they had come from their modest beginnings. And on another, their material advantages finally allowed them to appreciate the beauty of the island. Alfonso said, "Now that they've made money, they're living well, and they go back, it's like, 'Wow, this is beautiful.'" His father, said Alfonso, was even able to buy a house back on the island and for a time owned a security company there, well aware of the need to protect one's self and possessions in his still-struggling native country.

High Replicators

Catalina, a parent whom we interviewed, seemed like another example of the quintessential successful immigrant journey. In contrast to Alfonso's parents, however, Catalina came from a privileged position in Colombia, where she was a university graduate and a comptroller for the subsidiary of an American oil company. The journey she undertook with her daughter Judy during the mid-1980s, leaving behind Judy's father, resulted in a replication of her previously privileged status, facilitated by several advantages: Catalina was a documented immigrant, she was still relatively young (in her early thirties), and she had some English-language facility. Nonetheless, she did briefly work at what she called "immigrant jobs" in her first several months in Boston, doing temporary clerical jobs and even working in housekeeping ("fixing rooms") at one of the city's premier hotels. She could still remember the job's physical demands, which "almost killed me, my poor back." Eventually, thanks to her bilingual skills, Catalina started working at nonprofit organizations serving Hispanic immigrants, first as a basic education instructor for adults and later shifting to positions that allowed her to use her prior training in economics and administration. While working full time, she became more proficient in English and later earned a master's in business administration (MBA) through evening classes at a state university. At the time we spoke, she had achieved the capstone of her American career: she was serving as vice president of a regional bank.

Over the course of her nineteen years in the United States, Catalina had found everyday life to be peaceful, compared to Colombia, and a realization of her early dreams. Both her father and brother had been assassinated in the aftermath of El Bogotazo and the ensuing La Violencia, and considerable family land holdings had been lost.[5] When interviewed, Catalina lived in a condominium that she owned in a northeastern city, and she had an investment property in Florida. She had remarried; her second husband was a second-generation Colombian American who also had a master's degree and was a consultant. Although they later divorced, he was a father figure for her daughter. Judy was a graduate of Boston's top public magnet high school and an Ivy League university. In short, Catalina had met all the goals she came to the United States to achieve: to get a graduate education, to improve her daughter's educational and cultural horizons, and to enter another professional field. However, her account also spoke to the important themes of social and cultural marginalization, which I shall return to in the next chapter.

Limited Risers and Low Replicators

Mercedes, the mother described at the start of this chapter, had not done particularly well in the United States. Her journey had not resulted in more schooling, a better job, or home ownership. Interviewed in 2004, she had been unable to go beyond the seven years of schooling she received in Tenares in the Dominican Republic. Life in the United States had brought more work opportunities but also its own share of challenges. She had worked several years in factories, putting the glue on shoes, cleaning out camera pieces, before she injured her back and started to collect disability. In Lawrence, Massachusetts, Mercedes had lived in a "hectic" public housing project and, most recently, in private apartment complexes that took Section 8, a government housing program that at least gave her the relative luxury of choosing where to live.

Given her limited household income, everyday life revolved around basic survival (Hernández 2002). Mercedes said that she collected $592 a month after taxes from disability benefits and an additional $380 a month in child support when her husband, from whom she was separated; had a job, typically in factories or in the construction industry; or was collecting unemployment benefits. Her two sons also had part-time jobs, in the public library and the local supermarket, earning about $7 an hour, and contributed their earnings to overall household expenses.

Marissa's mother, one of the limited risers, had had somewhat more success. After developing some English-language proficiency through classes, she had been able to take vocational classes. She owned a car here, an impossible achievement for her in the Dominican Republic. Yet in other key respects, the life of Marissa's mother, who also lived in Lawrence, Massachusetts, seemed little different from Mercedes's life. Over the years, she too had been a factory worker, as well as a housekeeper and nurse's aide. Divorced from her Dominican husband, she lived with a white American man in his house, an arrangement that helped her financially. Although she said that crime in their working-class neighborhood had declined, many of the homes still had metal gates on the first-floor windows to keep out intruders.

The lives of nearly all the limited risers and low replicators were marked by this element of continuing struggle, but it was especially pronounced for the Dominicans. This is not surprising, given the group's relatively high poverty rates and the fact that the Dominican children in the study were more than twice as likely as their Colombian counterparts to report growing up in families that depended on some amount of public assistance (Hernández 2002; Schwartz and Stiefel 2005).[6] They lived with the poignant paradox captured by studies of transnational flows among working-class Dominicans (Grasmuck and Pessar 1991; Levitt 2001). For instance, Peggy Levitt (2001) found that Dominican immigrants in the Boston neighborhood of Jamaica Plain earned more money than they ever had before and owned the modern appliances that had seemed so out of reach when they were in their native Miraflores. At the same time work ruled their lives, and even with the long hours and toil, they found themselves unable to get ahead; they remained aware of their low socioeconomic status here and, given their limited English and isolation from mainstream American institutions, the likelihood that they would stay at that level. The theme of struggling hard just to exist on the economic margins was echoed in this study for the Dominican parents, whose immigrant journeys had brought them scant or few gains.

The Downwardly Mobile

Struggle also characterized the lives of the downwardly mobile. When she was not working at a nearby factory, Ingrid spent her days in a small second-floor apartment in a working-class neighborhood of Providence, home to Cape Verdean and Portuguese immigrants. Her father had sponsored Ingrid and her son José so that they could come to the United States in the early 1990s; during their first few months here, he had provided them with housing and with job leads for Ingrid, then thirty years old. In the end, however, her father had his own new family in the United States to think about; now, Ingrid said, she had little contact with him even though he lived only a few miles away.

In the eleven years she had been in the United States, Ingrid had relied mainly on earnings from her full-time job as a factory worker operating machines that put the tips on shoelaces and part-time jobs in "aseo" (housecleaning) when she needed extra money; occasionally, community-based organizations helped her when basic expenses, like gas bills, proved to be too costly. Her son's father, a well-to-do local government official in Colombia, had provided no financial support and scarcely communicated with her or José after they left the country.

Life in the United States, as Ingrid told it, was dominated by work and defined by loneliness. She was grateful that her employer had managed to stay afloat during economic downturns, providing her with "steady work," but she was well aware of the flat wage structure, noting that "the only thing that never changes are the salaries." In the United States, said Ingrid, she worked like a "burra" (donkey). She was friendly with her coworkers at the factory, who were immigrants themselves, from Portugal, Cape Verde, and Central America. But her son was her closest companion.

Life in the United States had evolved into a series of trade-offs for Ingrid. Migration had brought overall benefits, such as economic and political stability, and she had been able to study English for the first time. Now she could read and understand some, but speaking remained a challenge. In the end, her greatest achievement was her son—José had excelled in the face of what his mother knew to be considerable odds. The living room wall in the family apartment was lined with diplomas, soccer trophies, and pictures of José at the White House during an internship with a leading national Latino political organization, but the wall displayed only some of José's accomplishments. Surveying the markers of her son's educational journey, Ingrid noted, "The biggest payback that I have is my son. With God's help, he has one more year before he graduates. It is the greatest satisfaction that God has given me."

Her comment speaks to the heart of this book—namely, the sacrifices made by immigrant parents on behalf of their children by coming and staying here. The expected exchange is that the children will do well in school and get ahead in the United States (Fuligni, Tseng, and Lam 1999; Portes and Rumbaut 2001; Suárez-Orozco and Suárez-Orozco 2001; Suárez-Orozco, Suárez-Orozco, and Todorova 2008; Kao 2004; Louie 2004; Perreira, Chapman, and Stein 2006; Smith 2006). Ingrid's sacrifices had left her own personal and career goals largely unmet by migration. She had experienced downward mobility in occupational status and standard of living. Although she described her family as relatively poor in Armenia (her mother was a housekeeper and food server at the local hospital, and her father was a bus driver and mechanic), Ingrid had completed high school there.[7] Working full time as a secretary for local government offices, she completed a certificate in secretarial studies by taking night classes at SENA, a nationally recognized vocational postsecondary institute. The training gave her "intermediate career work," or "good jobs," in contrast to the manual labor she later performed in the United States. We asked her to compare her position in Colombia as a government secretary with her jobs here on the assembly line and in housekeeping. "My God. They do not compare," Ingrid responded. "Over there I was very well kept. Over there you would not see me like you do here, like a crazy person," she noted with a laugh. Ingrid had wanted—and still wanted—to pursue postsecondary education in the United States, perhaps specializing in a helping profession like nursing or in secretarial work, but she knew that she needed to improve her English. She remained hopeful about her possibilities here, but there always seemed to be obstacles, whether time or money. Back in Colombia, she could rely on family supports like her mother and grandmother to help with the child care responsibilities she shouldered by herself here as a single mother, as well as a network of friends for additional support. In the United States, she felt largely alone except for her son. Yet as much as Ingrid missed Colombia, her permanent return seemed doubtful, except in the unlikely event that she saved enough to retire there. Making enough to meet her basic needs had not been easy in Colombia, but it would be virtually impossible, she said, now that she was forty-one, an age when it was hard to start over in the labor market, particularly for a woman.

Like Ingrid, other downwardly mobile immigrant mothers highlighted the disjuncture between the higher wages they earned as unskilled labor in the United States and the benefits that came with their skilled jobs in the home country. Comparing her work as a typist of doctoral dissertations in Colombia and as a housecleaner in the United

States, one mother said, "I liked the duties I was doing over there more than the ones I do here; however, I like the pay here more than in Colombia. Just to give you an example, sometimes I can make $50 an hour in the U.S.; this would never happen in Colombia." A mother who had been a secretary for a Dominican state agency for more than a decade still spoke with longing of her old job. There she had "worked at a desk, had three months of maternity leave" per child, "plus fifteen days of vacations."

A Colombian mother was pointed in her dislike of the work she did in the United States. She had started out in factory jobs before switching for a time to housekeeping and live-in nanny positions, then finally settling for part-time nanny and security guard jobs. This mother said that she could not tolerate the lack of privacy and the expectation of around-the-clock availability that came with living in an employer's home (Hondagneu-Sotelo 2001). The demands of a live-in nanny position were too demeaning for her, a woman who had first learned to cook after coming to America. She noted that, although her family origins were modest, her own mother had been able to afford a cook back in Colombia, whereas in the United States she herself was often treated as a servant. She was appreciative of both the higher wages available to her and the educational opportunities afforded her children (the daughter whom we interviewed graduated from a top-tier liberal arts college), but this mother was also well aware of her decline in status.

Other individuals spoke of how painful it was to witness their loved ones' downward slide in status (Gans 2009). While Margarita, a mother we interviewed, never recouped the status she had had as a school principal in the Dominican Republic, she did rise over time in the United States—from working as a teacher's assistant to getting a job as a public school teacher after earning a master's degree in bilingual education. This was in contrast to her husband's different trajectory. A career naval officer in the Dominican Republic, he was reduced to working in hotel maintenance and then later as a building superintendent in the United States.[8] She remembered that he was "cleaning rooms, taking the garbage out, and well, as you can imagine, a whole tragedy."

Paola, the Colombian mother described earlier, was another example. After arriving in a Kansas suburb to live with relatives, she and her husband struggled to find employment and had spells of not working. Their son Javier, who was twelve when the family migrated, spoke of how his father's decline in job status affected himself and his older brother, then fourteen. The boys' difficulties with a new language, culture, and school were compounded by seeing their father, formerly a prominent businessman, unemployed and taking on "housewife duties" such as cooking. His older brother had difficulty making friends, said Javier, and was embarrassed when he brought home the few friends he did have, given their father's diminished position.

The parents' job situation brightened when they moved to Miami. There Paola occasionally sold phone cards to Colombian friends and had a temporary job driving children home from school. Her husband, meanwhile, sold used cars for a local dealership. Compared to their former lives in Colombia, however, even these positions represented a dramatic decline. Paola, a university graduate in business administration, had been a credit analyst for a leading Colombian bank before eventually purchasing a travel agency. Her husband, also a university graduate, had once studied in the United States for a year to learn English, and in Colombia he had had his own chemical distribution firm and also worked for his family's regional poultry firm. Of the couple's downward mobility, Paola said, "Of course, I lived much better there. Although I live happy here and I'm grateful to the U.S. because we have received a lot of things, you know, life in our country is quite different." She spoke of having two housemaids in Bogotá and belonging to a social club that demarcated status not only by income but also by social status (family lineage).

In the Dominican Republic and Colombia, these families had one or more of the following: servants, membership in an elite social club, tennis and music lessons for their children, multiple luxury vacations a year, a car, a home in a good neighborhood, and paid maternity leave. In the United States, the families found that none of this was possible for them, except possibly car and home ownership. (Even their compatriots in the study who joined the upper stratum here could not afford servants.) The findings on the downwardly mobile immigrant families presented here are consistent with the struggles that Katherine Newman (1988/1999) found among downwardly mobile Americans. The adults in Newman's study had to negotiate the differences between their previous middle-class identity as successful professionals and their present existence as low-level employees not making enough to pay the bills (Newman 1988/1999, 10). Their children, especially if they were young, looked on in confusion as their fathers, whom they had once looked up to, were unable to cope with the downward slide. As Newman writes, everyone in the family got caught in the difficulties of managing the status inconsistency: "Without any guidelines on how to shed the old self, without any instruction or training for the new, the downwardly mobile remain in a social and cultural vacuum" (10).

The same themes of isolation and confusion mark the experiences of the families we interviewed. The downwardly mobile immigrant parents lost the deference, authority, and autonomy of their old lives and felt they would never regain them. Their children found it painful to watch this process unfold. The families certainly believed that the descent down the social ladder would be permanent for the parents. The saving grace was moving from one nation to another: with the old and new lives of the parents neatly separated, the public dimension of the fall was removed. There were no physical reminders in America of what the parents had lost. And there was no need for immigrant parents to hide their fall from others here, since most people assumed that they had always been manual laborers and renters living on the economic margins.

In Two Worlds: Immigrant Optimism

Yet for all the struggles faced by the limited risers, low replicators, and downwardly mobile, these families shared the optimism of their counterparts who had either made great gains here or reproduced their previous high status. Overall, the parents believed that the immigrant journey had turned out well and that they were living the American Dream. How did this belief arise? To understand the contrast between parents' positive feelings about their lives and the challenging work and living conditions some of them faced, we need to draw on their dual frame of reference. The optimism of immigrant parents was born of having lived in two worlds.

Leaving Behind the Certainty of Closed Mobility

The parents were optimistic because they believed that they had left behind the conditions found in the Dominican Republic and Colombia that had leveled their aspirations and efforts: social class systems characterized by limited class mobility and, on a national level, intransigent economic and political uncertainties (Sawhill 2007, 2). Indeed, the children's parents tended to come from the capital and the second-largest city in each nation—Santo Domingo and Santiago in the Dominican Republic, and Bogotá and Medellin in Colombia. All four of these cities were grappling with similar challenges in the wake of economic downturns in Latin America.

During the credit crisis of the 1980s, for instance, the wage structure remained flat in the Dominican Republic and living conditions worsened, especially for the middle class; inflation reached 47 percent in 1985, and unemployment stood at 27.2 percent (Hernández 2002). Educated individuals also found themselves suffering from unemployment, and when they found jobs they were paid about the same as their less educated counterparts (Grasmuck and Pessar 1991). Meanwhile, basic social goods were difficult to come by. In 1988 drinking water was not available to more than half of the nation's residents, and a "covered sewage system" was out of reach for 59.7 percent of the population (Hernández 2002, 83). Owing to the rural out-migration to the cities that started in the 1950s, urban inequalities had increased, and city dwellers also lived without services that rural residents were used to not having, such as potable water, schools, and health care facilities (Hernández 2002, 61;

Hoffnung-Garskof 2008). Similarly, in 1999 urban Colombians were doing worse than in 1988, reversing an earlier decade's gains in per capita income.[9] The urban unemployment rate for high school dropouts and graduates alike was 23 percent, for college dropouts it was more than 18 percent, and 9.1 percent of college graduates were unemployed (Velez et al. 2002).

In both nations, education is thought to be a vehicle of social reproduction rather than upward social mobility, a perception with a strong empirical basis. Despite gains in primary school attainment during the 1990s, the Dominican Republic and Colombia continued to have gaps in schooling enrollment and completion between residents of urban and rural areas, residents of different regions, and residents of different income categories (Laserna 1988; McEwan 1998). Private schools are a significant presence in both countries and are typically of higher academic quality than public schools (Jimenez et al. 1991; Duarte 1998; Somers, McEwan, and Willms 2004; Mendoza 2007). In Colombia fewer than one-fifth of individuals in the lowest income quintile have attended university, compared to half of those in the highest bracket; cost is consistently raised as an issue for the less well-off in their stalled trajectories through secondary and postsecondary schooling (Gomez 2000).

Entering the Promise of Possibility

This backdrop of stark inequality and economic instability in the countries of origin helps explain why the families were surprisingly positive about their lives in the United States, even when their living and work conditions, by any objective measure, were difficult. Mercedes, one of the low replicators described earlier, said that life in her home country would have been harder still. In the Dominican Republic, her work helping out at her father's bodega had placed her in the informal sector, the most disadvantaged stratum in the nation's class structure (Portes 1985; Portes and Hoffman 2003).[10] While she looked forward to returning to the Dominican Republic, as she felt more culturally comfortable there, Mercedes doubted that she would ever go back for long, given the high cost of living relative to the wage structure and job availability. As she noted, the best that she could hope for was circular migration (Grasmuck and Pessar 1991; Hernández 2002).

A comparative frame on the educational system was another source of the parents' optimism, although they were careful to provide nuanced comparisons rather than over-inflate the merits of the American educational system (Menjívar 2008). The parents acknowledged that American schools did not teach students much about "urbanidad," or what one Colombian parent described as "good manners," and they saw that as detrimental to the students' well-being. Parents found the curriculum of the American educational system, on average, less advanced than in the

Dominican Republic or Colombia. Thomas's mother compared what she had learned decades earlier in a Medellin secondary school to what her son was presently learning in community college:

> My son attends college, and when I compare my high school books from chemistry, algebra, physics, and trigonometry, my books are at a much higher level. In Colombia courses are more advanced. Here, it seems courses are at a very minimal level. And worse, everyone here complains. . . . If a teacher assigns too much homework, students complain to the principal.

Still, the parents believed that the relative educational advantages in the United States far outweighed the drawbacks. They told us, as well as their children, that the American higher education system was not as dependent on family influence and provided more financial aid. Penny's father, a dramatic riser, related the story of two Colombian high school classmates: "They both visited the University of Cartagena, because they wanted to study medicine there, and what happened was that the smart one wasn't admitted and the lazy one was admitted. How can one explain something like this?" The answer, said Penny's father, had to do with the influence wielded by his "lazy" classmate's family. While he acknowledged that this kind of favoritism based on family money and social status could occur anywhere in the world, Penny's father underscored that it was a significant social problem in Colombia. He said that he had not had the necessary influential contacts in Colombia to get accepted into college. In the United States, however, he had found it easy to enroll in basic classes in mathematics and English as a second language (ESL) at a technical college; "second chances" for education, he said, were more available here (Holdaway, Crul, and Roberts 2009). The challenge here was working two jobs to send money home to his parents, which proved too much of a burden; in the end, he abandoned his educational plans and focused on his main factory job, eventually retiring as assembly line head operator. He pointed out, however, that his children were the beneficiaries of the relatively more open American educational system.

Andrea's mother, a limited riser, provided a similarly hopeful perspective. She held a GED, worked as a school bus matron, and lived an economically modest life: earning $17,000 in 2003, she rented a sunny but run-down apartment in Washington Heights, a neighborhood in New York City's upper Manhattan. In an interview conducted at her apartment—where she had laid out buckets to capture water leaking from the ceiling—she nonetheless framed her immigrant journey as a success because of the opportunities available to her children. Asked where she saw her children in ten years, she envisioned Andrea, recently graduated from Cornell, with another degree and in a professional job:

> I tell them that I come from a Latin American country, and over there we have to pay for an education like this, and over here there are many ways to get free education, or financial assistance. As a parent, you expend some money in their education, but it's not the same.

The Colombian families had another reason for optimism: freedom in the United States from the threat of systemic violence. Given that the Colombian families arrived in the United States well before 2002, the year when homicide and kidnapping rates started to decline in Colombia, security was a big theme for them. Eighteen of the thirty-seven Colombian children, or 49 percent, spoke of violence in the Colombian context, mainly experienced firsthand by members of their extended or immediate families. In contrast, only 10 percent of the Dominican children spoke of violence in the parental homeland, mainly with regard to street crime, riots, and the four-year civil war that followed Trujillo's assassination (Torres-Saillant and Hernández 1998). For the Colombian children and parents, the underlying threat of violence was posed by the guerrillas specifically, but also by a systemic web of kidnappings, carjackings, robberies, and extortion of businesses (Coatsworth 2003).

Freedom from such threats helps to explain the optimism of the Colombians who had not made many economic gains here. Sonia, a downwardly mobile mother, had left behind a comfortable life in Cali, with her own real estate business, a house she had inherited, a car, and the means to take several yearly luxury vacations abroad, because of the worsening and increasingly immediate threat of violence in the early to mid-1990s. To her, the sacrifices she made here were well worth it, because she knew what might have happened if she had stayed in Colombia. Sonia's stepfather, owner of a large farm near the coast, was killed after he refused to continue paying the guerrillas a monthly fee from his proceeds. The guerrillas then threatened Sonia and her son Pedro by casually remarking that her son "needed walking"—the euphemistic phrase for kidnapping, as victims were often made to walk along the mountains during their captivity (González de Perdomo and Moncayo 2008).

Even life in high-crime American neighborhoods did not seem as dangerous as the charged situations that the Colombian families had left. Herman's family had settled in the public housing projects of Lowell, Massachusetts, only a five-minute walk from downtown. The area was known to have the heaviest concentrations of poverty and immigrant settlement in a city characterized by crime and violence, partially owing to Asian and Latino gangs (Fry 2007; McDevitt et al. 2007). Herman migrated at the age of six, too young, he said, to have strong memories of Colombia, but he later visited as a ten-year-old and twice again in his early twenties. Herman came to conclude that life in Lowell was actually much safer than what he saw in Colombia: "When I went there, the things we have here, you know, we take for granted. It's incredible how unsecure this was in Colombia. Yeah. It's very dangerous. Growing up in Lowell was the best thing that could've happened to us probably."

Herman's parents spoke of the persistent danger they had felt in Medellin, engendering a fear strong enough to make them feel "almost scared to death over there." Interviewed in 2005, the retired couple had just started to go back and spend the winters in an apartment they had purchased in Medellin. The lower cost of living, the warm weather, and the cultural familiarity were strong attractions. Nothing had happened to them, but they continued, they said, to be "very cautious." Noting that they traveled along the coastline, where they felt it was safer, they highlighted the security improvements under the Uribe administration. They were happy to have their children visit Colombia but not to live there, out of concern for their safety. Their perspectives were similar to those of Central American immigrants who reported feeling safe in their high-crime neighborhoods in Phoenix, Arizona. The Phoenix immigrants evaluated their milieu not only by local standards but also by their experiences in their home country, where political violence had an impact on everyday life, including the lives of those who were not engaged in political activities (Menjívar and Bejarano 2004).

Living in the United States, freed from such strictures, intensified the promise of the possibilities. Even a limited riser could save enough money to buy a home in the United States or invest in properties in the homeland, retiring there to enjoy a lifestyle that would have never been possible without migration. An immigrant could actually see a small business flourish in the United States, where one did not have to deal with the extortion and corruption that made the same kind of enterprise so challenging in the Dominican Republic or Colombia. A woman could go to work here and not have to deal with the kinds of Dominican and Colombian gendered labor market norms that allowed male employers to exploit young single women and discriminate against married women with children (who are viewed as less sexually exploitable; National Public Radio [NPR] et al. 2004). The parents' optimism was fueled by the freedom from the strongly prohibitive barriers found in their country of origin and, on a related note, the sheer possibility for gain in the United States—more so than the extent and type of gains they actually experienced.

The Freedom to Become Somebody: The American Dream

Yet the parents did not merely view the United States as a welcome refuge from the considerable restrictions of their home countries but rather as a unique nation defined by self-invention (Hochschild 1995). Gain was regarded not only as possible in the United States but as more possible here than anywhere else in the world. In this, the parents subscribed to the American Dream, with its freedom "to become somebody," an outcome achievable by dint of individual effort (Deaux 2006). They understood, of course, that individual effort could not completely explain individual outcomes here either (Suárez-Orozco 1989; Clark 2003), but key to their optimistic outlook about the United States was what they perceived as the higher *likelihood* that individual effort would matter. To borrow from a Dominican young man's apt analogy, whichever aspect of "the American Dream wave" one was riding, there was a shared sense of its promise and hope (Hochschild 1995; Hochschild and Scovronick 2003, x).

This is how Javier, the son of the downwardly mobile Colombian parents described earlier, portrayed the American Dream—as offering the freedom to become somebody.

> This country was founded on people seeking a better life, and still to this day, that has a huge meaning to this country. That is why so many people come here. There is an American Dream, and it is the pursuit of happiness, just being able to seek a better life and having everything available to you to get a better life, to have a government that is willing to pay for education, that is willing to provide you certain services for you to be able to live this life.

The power of American individualism was a key theme in the interviews. Elena, whose Colombian parents replicated their high status in the United States, nonetheless underscored its limitless possibilities as a nation where one's best advantage was oneself. "Here you can sort of really start on your own and, you know, if you work hard, you can get it." Sally's Colombian parents, limited risers, highlighted their sense of good fortune to her: "I think they feel really privileged, really lucky, to live in the U.S." As Sally told me, her parents believed that the American advantages of peace and political stability buttressed by an opportunity structure largely dependent only on a person's motivation and skills proved a powerful combination, one that allowed them to do what they wanted. Such sentiments were similar to ones expressed by upwardly mobile families.

This is not to say that my respondents denied the existence of American shortcomings. Most of the children and the parents we interviewed spoke frankly about the downside of American life, particularly compared to their home countries and home cultures (Mahalingam 2006, 3). In the cultural realm, the consistent themes were lack of morality, manners, community, friendliness, and family cohesion. The immigrant families perceived an absence of overall morality in the United States, most visibly as embodied in the media, which showcased "improper" subjects such as flatulence and, more disturbing, violence and sex. Many of them assumed that media representations merely reflected the behaviors of individual Americans, whom they saw as more likely to be involved in alcoholism and drug use than citizens of other nations (Perreira, Chapman, and Stein 2006). Some complained about an atomistic way of life in which neighbors did not care to know one another, not even their names, and about a lack of strong community ties. This seeming atomism carried over to family life, in their view: American parents could not discipline their children, not even by setting rules to keep them from going out; families did not typically eat dinner together; and children moved out of the family home at the age of eighteen (Portes and Rumbaut 2001; Suárez-Orozco and Suárez-Orozco 2001; NPR et al. 2004; Kasinitz et al. 2008; Massey and Sanchez R. 2010). Much of this sentiment was captured by Rafael: "Like, values aren't given as much attention in the United States as there is in D.R. [the Dominican Republic] Like, family life is more important in D.R. Like, here kids tend to think that, 'Oh I'm turning eighteen, I can move out.' In D.R., people are thinking, 'Oh, once I'm eighteen I can get this job so I can help my mom out,' you know?" Several interviewees mentioned coldness, not only in the weather (although that was frequently cited) but also in the cultural climate. As Julian, whose parents were natives of Colombia, put it: "Like, the people are cold, nobody says hi to nobody. I mean, I'm used to it, 'cause I grew up here, but they're not."

Nor did the immigrant children and parents hesitate to criticize the United States for what they saw as its institutional shortcomings, including its self-appointed role as the world's policeman in the international arena and persistent inequalities in the domestic arena along the lines of race, ethnicity, language, social class, and immigrant status. Sally grew up hearing this kind of critique from her Colombian mother, and she still heard it:

> Like, I mean, I think my mom is really critical of the government in the U.S. I mean, she's very socialist in her way of thinking. And so she's very critical of how the U.S. funds are divided so unequally among people and how, you know, she just appreciates a more socially conscious way of dealing with your population. She's critical of the politics, especially their politics abroad, and the American arrogance—the arrogance of the American people. She's very hard.

Both the parents and children were well aware of the constraints in the opportunity structure, for others and for themselves, and some wished that they had done better. Nonetheless, the overwhelming optimism expressed by the first-generation parents and their children was striking and well aligned with the cultural power of the American Dream. In feeling that they had participated in the American Dream, which hinges on the idea that "everyone may participate," the immigrant families were becoming American (Hochschild 1995). The majority of Americans, including the poor, do not believe that social class or family background matters in who gets ahead in the United States, despite evidence that the American Dream has been and remains a contested concept (Newman 1988/1999; Hochschild 1995; Lareau 2008). Intergenerational mobility is not universal, especially for individuals from modest family origins.[11] Owing to discrimination in the labor market and other domains, black Americans have had a long history of exclusion from the promise of the American Dream (Lieberson 1980; Hochschild 1995). Even after the removal of legally inscribed barriers to mobility in the wake of the civil rights movement, the chances of mobility for black children who grow up in poverty are still lower than for their white counterparts.[12]

To sum up, the interviews revealed that immigrant families, who made varying material gains in the immigrant journey, nonetheless came to conceptualize the United States and frame the success of their journeys in very similar ways. As all the parents noted (whether to us or to their children), mobility was more than a matter of wages or a family's standard of living, important as those were; the chance to live in a nation where the succession of political leaders was orderly and assured and the currency stayed within a bounded valuation range represented another kind of mobility in and of itself, one that was not easily quantified (Hochschild 1992; Sawhill 2007). The immigrant families believed that more than most nations, including their home countries, the United States offered more everyday security and a greater possibility for advancement, along with greater social and political freedoms, and that counted for a lot. Certainly, there was the universal expectation, strongly felt, that the children would not face the economic challenges of their parents, whether short or long term. Since they had been born and/or raised in the United States, the children could actualize the promise of possibility here, and a key way of doing that was thought to be through education. Although this expectation was more pronounced among parents who had not done as well as they would have liked, all parents held on to it.

What these accounts have shown is that our understandings of immigrant mobility should include both economic and non-economic dimensions. In the latter dimension, it is important to understand how immigrants themselves make sense of their mobility paths in the United States, especially nuances of social standing and the related rewards from a dual-nation perspective; it is precisely such nuances that are not always well tapped in analyses that use "objective measures of socioeconomic position" (Nicklett and Burgard 2009, 10).

The accounts of the immigrant journey have so far pointed to a picture of relative optimism tempered by the crucial vicissitudes faced by some of the families. However, only one part of the immigrant journey can be understood in terms of immigrants' belief in the American Dream and their relief from having escaped the strictures that blocked mobility in their country of origin. The story of immigrant Americanization, as Gary Gerstle (2000) has written, is at once about *both* emancipation and coercion. As we shall see in the next chapter, the families in our study perceived a status decline that came from being an immigrant and thus, on some level, foreign and unwelcome in the United States, and they believed that this decline was more especially felt by Latinos. This belief in immigrant marginalization is the other equally powerful part of how immigrants themselves understand the immigrant journey and frame the immigrant bargain.

Chapter 3

Being an Immigrant: Alone in America

> Imagine it—I was all by myself, I was struggling on my own and making all the decisions alone.
>
> —Gina, fifty-one-year-old urban Dominican mother

> We have lived in a foreign country. [My children] haven't had a family. I mean, we go during the holidays, but it's not like a family in moments of crisis, do you understand? You can't say, "I quarreled, so I'm going to my grandmother's." We have lived on our own, lonely, that kills me.
>
> —Ines, forty-two-year-old suburban Colombian mother

THE PARENTS in our study experienced bifurcated immigrant incorporation—they were optimistic about their mobility regardless of their actual economic gains or losses. And they shared an abiding faith in the American Dream and the promise that the next generation would achieve what had remained out of the parents' reach. Yet they were also pessimistic about their assimilation. As the parents learned who they were in the United States, they grew to understand that regardless of how they felt or how much success they had, they would never be accepted by others as American.

The immigrant parents conceived of mainstream American culture as narrower than it really is, for example, as embodied by white, middle-class, and native-born individuals—indeed, as embodied by several generations of such individuals in the United States. It was through this lens that they believed Americans saw *them* as not being American. According to the parents, they were seen as immigrants and thus as foreign, not American. The bifurcated incorporation of the parents in our study differs from the more positive parental accounts of other studies (Portes and Rumbaut 2001). Because our dual-generation approach compares how the children and the parents *each* understood the immigrant journey, for themselves and for the other, we are able to draw a finer-grained picture that includes both the parents' optimism about their mobility (and their children's) and their pessimism about their assimilation.

Even middle-class parents, who would appear to be quite assimilated, shared this pessimism. The parents' pessimism about their own assimilation is important to understand because it is central to the immigrant bargain: children feel the need to make up for their parents' sacrifices by achieving academic success.

To understand this pessimism, we need to know more about what it is like to be an immigrant alone in America, never quite fitting in or even knowing how to belong. Let us turn to Gina's and Ines's accounts. Gina felt alone and without adequate supports even though she had family in the United States; lived in largely Puerto Rican and Dominican immigrant communities in New York and the greater Boston area; and worked with Dominicans, first in the factory and later in the hospital among the nurse's assistants. Ines had no family nearby and lived and worked as a professional among native white Americans in the greater New York area and Miami. She was married to a native white American, although she felt that she could not turn to him for support when she was facing the psychological challenges of being an immigrant. Despite their very different modes of incorporation, these two women both felt isolated in America, particularly from native white, middle-class America—in Gina's case by virtue of social class, and for both women by virtue of social and cultural differences. Nor did they believe that this lack of acceptance would change, at least not for them. Gina lived and toiled in working-class coethnic and panethnic contexts and rarely had firsthand knowledge of other American contexts, and what she did know certainly did not seem promising. Even though Ines's daily life was deeply embedded among middle-class whites, she did not think that she was American or that she could ever be accepted as American.

In contrast to the dominant melting pot metaphor, which describes immigrants as having the chance to melt into mainstream American culture despite being culturally different (Deaux 2006), the families we interviewed believed that certain key cultural distinctions would be difficult to overcome, at least for the first generation. Although the immigrant parents believed that they could participate in the American Dream, they still did not feel themselves to be a part of America—and not by their own choice but rather because of the constrained choices available to them. Immigrant pessimism about assimilation is derived from the parents' perceived lack of competency about knowing who they are in the United States and how others see them. Since the parents were not native English speakers—and their proficiency varied (Deaux 2000; Jiménez 2011)—they could not grasp the meanings of many American cultural norms and were especially uncomfortable with the American racial and ethnic classification system, which typically did not match up with how they viewed themselves. Instead, they were classified by others as Hispanic or Latino, labels associated with negative stereotypes (Falicov

2002; Deaux 2006; Massey and Sanchez R. 2010). By all such indicators, the immigrant parents felt themselves to be marked as foreign and thus felt stigmatized as they interacted with their environment. Their accounts, which give us a sense of how they produced meanings from the social conditions in which they lived, point to a shared immigrant cultural identity of foreignness and stigma (Lamont and Small 2008).

There were class distinctions, however, in how this immigrant cultural identity was experienced in the immigrants' different workplace and neighborhood contexts (Deaux 2006). Our comparison of the Colombians and Dominicans also reveals ethnic-class distinctions, mainly because the Colombians were less residentially segregated. Nineteen of the Colombians, or more than half, reported growing up in mostly white areas, whether in suburbia or urban areas, some with a "suburban feel" to them. By contrast, only six Dominicans reported the same, and of those, three lived in the mostly white pockets of a predominantly Latino urban area. The working-class, urban Colombians still tended to live in more integrated areas with less poverty and crime than did their Dominican counterparts. Thus, the Colombians and Dominicans of the same class background did not always have the same experiences with immigrant cultural identity, given the demographic differences in where they lived.

Meanwhile, the experiences of the middle-class Colombian parents warn us not to rely exclusively on traditional indicators of assimilation. On such indicators, they were mostly quite assimilated—socioeconomically, residentially, and linguistically—yet they nonetheless wrestled with immigrant pessimism *about* their assimilation (Louie 2004). What is interesting is that although the parents felt that all Latinos were stigmatized, some—especially those who were better off—did not necessarily feel solidarity with other Latinos. Rather, they spoke of certain Latino groups being inferior and more deserving than others of the negative stereotypes attributed to all Latinos (Tajfel and Turner 1985; Perreira, Chapman, and Stein 2006).

A final point about length of residence. I look at what it means to be an immigrant eight or more years after arrival in the United States and after the achievement of a measure of economic and social stability. When we spoke with the parents, the initial disorientation around geography, language, and culture was a thing of the past. Social isolation and cultural alienation, however, remained very much a part of their lives (Mirdal 2006). The parents' perception of still feeling like foreigners was not just about having lost their old identity but also about feeling unaccepted in the United States and pessimistic about the possibility of ever being accepted. A symbolic boundary separated immigrants and Americans, and it was especially resonant for Latino immigrants (Lamont and Small 2008; Cornell and Hartmann 1998; Massey and Sanchez R. 2010). The immigrant parents perceived a "bright" immigrant and ethnic boundary, and they knew "at all times which side of the boundary they [were] on" (Alba 2005, 22).[1]

Immigrant Identity: We Have Been Alone

Language

While English is not the official national language of the United States, it is nonetheless part and parcel of the American identity. Although we did not directly ask about the parents' English-language skills, we asked the children about the language used in the home, whether their parents preferred that a specific language be used, and if so, why. According to the children's surveys, most of the parents used Spanish to communicate with their children, the remainder did sometimes, and most of the children also spoke in Spanish with their parents. These patterns were due to both preference and ability. The parents preferred to use Spanish in the home (while fully expecting their children to learn and use English outside the home) because of their own comfort level with Spanish and their ability levels in English. It is interesting that even children whose parents were fluent in English reported this pattern.

We should not think that the families placed little value on English: they knew that English-language proficiency would help members of their family more fully realize the American Dream and feel more accepted. That said, there were also clear challenges for the parents in learning English. Unlike barriers like financial resources or education, which native-born Americans might also face, language was seen as a challenge specific to being an immigrant. It was thought to be more difficult for an older newcomer to learn a second language as compared to the 1.5 and second generations, a perception supported by research showing the importance of age of arrival and nativity status in English-language proficiency (Jia 2007; Rumbaut 2004). It was also argued that adult English-language learners faced scarce educational opportunities. Although the parents were motivated to learn English, and in some cases had even taken classes, they were held back by the difficulty of working classes into their work and child care schedules.[2] It was also difficult to build from basic ESL classes to more advanced competencies (Tucker 2006, 1).

Finally, the stakes around English-language acquisition were very high, because without it social mobility was thought to be limited (Louie 2004). Most of the children expressed this view, saying that immigrants could be kept out of higher-paying segments of the labor market and precluded from occupational mobility within a particular segment (McManus 1985; Stolzenberg 1990; Chiswick 1991; Davila and Mora 2001; Portes and Rumbaut 2001; Boston Foundation 2011).[3] To fully realize the payoff to English fluency, according to my respondents, one had to speak the language without a discernible accent, a less likely prospect for adult second-language learners.[4] Sally said that her Colombian mother was "humiliated" by the way her accent limited her employment opportunities in secretarial assistance and data entry, fields in which she had already worked in Colombia (Sato 1991; Derwing 2003; Moyer 2007). Said Sally: "It's very clear to people that she's not native. And I think that makes it also very challenging to find a job, even in New York, where no one's native."

Some parents and children acknowledged that it might be reasonable for employers to expect such highly developed linguistic skills. Billy, a U.S.-born Dominican working in the greater Boston area, highlighted the concrete ways in which speaking accented English could serve as a problem in the sales field. He told Silvia Covelli, our Colombian interviewer, that native-born American customers would have an easier time comprehending him than someone who spoke accented English: "They understand me the first time I say something. Because some people are Dominicans and have the heavy accent and the customers will say, 'Say that again. Say that again.' You can't hear [the accent] because you're Hispanic but Americans can."

It is worth noting that the respondents' keen awareness of accent might actually have to do with their perceived lack of voice as immigrants. In other words, their worries about speaking accented English might be a proxy for their deeper sense of not being accepted in the United States, another trade-off of the immigrant journey (Suárez-Orozco, Suárez-Orozco, and Todorova 2008). The respondents mostly described the linguistic power relations between immigrants and native speakers as marginalizing immigrants (Peirce 1995, 12). Social interactions highlighted the vulnerability of the immigrant parents, whether they spoke little English, some, or a great deal, and/or with a perceived accent. Calida's Mexican father told her stories of working with white Americans who assumed that he could not speak English. Sometimes, before he could correct this impression, his coworkers had already ignored him, tried to take advantage of him, or insulted him. Calida said, "Since he works with a lot of Caucasian people, they'll kind of look down on him, but once he opens his mouth and you know he's a strong man, so he's not going to let someone let him feel smaller than anybody else."

Nor were immigrants with greater facility in English exempt from such power dynamics, albeit in a different form. This theme is evident in the accounts of two mothers who, while relatively skilled in English and living in white, well-to-do suburban communities, nonetheless felt anxious when speaking English. Alegria was a high school graduate in Colombia and in seven months of English and math classes at a greater Boston college learned enough English to get a bank job through a family connection. However, she asked not to do sales, preferring tasks that relied on her math and reading skills, such as coding checks and counting money in the currency department. At the start, she had to read documents several times to ensure that she had correctly grasped the meaning. However, it was speaking that really proved disquieting. Alegria recalled some occasional anxious moments with native-born American coworkers who were impatient with her and struggling to stay on an equal footing in their exchanges.

> Because we cannot speak English fast or get confused, they think we do not understand. That has happened to me at my work. Because a person knows English or can speak it at full speed or they can respond faster, it does not mean that I did not understand. I can say it slower if they give me time. I can say the same thing.

For a brief while, her husband was doing so well that she did not have to work outside the home. But after her husband's unexpected death, Alegria went back to the bank. Because of her strong interpersonal skills, she was tapped to work with customers, but although she had been in the United States for nearly nineteen years, she was initially apprehensive because of her English. This time, however, she drew support from her coworkers, many of whom were immigrants like herself for whom English was a second language; hailing from Cambodia and Brazil, they had banded together to help one another.

Ines, a university graduate in Colombia, took English-language and graduate-level courses in the United States, was married to a white American, and lived in upscale, white communities. Yet in reporting on her anxieties with English, she spoke about her literal lack of voice (Peirce 1995). She chose to pursue computer programming because verbal communication is not an issue in that field, and in multiple contexts she chose to be silent even when she understood what was going on and had something to say.

> I would have liked to work on something else, but in programming you don't have to talk to anybody. You just have to understand what people want and do it. They drew or showed me more or less what they wanted, and I did it. It frightens me to speak English in public because I don't want to make mistakes. I make mistakes in English. I understand and speak, but I make mistakes. I don't speak perfectly, so it's a pity. So I try to speak as less as possible.

These mothers' narratives underscore that after a long time in the United States—thirty-one years for Alegria and thirteen years for Ines—they still thought of themselves as "illegitimate speakers of English" (Peirce 1995).[5] Although they were among the more privileged parents in the overall sample, including in linguistic assimilation, their experiences highlight how language negatively defined their lives and structured their identities (Suárez-Orozco and Suárez-Orozco 2001). Both struggled with the loss of their linguistic competence and their belief that only "perfect" English speakers are truly accepted as American.

Beyond language, there was the matter of cultural belonging. While the two are linked, they are not one and the same. A few respondents noted that even immigrants who were proficient or fluent in English could not grasp the meaning of mainstream cultural nuances, since they had not grown up here and thus still felt a lack of competence (Louie 2006b). Although speaking English is definitely crucial to an immigrant's adaptation, linguistic skills alone do not make an immigrant feel American. Such themes were evident in Peggy's efforts to understand her father's downward occupational trajectory in the United States, which she witnessed with great distress (Gans 2009). Peggy's father, a university graduate in the Dominican Republic, had served as director of health there before political turmoil and economic instability resulted in the loss of his job and much of the family's savings. To cut their losses, the family migrated to the United States. For about fifteen years, Peggy's father worked as an engineer at a top defense and aerospace systems supplier before getting laid off; after spending a long time looking for work, he finally landed a position as a security guard. His friends back in the Dominican Republic who had successfully weathered the period of national instability were in prominent positions—in stark contrast to his own downward slide.

To account for her father's steep decline in occupational status, Peggy mentioned phenotype (he was dark-skinned), language (he spoke English with a strong accent), and age (he was already in his fifties). In addition, in her view, her father was disadvantaged because he did not know the culture well enough *despite* knowing English. Peggy could understand that age discrimination affects "regular white people" as well, but she believed that language and cultural barriers are added disadvantages for immigrants. Conceptions of language as a marker of not belonging were shaped by the very exchanges that immigrants had with native English speakers. In these exchanges, Dominican and Colombian immigrants felt excluded from full acceptance as English speakers, just as they felt excluded from certain cultural norms that are learned through growing up in the United States (Norton 1997, 423; Louie 2004, 2006b).

The parents' sense of who they were in the United States was also complicated by the ways in which language and race are linked here. This was especially the case for those parents who tended to be identified by others as black or white American on the basis of their skin color, hair texture, and hair color. According to the children and parents we interviewed, such physical characteristics are a necessary but insufficient condition of being black or white American: one also has to be a native English speaker from a non-immigrant family background. So even though many of the Dominicans had African ancestry and could be classified as African American by that criterion, the fact that they were foreign-born and/or native Spanish speakers excluded them from being seen as black American (Davis 1971; Bailey 2002). Some of the lighter 1.5- and second-generation children and their parents found themselves in a similar situation.[6] These children were often phenotypically and linguistically identified as white American by others, but not on the basis of family background: their immigrant parents could not linguistically "pass" as white. This contradiction was made clear when Sara, a U.S.-born Colombian, described her mother as someone who was "white, white," but who could never be seen as white in the United States: "Nobody ever knows my mom is Hispanic. Except, once she opens her mouth, you hear her accent."

Skin Color, Race, and Ethnicity

This conflation of language and race was only one of several "traumatic racial experiences" for the first-generation parents—like both earlier and contemporary waves of immigrants, they needed to understand and locate themselves in the alien racial hierarchy of the United States (Alba and Nee 2003). As with mobility, these identity experiences were influenced by the immigrants' dual frame of reference. The parents found that their home country labels did not apply in the United States. Their difficulties with this experience evoke the dialectic between the internal and external components of identity, namely, how identity construction depends in part "on the kinds of person available in one's society" (Appiah 2001, 326). These experiences were complicated by the fact that "raza" in contemporary Spanish does not have the same meaning as "race" in English. Rather, "raza" also connotes feelings of a common culture and belonging (Kaminsky 1994).

To understand the difficulties faced by the immigrant parents, we need to map the home country contexts and how they were similar to or different from that of the United States. Although racial mixing among Europeans, blacks, and Indians occurred in both the Dominican Republic and Colombia, blacks were systemically marginalized in conceptions of national identity (Green 2000; Candelario 2007; Roth 2008). Trujillo tried to set the Dominican Republic apart from Spain, Haiti, and the United States (all would-be colonizers) by highlighting the Spanish and Native American (Taino) aspects of the nation's demographics and denying its African ancestry (Bailey 2002). The Dominican Republic does not acknowledge blacks as a significant racial category within the nation unless they are foreign; Haitians are black and seen by Dominicans as subordinate, wild, and alien. Dominicans are seen as mostly a mix of white and Indian descent—an ideological view that runs counter to the nation's historical and demographic record: the Spanish conquest and illnesses brought over by Europeans drastically reduced the Taino Indian population; indeed, some would argue that it was virtually decimated (Duany 1998).

In Colombia, blacks are more readily acknowledged as a substantial native racial category; areas such as Choco are thought of as majority black and mulatto and Antioquia is perceived as majority white (Wade 1993). Yet the history of Colombian nation-building also privileged whiteness and marginalized the Indian and black populations (Green 2000). Afro-Colombians were seen as ugly, backward, and animalistic, sometimes even by Afro-Colombians themselves (Streicker 1995; Green 2000; Rodriguez 2001). Within this racial ideology, it is logical that Choco is largely poor and undeveloped while Antioquia is economically thriving (Wade 1993).

Both nations differ from the United States in that they offer intermediary racial categories between black and white in a color-calibrated "continuum" (Wade 1993, 233; Duany 1998; Itzigsohn and Dore-Cabral 2000; Candelario 2007). This racial classification system was evident among the immigrant parents when we asked them how they would describe their skin color in the homeland. Dominican parents referred to themselves as white, mestizo/a, Indian, Triguena, or "marilla jabao" (yellow), the last three terms falling under their home country's white-mulatto or mulatto racial categories (Candelario 2007). Colombian parents also reported being white along with the intermediate categories of Triguena, "morena" (olive), medium, and olive-cinnamon-colored.

Leaving behind such relatively fluid systems, the immigrant parents encountered the apparently unambiguous American racial ideology—there are only whites and blacks, and one cannot be the other. Racial mixing, of course, occurs in the United States, but theoretically at least it does not threaten the white-black dichotomy because anyone with black ancestry is classified as black (Davis 1971). There is a clear American "black-white division" (Wade 1993, 233). Historically, immigrants to the United States have had a contentious relationship with this black-white color line. In contrast to non-Europeans, the European newcomers were always legally regarded as white (Foner and Fredrickson 2004), but exactly when they and their descendants became socially and culturally accepted as white has been debated.[7] Writing in 1899, W. E. B. DuBois noted that most immigrant groups were eventually accepted as citizens by Americans, while blacks continued to be denied access to the rights to which they were entitled: "We grant full citizenship to the Anglo Saxon, the Teuton, and the Latin, then with just a shade of reluctance, we extend it to the Celt and the Slav. We half-deny it to the yellow races of Asia,

Table 3.1 Self-Reported Parental Phenotype Categories—Dominicans

Phenotype in the Dominican Republic	Phenotype in the United States
White	White, Indian,[a] brown[a]
Mestiza/o	Mestiza/o,[a] black
Triguena/Indian	Triguena/Indian[a]
Indian	Indian, indigenous,[a] black
Marilla jabao (yellow)	Does not know

Source: Author's compilation based on data from the Dominican and Colombian Immigrant Family Study (2009).
[a]A category not commonly used in the United States.

admit the brown Indians; but with the Negroes of Africa, we come to a full stop" (DuBois 1899/1996, 387). For many newcomers arriving in the midnineteenth century and into the early twentieth century, the process of becoming accepted as American meant acceptance of the black-white color line and active resistance to being identified—and stigmatized—as black (Lee and Bean 2010). Especially now in the post-1960s period of immigration, this social distancing from African Americans continues, particularly among black and Latino immigrants, who learn to contrast their work ethic and optimism with the supposed lack of the same among native black minorities (Waters 1999; Perreira, Chapman, and Stein 2006; Smith 2006; Vickerman 2007). Yet like their predecessors, the post-1960s immigrants can find it challenging to situate themselves in the nation's racial and ethnic classification system.

Our interviews gave parents the chance to offer their interpretation of what it was like to encounter the American racial classification system and to express how they would like to be seen. Tables 3.1 and 3.2 show the complex range of answers that parents gave when asked to describe their skin color in the country of origin compared to the United States. Only three of the thirteen Dominican parents said that they were white in the United States. Six reported a change, mainly from being white in the Dominican Republic to a darker phenotype here (such as Indian or brown), or from Indian-mestizo to black. The Colombian parents, meanwhile, were nearly twice as likely to identify as white here: eight of the eighteen respondents did so. The Colombian parents were also less likely to report a change in how they identified their skin color with migration; only six did so, and of these, two lightened, going from morena to white in the United States, and two darkened, from white and chestnut to Indian and black here, respectively.

Thirteen parents said that they were neither black nor white in the United States, a response consistent with what Robert C. Smith (1994; 2006, 35) has called doubly bounded solidarity—"bounded on one side

Table 3.2 Self-Reported Parental Phenotype Categories—Colombians

Phenotype in Colombia	Phenotype in the United States
White	White, Indian/indigenous[a]
Triguena (brunette/light brown/café latte), Triguena/Morenita (wheat/tanned)	Brown[a] or white, Spanish, don't know, Triguena[a]
Morena (olive)	Hispanic or white
Castano (chestnut)	Black
Medium	Medium
Olive-cinnamon-colored	Olive-cinnamon-colored

Source: Author's compilation based on data from the Dominican and Colombian Immigrant Family Study (2009).
[a]A category not commonly used in the United States.

by not being white and on the other by not being Black." Rather, they tended to report an American skin color that did not popularly exist, such as brown, medium, or Indian, thus borrowing from homeland conceptions (Mahalingam 2006). The following responses speak to the theme of doubly bounded solidarity and highlight the ways in which the parents employed home country categories to frame their discussions of U.S.-based labels and the disjuncture between the two.

> Marissa's mother, who said she was Indian here: "Since my family was light-skinned, I never identified as black."
>
> Isabel's mother, who said she was brown here (in the process, painting an idealized picture of the Dominican Republic as having no color distinctions): "No, because in my country this doesn't matter that much. We learn about skin colors here in the U.S. Here they pay a lot of attention to that."
>
> Elias's mother, who said she was Triguena/Indian here (upholding the Dominican Republic's mythology that its population is largely a mix of European whites and Taino Indians): "No. Because in my country the white is white, the black is black, and those in the middle like myself are Indian or 'mestizo.'"
>
> Shirley's mother, who said she was indigenous in the United States: [*Why not white?*] "Because I am not tall, and I do not have blue eyes. My father is Indian, very indigenous. My mother is tall and had brothers who are blond, but I think we are very indigenous."

It is worth noting that the mothers of Marissa, Isabel, and Shirley all said that they were white in their country of origin. Shirley's mother, the only Colombian represented in this cluster, believed that the white racial category was not an option for her because it was far narrower in scope in the United States, with American whites understood to have blue eyes and to be tall.

Even a few of the parents who chose black or white were clear that they did so by default. The tendency among this small number of cases was for the Dominicans to choose black and for the Colombians to select white, even though each group believed that the labels did not adequately capture who they were. Angel's mother, who said she was Indian in the Dominican Republic, told the interviewer, "I think, for the United States, I am black because I am not white. Here there aren't middle grounds, because you are one or the other, so I think I would be black, what do you think?" Although she never saw herself as white or black in the United States, Angel's mother said that if pressed—for example, in filling out a form—she would choose black. Judy's mother, who said she was Triguena and morena in Colombia, felt that a similar set of dynamics would persuade her to choose white:

> I would definitely have to discard "black." If the word "brown" does not exist, then I have to put "white," because there is nothing else to do, because black is not an option for me. Because black refers to the black race, and I am not from the black race. My race is a mixture of white and Indian, so I have no Afro genes.

Overall, many of the parents said that they were neither white nor black, or they chose one of the two as a default category. Regardless of the labels chosen (or not chosen) by the parents, the interviews underscored that for a substantial number of them the underlying processes around choosing a racial classification in the United States signaled a thoughtful resistance to the American racial system, followed in some cases by resigned acquiescence. It was certainly difficult for the parents to believe themselves to be part of the American racial system, given that it did not leave room for their interpretations.

The panethnic terms "Latino," "Hispanic," and "Latin American" were relevant categories for many of the parents, though typically secondary after national origins (Jensen et al. 2006; Passel and Taylor 2009). Several themes emerged from these accounts. Unlike conceptions of race, the parents found panethnicity to be less alienating and to correspond better to how they saw themselves. Panethnicity signaled an identity based in a common language (Spanish) or a common region of origin (Latin America). For a few parents, the national and regional aspects of their identities were fused and thus inseparable. These immigrants deployed the linguistic and geographic logics employed by Americans "to define the boundaries of Hispanic/Latino panethnicity in the United States" (Marrow 2003, 432); it is unclear, however, whether the parents brought such logics with them or absorbed them in the United States, or whether there was a combination of both processes. Finally, a few parents did express confusion about the differences between the terms "Hispanic" and "Latino."[8] The concern voiced by these respondents was that "Hispanic" is associated with Spain, which they felt is too narrow and denies Latin America's multifaceted cultural history, including that of its indigenous populations (Fears 2003; Diaz 2004).

Some parents recast American panethnic and ethnic terms—"Latino," "Hispanic," "Colombian," "Dominican," "Spanish"—as intermediate racial categories to describe themselves (rather than draw on familiar homeland ones).[9] Nearly all of them also said that they were neither white nor black, or that if they chose one of these labels, they did so by default. These parents turned to "Hispanic," "Dominican," or "Colombian" as racial labels because they thought that they did not fit the traditional U.S. bimodal racial typology (Itzigsohn and Dore-Cabral 2000; Jensen et al. 2006).[10] Angel's mother, who was Dominican, provided the fullest elaboration of why this "other race" was a necessary classification. In her view, the physical diversity among Hispanics due to a history of intermixing was far too complex to be accommodated by the metric of American racial categories. As she told Silvia Covelli, who had light brown hair and pale skin:

> I think the world has a general idea that Hispanics are not black or white. My youngest son is like you and has green eyes because my dad was white with green eyes and my mom was Indian, so we are a mix. My sister is completely like you. My brother is Indian like me. For us, our skin color is called "Indian," but I don't think it is Indian for the Americans because when they hear that word they think of [Native Americans].

The findings presented here coincide with what Nancy Foner (2000, 156) documents in the New York City context; quoting George Fox (1996, 33), she points out that the term "Hispanic" "generally means someone who is 'too dark to be white, too light to be black, and who has no easily identifiable Asian traits.'" In sum, some immigrant parents made sense of how they were distinct from black and white Americans by thinking of "Latino" as having a skin color between black and white, speaking Spanish, and coming from Latin America or the Caribbean, while a few others further thought of Latino as a separate race.

Nevertheless, the following reflection by Jorge's mother highlights how complicated it could be for parents to figure out what they meant by "Latino" and how it differed from "Hispanic," much less what the American classification system said about the distinction. While Jorge's mother had managed to replicate much of the privileged lifestyle that she enjoyed in Colombia, where she was considered white, she could not replicate her racial privilege in the United States. Exclusion from the white American category was especially challenging for some of the high replicators. While emphatically declaring, "I am whiter than many here who say they are white," Jorge's mother said that white Americans did not accept her as one of them (Deaux 2006). Most Americans she knew did not share her belief that Latinos can be of any race (even though this is consistent with the U.S. census classifications).[11] She further understood "Hispanic" to be a marker of a common language, Spanish, similar to Italian. If Italian Americans were considered white in the United States, why were not Hispanics? This was how Jorge's mother learned that American cultural norms racialize Hispanics as nonwhite and leave no space for how she actually viewed herself:

> I wrote down "white" [on a form] because to that day I didn't know I was Hispanic. A man who worked with me, of Italian origin but an American citizen, told me, "You aren't white, you are Hispanic." I told him I wasn't, that I spoke Spanish. I held his arm and I told him, "I am whiter than you—you are darker, more black than I am." And I asked him why he was white, and he answered that he was white because he was Italian. Hispanic is a language. Hispanic is not a race, it's a wrong use of the word. . . . I really hate writing "Hispanic" [on forms].

The findings presented so far demonstrate that answers to survey and census questions about race and ethnicity can be misleading or overly simplified. For instance, 48 percent of Hispanics chose to identify as white in the 2000 census (Tafoya 2004); however, a limitation of such data is that they do not provide a nuanced sense of the meaning of that identification (or others) to Hispanics, especially the first and second generations. Just as important as what race Hispanics say they are (for example, the box they check) is how they arrived at that decision. Qualitative methods, like the ones used in this study, can help elucidate these processes. Certainly, the responses of the parents we interviewed shed light on their use of a dual frame of reference to answer a survey question about race and on how the survey answer left uncaptured what they really meant (Chan 2006).

"They Always Call Me Hispanic"

Regardless of how the parents self-identified and why, one of the migratory lessons that stayed with them was that mainstream America views them as Latino or Hispanic. The dominant definition of Latino or Hispanic was understood to have negative connotations, quite different from the more neutral ways in which the parents themselves understood such identifications (Falicov 2002; Rumbaut 2009; Massey and Sanchez R. 2010). Thus, despite the common experiences accompanying migration, both the children and parents pointed out that there was particular stigma attached to being a Latino immigrant (Suárez-Orozco and Suárez-Orozco 2001; Deaux 2006). Alexsa, a U.S.-born Dominican, discussed negative media portrayals of Latinos, which she said tended to aggregate all ethnicities into one murky, deviant "brown" category (Liberato et al. 2009):

> If you are portrayed on television as being a drunk or like somebody who cheats on their wife, or a drug dealer, people are going to look at you and indirectly they're going to stereotype you. They're going to say, "Oh, a Spanish person." And even if they don't say it, but of course in their minds they're going to be like, *Drug dealer, alcoholic, lazy person, somebody who's on welfare.*

Along with the black poor, contemporary immigrants, at least those from economically disadvantaged backgrounds, are blamed for a host of social ills, from rising crime rates to depleted public resources, particularly the welfare system. But while nativist and racial discourses clearly intersect, the former invokes a distinct "fear of foreignness" (Sanchez 1997, 1018).

However, the children's perceptions of Americans' negative view of immigrants, and especially Latinos, were somewhat at odds with how Americans actually view these groups. It is true that immigration has at times spurred mainstream fears of newcomers as a strain on American resources, such as jobs and housing; as a catalyst for rising crime rates; and, in the case of some groups, as bearers of inferior cultures incompatible with American norms (Jaret 1999; Simon and Lynch 1999; Menjívar and Bejarano 2004; Ochoa 2004; Deaux 2006; Kohut et al. 2006; Chavez 2008; Massey and Sanchez R. 2010).[12] Still, while Americans have been increasingly worried that immigrants are an economic burden (52 percent in 2006 compared to 38 percent in 2000), their view of Latinos has grown more positive over time. Latinos have been seen as less likely to collect welfare and increase crime than in the past (Kohut et al. 2006). To the children and parents we interviewed, however, there was little distinction between negative views of immigrants and negative views of Latino immigrants in particular; the two tended to blur together. A small number of the children and parents we interviewed explicitly elaborated on the similar challenges around being seen as foreign and marginalized faced by immigrants of other national origins, not only Latinos.

For some families, the parents' immigrant optimism, especially their faith in the American Dream, was combined with immigrant pessimism about the specter of discrimination (Devos, Gavin, and Quintana 2010). Half of the children said that their parents told them that being Dominican or Colombian would limit how far they could go in life or that unlike white Americans they could not afford to slip up or fail and still expect to get ahead. These children were often charged by their immigrant parents to overcome discrimination and thus to disprove negative stereotypes about Latinos (Perreira, Chapman, and Stein 2006). The children were told that they would have the advantages of cultural familiarity and English-language proficiency, not to mention the educational skills, to have a clearer path to success (Portes and Rumbaut 2001). The children could not be seen as foreign and thus would avoid—or would at least have a fighting chance against—the disadvantages faced by the first generation. Such themes were evident in Rafael's recollection of his Dominican parents' framing of the American opportunity structure and its potential obstacles:

> My parents always said that you have to always watch out for white people. They try to take advantage. They try to make the Spanish guy work and then take the credit for it. You know? They always said, they always said, never to think that you can't do something because you're Spanish. You can do whatever you want. You were born here. They just said, make sure you work hard. Because a lot of people think that Spanish people are lazy or Spanish people can't do something. So they said, just work to prove them wrong and be successful so you can stand up and say, "Hey I did it."

The parental interviews lent additional support to this interpretation. Most of the parents reported that discrimination existed against their national-origin group and/or Latinos. Like the children, the parents framed discrimination as an immigrant phenomenon, but one that was more pronounced for Latinos. The prevailing theme was that Latinos are thought of as ignorant drug dealers (especially in the case of Colombians) or general criminals and are consigned to inferior jobs or not promoted as readily as non-Latinos (Chavez 2008; Maldonado 2009). Discrimination was a part of the cultural and social milieu that most parents inhabited, including those who had not personally experienced intergroup bias, owing to their limited contact with non-Latinos; even they said that they saw Latinos being framed as criminals in the media (Chavez 2008) and had heard of friends and relatives who had experienced difficulties getting a job or an apartment because they were Latino (Massey 2007). The following account provided by Thomas's mother speaks to this theme. A joyous family occasion marking the parents' legal residency in the United States instead became a cause for denigration and was symbolic of her lack of voice as an immigrant. A simple misunderstanding about a Colombian tradition that had allowed her to keep her natal surname devolved into a referendum on supposed Latino inferiority:

> The woman from immigration insulted us—she said I was "stupid" and "ignorant." Remember that when one comes, they come with their traditions. So when I came, I used my father's last name. Usually one uses both

> last names. She would ask me, "What is your last name?" and I would reply, "Sanchez." Then she asked me for my husband's last name, and I replied, "Gomez." "What is your husband's name?" she asked again, and I replied, "Andres Gomez." With the little English that I understood, I remember her turning to another female officer, and she said, "Hispanic people are stupid, they don't understand anything." She then erased all of my information and wrote down my husband's last name. So then my last name became Gomez.

Such disparagement could be especially painful for the families who had experienced downward social mobility in the United States, as it only compounded their decline in status (Gans 2009). These members of the lower, middle, and upper-middle classes in their country of origin found themselves transformed by immigration into both manual laborers with lower standards of living and mainstream objects of scorn. In contrast to the high replicators, who were able to reproduce their economic status and could draw on their American occupational prestige and standard of living as buffers against a stigmatized, immigrant, Latino identity, the downwardly mobile lacked such supports.

The poignant advice that Jose's mother Ingrid shared with Claudia Pineda, the Harvard doctoral student interviewer, is an example of the kind of exhortation that half the children reported hearing from their parents—namely, to disprove the stereotypes about Latinos. Since José was a Brown University undergraduate, his mother viewed Claudia and her son as kindred "Ivy League" souls coping with similar dilemmas: "Hispanics like you face a lot of struggle. It is not easy to get to where you are. But you continue and continue, you have to demonstrate that you are 'berracos' [tough] when it comes to struggle." Declining to discuss the kinds of struggle that she herself had experienced in the United States as a former secretary who was now a factory worker and part-time housecleaner, Ingrid nevertheless had hope for the upward trajectory of all Hispanics, regardless of their level of education, English-language fluency, or occupation:

> That we are a people—and I am not only talking about Colombians—that we are the ones that do the work that people from here do not want and will not do. We are the ones that wash, and in our factory we are the ones that struggle a lot. We are here, and we are getting ahead. I think that if we unite we will be a strong, strong force.

Class Distinctions

Marginalized in the Workplace

This immigrant cultural identity that informed the parents' pessimism about their prospects for assimilation, though strongly tied to being seen as foreign, inferior, and Hispanic, was experienced differently by class. In workplaces where employees were mostly low-skilled, the parents spoke of employers assigning more tasks to Latinos, even if they held the same position as white or black Americans, and putting Latinos in the less desirable jobs. Regardless, Latino workers were expected to keep silent and be happy with whatever treatment they received. Sergio's stepfather, who was blond and blue-eyed and often mistaken for being "gringo" (except for his accented English), spoke of Latinos routinely being placed in the "back of the house," a phrase commonly used in the restaurant industry to refer to employees who do not have much contact with customers. At the golf course restaurant where he had worked for five years, his former supervisor, a Peruvian immigrant, was replaced by a native-born American woman who "did not want Hispanics in [the] front of the house." The stepfather found his hours as a bartender, a front-of-the-house job, cut in half despite his employment contract. He noticed that his fellow American bartenders were not asked to take a reduction in hours. Given two choices by his new supervisor, leave or work in the kitchen as a cook, he chose the latter.

The distinctions that marginalize nonwhite Americans in professional workplaces were viewed as far more subtle and as also involving gender. Let us revisit Catalina, Judy's mother, one of the high replicators described in chapter 2. Despite her success, or perhaps because of it, Catalina said that she had seen firsthand the opportunities that remain closed to skilled immigrants like her—women and native racial and ethnic minorities (Neckerman, Carter, and Lee 1999). An executive at a financial corporation, she noted that workplace discrimination according to race, nativity status, and gender still exists. Her comments speak to what might be called a minority striver analogy, for example, immigrants identifying with the racism that middle-class blacks continue to encounter, despite their success (Zweigenhaft and Domhoff 1991; Lawrence-Lightfoot 1994):

> You begin to see who is on top, you begin to notice an extremely reduced nucleus of people, they are always white males. At the next level, you will find white men and white women. Once in a while you will find a black person. At the next level you will find a few more black men, women, and a few black women, and so forth and so on. Near the bottom you will find a multitude of blacks, Latinos, and Asians and others. Those circles are reducing as you move up, they are becoming more pure, they become cleaner. That is the reality.

According to Catalina, the reasons for the homogeneity among top officers are not difficult to understand. Despite the nation's increasing diversity, a large proportion of the population still does not really understand social difference. Individuals in the upper echelons continue to maintain preferential treatment for themselves and strongly seek a system that will "always open its door to them" and not others. In her words:

> To those that are on the outside, we must figure out how to filter in somehow. I am very clear that we, any person of color that does not belong to that nucleus or to that base, we will never reach the top. We may have a position, but it is an extremely limited position. Someone will always limit you.

As a Hispanic woman, Catalina realized that her opportunities for further advancement were thus limited, despite her credentials, but she said that she resented the situation less than a U.S.-born individual would. Although she did not mention her former husband, a U.S.-born Colombian, her daughter Judy clearly remembered that he had advised the children that "Latinos have to work five times as much as another person" for the same reward, owing to racism. Catalina simply said:

> I think discrimination is absorbed differently between those of us that come from outside and those that were born and raised here. I came here at thirty. I know who I am and where I came from, what my history is, and I know exactly what my purpose is. So I will never aspire to be a great businesswoman for [this firm].

Instead, Catalina focused on the opportunities that she did have in the United States. The dual frame of reference born of being a first-generation immigrant allowed her to compare what she had now to what she had had before rather than to what she *should* have had in the United States (Gans 1992; Kao and Tienda 1995; Waters 1999; Portes and Rumbaut 2001; Suárez-Orozco and Suárez-Orozco 2001). It was in that spirit—aware of and having experienced discrimination in the United States vis-à-vis immigrants, people of color, and women, and yet opting out of the competition, at least at the highest levels, and thus its potential injuries—that Catalina noted, "I never feel sour or discriminated against because, on the contrary, I have been able to do many things here."

Alone in the Neighborhood

There were also differences in how neighborhood context informed the parents' pessimism about assimilation, given how much of where one lives has to do with race, ethnicity, and class. Similar to other immigrant and native-born minority groups living in middle-class suburbia or cities with a "suburban feel," the Colombian families remembered the communities as being safe and having high-quality public schools and well-tended public spaces (Louie 2004). Here again, however, the immigrants and their children were undergoing a variant of the minority striver analogy: even moving to the suburbs or to a luxury city building did not necessarily gain them sufficient distance from racism (Patillo-McCoy 1999; Wilson 2009).[13] Although these families had the financial means to live in quintessentially American middle-class neighborhoods, they found that a sense of belonging was much harder to acquire. Children and parents alike spoke of occasionally being marked as possible thieves by their new neighbors and very often stigmatized for speaking Spanish in public and at home. Carmel's parents, along with a few other Colombian families, were part of a middle-class exodus of Latinos to New Hampshire (Camayd-Freixas, Karush, and Lejter 2006). The parents reported on the envy of their white coworkers and suburban neighbors, who could not understand why the couple was doing so well financially, unless they were selling drugs, and who disparaged Colombia and Latin America as backward places (Guarnizo, Sanchez, and Roach 1999). It was obvious to the couple that the whites making such remarks believed that they were "superior than Hispanics." At the least, the families knew that they were distinct, if only for celebrating popular American holidays with an ethnic flavor. In a small but telling example, Sally recalled that her family observed Christmas in ways both similar to and distinct from the celebrations of her Italian and Irish American neighbors in Long Island: "You know, our presents growing up were always from El Nino Dios (the Baby Jesus) *and* from Santa Claus. We always got both of them, because in Colombia the Baby Jesus always brings you your presents. El Nino Dios."

Let us return to Ines, one of the most economically privileged parents in the sample. When she was still living in Colombia, her parents owned a condominium in Florida, and the family would go once a year to visit. She had also vacationed in San Francisco, New York City, and Boston before migrating to the United States. She had met her first husband, a dentist, while they were taking private flute lessons as teenagers. She had left Colombia after her brother and then her first husband were kidnapped and killed. Here Ines was able to replicate her economic status. She lived with her white American husband and two young Colombian children in a Westchester County suburb of New York City before building a house in an exclusive enclave of Palm Beach, Florida, three minutes from the beach. Ines partly understood her decision to live in mostly white communities as necessary given the association between whiteness and a high-quality neighborhood. Still, she admitted to having negative views of blacks, many of whom, she said, were "uneducated dirty people, they destroy things." Certainly, it was alright for the family to be friendly with more cultured blacks, but they were not suitable dating partners for her children (Waters 1999; Kasinitz et al. 2008). And yet, Ines expressed some ambivalence about distancing herself from blacks: she said that she knew what it was like not to be given a chance by white

Americans, to be discounted without ever being known. Ines knew this because she was an immigrant.

The theme of immigrant isolation due to lack of acceptance by native white Americans punctuated her interview. In Westchester, with her light eyes and what she described as "yellow" skin, not "white, white" skin, and hair dyed lighter than her natural brunette, Ines knew that she could pass for American except when she spoke. Although fluent in English, she had an accent, and she quickly learned that her neighbors did not appreciate having a Colombian in their midst.

> That happened to me at the bus stop in New York. I said, "Hi, good morning," because at the beginning I didn't know the mothers. Once, the third week, everybody smiled at me, then they asked me where I lived. I answered, and they asked me, "Where are you from?" I said the words, "From Colombia," they said, "Okay," and they didn't even say hi to me the following day. They made their own little circle, and I stood there by their side like an idiot.

Yet in the Palm Beach enclave the neighbors, all white Americans, sometimes thought Ines was one of them—or at least it seemed that way when they started engaging her in conversations that she felt had anti-immigration overtones. Or perhaps their remarks stemmed from the fact that Ines's second husband did not speak any Spanish, disliked the language's prevalence in the United States, and openly supported anti-foreign rhetoric (Sanchez 1997). Ines never expressed her differing viewpoints to her neighbors, who nevertheless left her feeling, in the end, that she and her children would always be seen as foreigners.

> You understand, they don't see me as a Hispanic person anymore. But you hear their comments about political asylum, about all the help, all the U.S. benefits. People say, "Why are those grants given to Hispanics or blacks if my children are better or more intelligent students?" I've heard my friends, my neighbors, say this many times, you hear people talking. I don't get involved in those subjects, but if you hear these comments you feel cast aside. I feel I don't belong here completely. We became citizens in '95, when I came here, but I don't feel like that. I love this country very much, but you really feel uncomfortable at times.

Ines's experiences speak to Claire Jean Kim's (2000) concept of American racial ordering as a field structured along at least two axes: superior/inferior and insider/foreigner. Blacks and whites serve as the anchors, with blacks at the bottom, and newcomers are positioned relative to them. Ines wanted to be seen as white (which she learned was not possible) and was sometimes seen (and saw herself) as superior to blacks. Ines learned that she was neither white nor black because whites and blacks were both positioned as insider groups and she, as a foreigner, would always be positioned—and seen—as an outsider.

The urban families had different issues, and again, it bears noting that the Dominicans had a more difficult time with them, since they tended to grow up in more segregated and hardscrabble settings. The urban families were well aware of the effect of residential segregation on working-class Latinos like themselves, and they knew that the only places they could live were with other working-class and poor Latinos in areas that had substantial poverty rates and relatively few institutional resources (Massey 2007). They did not see that living in more integrated settings with more resources was an option. Living with coethnics and panethnics in these kinds of residentially segregated settings brought cultural and linguistic familiarity, but these settings were also subject to certain dangers, from vandalism, car break-ins, and youth idling (loudly) on street corners to, in a more serious vein, abandoned houses, gangs, stabbings, drive-by shootings, rapes, and shootings at parked cars (Sampson, Raudenbush, and Earls 1997; Portes and Rumbaut 2001; Suárez-Orozco and Suárez-Orozco 2001; Stanton-Salazar and Spina 2003). The latter dangers were typically linked to a thriving drug trade that reduced neighbors to selling CDs and stolen car radios for cash to buy drugs and brought strangers to the neighborhood as potential buyers. One-quarter of the Dominican children reported that violence had occurred in the K-12 schools they attended and that they had witnessed or been the victim of nonfamily violence.

The children and parents tended to differ in their responses. The children said that they rarely felt unsafe because they knew who to avoid and how to avoid potentially dangerous situations. Although Angel described the mid-1980s drug trade in Boston's Jamaica Plain as an episode straight out of the TV police series *Miami Vice*, he also said, "There was never a real sense of danger. Man, we knew everybody. I mean, we grew up with everybody." The comfort that parents felt from living in a culturally familiar setting was frequently undercut, however, by the high levels of crime. Their accounts, whether relayed directly or via their children, spoke to the perceived lack of social cohesion, trust, and informal social controls at the neighborhood level (Sampson, Raudenbush, and Earls 1997).[14] Families tried hard to shelter their children from risk factors (Elder et al. 1995; Guilamo-Ramos et al. 2007). One strategy was to stay put in the neighborhood but to decisively mark the boundary for their children. Occasionally, the marking of the boundary was physical: parents literally barricaded their homes behind forbidding gates, fences, and even barbed wire, and those living in apartment buildings would deliberately choose units in the back of the building, away from the street violence that could penetrate the home. More often, however, parents just kept their children inside the home. Sometimes random threatening encounters outside the home could not be avoided. Aurora's mother, who had lived in East Boston and Chelsea, reported on an apparently mentally ill Central American man who followed her on the bus every day, insulted her in Spanish, and brandished a knife, until she changed her route. Asked how she felt about living in these neighborhoods, Aurora's mother replied, "Well, I was content with whatever I had."

Another strategy adopted by parents was to keep looking for a better neighborhood; for many, however, given their limited options, the dangers of the old neighborhood would literally catch up with them in the new one (Massey 2007). Rafael's parents left Jamaica in Queens, New York, for Lawrence, Massachusetts, because they had heard that Lawrence was a "calmer" place for their children and a place where they could leave their apartment door unlocked. Among Massachusetts cities, however, Lawrence has one of the top ten highest individual poverty rates (Lavan and Uriarte 2008). Even though they lived in one of the safer parts of Lawrence, Rafael's parents were alarmed by the town's overall rise in crime over the last ten years. As they saw it, the rising crime was directly linked to the increase in the town's Latino population. Rafael's mother said, "This city is now ugly and dangerous. People look for towns where police are paying less attention, where things are quieter, where there is less robberies." And the father added, "It is our own race, the one who does this."

The Other Latinos

While the parents did not believe that the negative associations with being Latino applied to them, some thought that other Latinos did embody those characteristics. These parents were pessimistic about their assimilation because they believed that they had to pay the price for the actions of "the other Latinos." The concept of the "other" Latinos—the ones who were poorer, less educated, and less cultured—was especially salient for the immigrants from better-off backgrounds (Perreira, Chapman, and Stein 2006; Vallejo 2009). In some of the children's and parents' accounts, Puerto Ricans were particularly criticized for being able to enter and leave the United States with ease, owing to the island's commonwealth status, and having greater opportunities because they had arrived earlier and received access to public goods, such as public housing and welfare subsidies. The prevailing sentiment in these accounts was that Puerto Ricans created a generally negative reputation for Latinos and that other groups then had to suffer the consequences of this reputation without having any of the benefits that the Puerto Ricans enjoyed.

Carmel's Colombian parents were mortified that their daughter, who had grown up mainly in white, middle-class suburbs, chose to move to Lawrence, Massachusetts, a largely low-income, Puerto Rican, and Dominican town, because the rents were cheaper. This is how Carmel's father framed the contrast between Colombians and the Latinos in Lawrence.

> Their culture is very much below ours. Their values and principles, and many things that affect the normal upbringing of children, [are not good], and we didn't want that bad influence in our children. People over there live a lot on the government, people live together without being married, they get divorced, so this is not really the culture and the principles that we have. Even though we live in this country, we have our Colombian principles from thirty years ago.

In his use of the word "culture," Carmel's father was drawing on the Colombian concept of "cultura," which, as Peter Wade (1993, 20) discusses, refers to "culturedness or cultivation" and encompasses a broad range of phenomena, including "lifestyle, material style of living, education, manners, speech, and family structure." Cultura translates into the norms and behaviors of respectability and is associated with being white and/or middle- to upper-class (Streicker 1995). Carmel's mother said that she used the term "Latina" to describe herself because it was used more often by South Americans to distinguish themselves from Central Americans, whom she felt had lower status in the United States. "We Colombians come from the Spanish, who were not illiterate, but people with education."

Nor was this emphasis on cultura strictly a Colombian sensibility (although Colombians were seen as being more elitist by both coethnic and Dominican children). Natalia's Dominican parents raised her in predominantly white suburbs and socialized with more well-to-do Dominican immigrants who, like themselves, were able to send their children to Catholic schools. Natalia knew there were Latinos who moved into poor, native black neighborhoods; she said that these Latinos adopted "ghetto culture" and rejected the culture of their parents' home countries, expressing views consistent with segmented assimilation theory (Portes and Zhou 1993; Portes and Rumbaut 2001). It was these Latinos that Natalia and her sister were not allowed to know. For that reason, although they lived near New York City, the parents would not let the children attend Dominican parades or festivals. Natalia said, "The fact that it was dangerous, and the bad stories, and also the fact my mother wasn't interested in mixing with ghetto Dominicans."

Although no particular ethnicity was mentioned in seven parental accounts, the parents were nonetheless comparing themselves to the less well-to-do Latinos, whose limited mobility they attributed to a lack of individual responsibility. Rafael's father aptly articulated this view when he said that there is no discrimination in the United States. Individuals who talk about discrimination, he believed, need to look first at their own behavior:

> It is the person itself that makes the discrimination. I have seen people that says, "I got discriminated for this or that," and I think that it is inside of you, because I have never felt discriminated in this country. . . . For example, if I am walking in the street with a bottle of beer and I break it in the street and someone reprimands me for being Hispanic, then this is something that I caused it. It depends on what you do, it depends on your behavior.

Interestingly enough, a few of these parents made contradictory statements. They believed that discrimination against Latinos exists, a claim they supported with quite detailed accounts, and yet in other parts of the interview they were equally emphatic that discrimination against Latinos does not exist. In making the latter point, they used an interpretation similar to the one offered by Rafael's father—that Latinos are more likely to see and claim discrimination than to actually suffer from it. Thus, Angel's mother warned Latinos not to attribute the group's social mobility to structural barriers alone. The reality, she said, is far more complex, and individual agency has to be taken into account. Her words reflected hope rather than pessimism.

> [Discrimination] does exist, but I don't believe it is something that stops you from achieving what you want. I don't think so because why are there some who make it and some who don't? Yes, it is true that racism exists, but I think many Hispanics use it as an excuse for their failure. I am not denying it exists, but it is very easy to say that things are the way they are because I am Hispanic.

These parents' responses suggest three different interpretations, each based on a status they held: as participants in the American Dream, as Caribbean immigrants with a dual frame of reference, and as members of a disadvantaged group.

The first interpretation is that *these people failed because of their own individual shortcomings*. This interpretation is consistent with American conceptions of upward mobility. Individualism is enshrined in the American Dream, which does not leave room for failure and obscures our view of institutional factors when people do fail (Newman 1988/1999; Hochschild 1995; Deaux 2006).

The second interpretation allows that *there is discrimination, but these people failed because of their own individual failings, not because of discrimination.* This interpretation acknowledges institutional discrimination but still says that the decisive factor is an individual's shortcomings. This interpretation is consistent with Wendy Roth's findings among Dominican and Puerto Rican working-class respondents in the United States: they firmly denied the existence of color discrimination, but many of them said that Latinos confront real obstacles. Claims of color discrimination were attributed to people "making excuses for individual failings that can be overcome" (Roth 2008, 227–28). The key, she argues, is the framing of color discrimination in much of Latin America as a kind of personal failure of the victim for coming from a family that failed to lighten via intermarriage.

The third interpretation is that *these people failed because they are Latinos, and some Latinos do things that make them fail (but I'm not one of them).* This interpretation legitimizes the derogatory status of (some) Latinos in the United States but rejects the idea that this status includes the parents. This interpretation coincides with the findings of social psychologists John Jost and Mahzarin Banaji (Jost and Banaji 1994; Jost, Banaji, and Nosek 2004), namely, that disadvantaged group members can have conflicting motives for understanding the existing social order. Rather than resisting the system that keeps them at the bottom, disadvantaged group members can in fact justify the system, or rationalize the status quo. Jost and Banaji argue that motives to justify the system can sometimes be stronger than the tendencies to protect individual or collective interests. In short, the respondents were drawing on their perspectives as an American, as a first-generation immigrant, and as a lower-status individual.

It is clear that there is cause for both optimism and pessimism with the immigrant journey. Upward mobility and the optimism of the American Dream indeed figure strongly in the stories of parental mobility told by the children and parents. The parents of the children we interviewed had experienced at least some success.[15] All had at least one child who transitioned to postsecondary education (for example, the focal child of the study), virtually all were documented, and even those who were in the lower social strata of the United States had benefited from the wage-job differential with their country of origin. But there was more variation in mobility than popularly thought. There was also a surprising pessimism about assimilation among the parents, derived from a shared immigrant identity and perceived decline in social status. Regardless of how much economic success the parents had here, they expected that this exclusion would remain a part of their lives. Even very upwardly mobile parents who worked and lived in non-ethnic institutions and neighborhoods felt a lack of acceptance from Americans whose families had been here generations. Even they felt constrained in some ways by being an immigrant and Latino and deferred their hopes for acceptance to their children.

Chapter 4

Children on Their Own in School

> Carmen Merced has had two sons in the Boston Public Schools. [A] teacher accused Merced of being a bad parent, and this, says Merced, is how many teachers view Latino parents. It's always the parents, says Merced. The parents are always at fault, never the school. She'd be surprised to know that Boston Schools' superintendent Carol Johnson agrees with her.
>
> —Claudio Sanchez (2009)

THE COMMENTS of Carmen Merced, the mother of two sons in public schools, underscore the widespread views that Latino immigrant parents are not involved in their children's education. Low-income Latinos who do not speak much English are thought to be especially disengaged. In this chapter, I argue that such views are overly simplistic and inaccurate. The immigrant parents offered crucial supports to the children we interviewed, just not in ways that were visible to or valued by schools. We need to understand the parents' access to the appropriate guidance and capacities to develop concrete and effective steps for their children to do well in school.[1] We also need to understand what the mismatched relationship between families and schools meant for the children. The argument presented here moves us beyond the static image of the uninvolved immigrant parent to a new and more dynamic understanding of involvement that considers what is possible and what is not, given the social conditions faced by immigrants. Just as important, the argument brings into the picture the voices of immigrant children, many of whom end up believing that they must orchestrate their own schooling and taking the steps, from a young age, to do just that—with varying degrees of success and shared feelings of frustration and even resentment.

The long history of parental involvement in American schools is intertwined with social class and race (Hiatt-Michael 1994). According to popular definition, an involved parent is someone who attends parent-teacher conferences, helps with homework, advocates for their child in school, volunteers with the parent-teacher association (PTA), and raises funds for school enrichment services (Epstein 1995; Lopez 2001; Garcia

Coll et al. 2002). Educators and policymakers have tried to increase this kind of involvement among the parents of poor and low-achieving children since the mid-1960s (Goodwin 2005), most recently with the No Child Left Behind (NCLB) Act (Hill and Torres 2010).[2] Typically left unsaid is the fact that such practices, either based in schools or at least visible to them, represent the norms of middle-class families and, historically speaking, white middle-class families (Lawrence-Lightfoot 1978; Delgado Gaitan 1991; Valdes 1996; Auerbach 2006; Lopez 2001; Suárez-Orozco 2001; Zarate 2007; Koretz 2008). What we do hear is that poor, working-class, and/or native minority parents who do not adhere to such norms do not value their children's education enough and do not provide enough support in the home and at school (Lawrence-Lightfoot 1978; Luttrell 1997; Ramirez 1999, 2003; Mapp 2003; Stein 2004). These parents are framed as deficient compared to their middle-class, white counterparts (Koyama 2006) and as potential obstacles to their children's academic success (Stein 2004).

In counterpoint to this so-called deficit model, a line of research has focused on *why* low-income and/or minority parents do not engage with their children's schools in the ways that middle-class, white parents do (Lawrence-Lightfoot 1978). We have learned that for low-income parents their labor-intensive jobs, child care arrangements, and transportation issues do not readily align with the scheduling of school events. Low-income parents may also be put off by a school environment that they perceive as less than welcoming to their needs and presence; indeed, the parents may view schools as having a structure characterized by "power over others" rather than a "relational one" emphasizing collaboration (Fine 1993; Mehan et al. 1996; Lareau and Horvat 1999; Diamond and Gomez 2004; Warren 2005, 138; Pollock 2008b). As Sara Lawrence-Lightfoot (2003) argues, the broader social, cultural, and institutional frames informing the emotions of parents and teachers in their interactions are central to a fruitful dialogue and thus need to be made visible.

How does class shape the involvement of immigrant parents, and how does being an immigrant matter? Similar to their native counterparts, the working-class immigrant parents in our study had a hard time learning how educational bureaucracies function here and developing the kinds of social networks that would furnish them with useful information (Stanton-Salazar 2001), although some were able to find a few supports. Parents who had greater facility in English and economic resources knew and could do more. Still, because they were newcomers, even these parents faced language and cultural barriers that native-born parents would not have had to face. Despite their advantages, even highly educated, middle-class parents had a tough time, especially in the beginning. There were also ethnic-class differences in school access. Because the Colombians were more residentially integrated, they could send their children to better public schools. Half of the Colombian middle-class children and several from working-class families went to high-performing suburban public schools.[3] Few of the Dominicans lived in the suburbs, and none went to public schools there. Even when Colombians attended urban neighborhood public schools, these schools were typically better than the ones attended by Dominicans.

The immigrant parents, however, are only part of the story. What existing theories do not really capture, and what practitioners also need to know, is how the children of immigrants take ownership of their own educational experience quite early on. This is a story not simply of parents' involvement but also of the children's; both kinds of involvement have largely been invisible in the discourse and need to be addressed. Finally, this is not only a Latino story: a comparison with working-class second-generation Chinese from my own earlier research points to a shared working-class immigrant model of education with levels of parental involvement that are low by conventional measures. This is an important comparison, since Latinos are often typified as underachievers due to lack of family involvement and the Chinese (and Asians generally) as overachievers due to an abundance of parental attention to their education.

Parental Involvement

Learning About American Education

The first step in our immigrant parents' involvement in their children's schooling was learning the new American landscape of educational inequality. Here the divide was not as straightforward as it had been in their home countries, where, as we have seen, substantial educational inequalities prevailed and the primary divide was between public and private institutions. Free education was almost always associated with lower quality, and so only people without the financial resources went to the public schools (Jimenez et al. 1991; Duarte 1998; Somers, McEwan, and Williams 2004; Mendoza 2007). In the home country, private institutions for the most part were Catholic schools, and the parents knew which ones were good. In the United States, the parents were bewildered by the dazzling disparities between schools. For example, in the private school universe, American Catholic schools are joined by small Christian-based schools along with private, nondenominational day and boarding schools. It took most immigrant parents a while to realize that there is also variation in quality and that an expensive tuition is not always a reliable indicator of quality.

As the parents tried to grasp these private school distinctions, they sometimes made decisions that ran counter to their intended goals and, in retrospect, reflected their lack of knowledge. Hence, a few of the parents who lived in suburbs with good public schools nonetheless enrolled their children in small, private Christian academies. Their hopes were that these academies would pay attention to their children's moral development and offer greater academic opportunities than the public schools. The parents were not aware, however, that private religious schools are often constrained by their small student size and modest budget; only later did they realize that their children might have been better served by the local public schools. Carmel's parents enrolled her in Christian schools because they offered her "superior spiritual guidance." But they came to regret that she had missed out on the sports facilities and computers available at North Andover High School, the suburban public school that she later attended after her Christian high school was moved to a different city.

The differences in quality between public schools was another major lesson. According to the parents, the key was to avoid what they viewed as the low-performing, overcrowded urban public schools, where discipline rather than learning was the primary objective. Regardless of whether the schools were located in Lowell (Massachusetts), Miami, Boston, or New York City, the picture painted by the parents was much the same. Violence between students was common, as was student insubordination against teachers; the teachers lacked dedication, and most of the children simply did not study and were still being passed from one grade to the next without learning anything (Waters 1999; Lopez 2003; Suárez-Orozco, Suárez-Orozco, and Todorova 2008; Kasinitz et al. 2008). The parents also came to learn that avoiding these schools was not often a decision they could easily make, given where they could afford to live and the little they knew, in some cases, about other good public school options.

Paola's account of American disparities in public education was evocative (Kozol 1991; Hochschild and Scovronick 2003). When the family first migrated, they lived with her husband's sister in a Kansas suburb, where the children attended the "superb" school system. While culturally different from the private boys' school the parents had sent the children to in Colombia, the standards were similarly high. Of the Kansas public high school, the mother noted, "That place was better than a university. Each classroom was a lab, each desk had absolutely everything you may dream of." However, the parents found it difficult to adapt to suburban life, having lived all their lives in Bogotá, a cosmopolitan city. The parents could not get used to living in a place that the mother called a "ghost city": people rarely walked the streets, there was little public transport, and even a taxicab had to be reserved a day in advance. The parents decided to move to Miami, where they had family and could find the communal vibrancy of urban, ethnic life. The unfortunate trade-off was the Miami public school system, which was so unlike what they had experienced in the Kansas suburb that the two systems hardly seemed to belong in the same universe. Paola quickly got the idea that the influx of immigrant families had overwhelmed the Miami school system, where the atmosphere was one of crisis management rather than learning.

> I was shocked because the schools are overpopulated. I don't know how to explain it. It's as if a school was prepared for three thousand students and received five thousand or six thousand students. So classrooms are similar to train cars. They place those cars in the basketball court, in the backyard. There isn't enough room for students, so the classrooms are those cars. . . . The impact was at all levels, the premises, the teachers, the academic level, the people, all of it. Everything shocked me. In Kansas my children had to study to get good grades, here they didn't touch a book.

Choosing Schools

What kinds of high schools did the parents help choose for their children? Class and residential incorporation shaped different patterns for the Dominicans and Colombians. The majority of the Dominican children, including most of the middle class, went to urban public high schools, mainly of lower quality than the suburban and urban schools attended by Colombians. Nine Dominicans attended Lawrence High School, a school in the greater Boston area that had a history of academic problems, culminating in the loss of its accreditation from 1997 to 2004.[4] This pattern is consistent with the findings of the Immigrant Second Generation in Metropolitan New York Study (ISGMNY)—namely, that South Americans tend to go to better public schools in New York City than the Dominicans do (Kasinitz et al. 2008). The remainder of the Dominicans and Colombians we interviewed went to high schools that generally required examinations or maintained other rigorous entrance criteria, such as grades and referrals—for example, magnet public, Catholic, and private high schools.

In short, many of the working- and middle-class Dominican parents tended to be "nonchoosers," a term used by John Diamond and Kimberly Gomez (2004, 398) to describe working-class African American parents who choose local neighborhood schools that tend not to be high-performing. Meanwhile, a greater number of the Colombian parents were like Diamond and Gomez's (2004) "skilled or privileged choosers"—middle-class African American parents who were cognizant of and able to negotiate school choice with more success because they knew which areas had good schools and could afford to live there. Not surprisingly, the six middle-class families who had replicated their status with migration sent their children to top magnet or suburban public high schools; their suburban schools were better than those attended by Colombian children from upwardly mobile, middle-class families.

The paths to Catholic schools among twenty-four of the 1.5- and second-generation individuals we interviewed reveal the interaction between their family's financial capital and access to social resources, which provided valuable information about the educational system. Their families tended to rely on extended family members of similar social class locations for information about Catholic schools. However, some of the children had to leave the schools, mainly owing to family difficulty with paying the tuition (Louie and Holdaway 2009). Dominican families faced a particular dilemma: they understood that certain public schools, notably the ones in their neighborhoods, were underperforming, but they did not realize that the system had better schools that their children might be able to attend. For many, Catholic school was seen as the only "exit" option available from poor neighborhood schools, but their family's lack of financial resources prevented a few of the Dominican children we interviewed from being able to stay in Catholic high school. Such choices were similar to what Jennifer Holdaway and I (Louie and Holdaway 2009) found in the Dominican sample of ISGMNY.

A few of the working-class families in this study were able to choose better schools for their children by linking with higher-status individuals who had more knowledge and resources. Nelson, a Harvard student, came from a downwardly mobile Colombian family. His father, a former industrial engineer, worked as a kitchen staff employee, and his mother headed a maintenance staff, both in a New Jersey suburb. Nelson's parents happened to work for prestigious schools and were able to enroll their son in them. Nelson thus came to know his Montessori preschool as a student in the daytime and as a child tagging along with his parents when they cleaned the facility in the evenings. Nelson later attended the elite private high school where his father worked. His parents' school choices exemplify the ability of immigrant service providers to develop trust with a higher-status employer, facilitating crucial exchanges of information, especially around children's education (Fernandez-Kelly 2008). Since Nelson's parents came from a higher-status background in Colombia, it might also have been the case that they had cultural capital that served them well in this context. As newcomers and members of the working class, Nelson's parents were probably not familiar with higher-status cultural knowledge in the United States; yet as former Colombian high-status individuals themselves, they might have been comfortable with relating to middle-class Americans and getting their help.

A key turning point in Sara's life occurred when her mother met the Murphys,[5] a middle-class Irish American couple with children. In fact, it was through the children that the two families first met. Sara and her brother joined a local, largely Irish American children's marching band in Queens, New York, and the mothers as well as the children became fast friends. As with Nelson, Sara's mother was downwardly mobile—she was a Colombian medical student vacationing in the United States when she met and married Sara's father, even though he was a factory worker and came from a lower-status family. Her familiarity with privilege—she had grown up with maids, spacious houses, and exclusive social club memberships—may have been helpful in her interactions with the Murphys. A key talking point between the two mothers was their dissatisfaction with the local public schools. The friendship flourished even though Sara's mother was still struggling with her English, and the Murphys became her mother's first American friends.[6] Soon Sara and her brother joined the Murphy children in forgoing the public intermediate school for a well-regarded Catholic institution that served as a springboard for her Catholic high school.

In sum, the parents knew that their college-going goals for their children could be best met if they themselves took actions that furthered those goals. To do that, some of the families, especially the working-class families, were able to use social networks to learn about and choose higher-quality schools for their children. The ability to get valuable information from like and higher-status individuals was an advantage (Kim and Schneider 2005). Yet social class continued to matter because families did not always have the financial resources to take or complete the actions they learned would be helpful.

Even when parents could send their children to better precollegiate schools, their own learning process—what they needed to know to adequately monitor their children in school—did not end. One lesson had to do with tracking or ability grouping (Oakes 1985; Lucas 1999), and immigrant parents also struggled to comprehend and successfully navigate the varied "nested structures of inequality and separation" in America's public schools, embedded within and across localities, districts, and schools (Hochschild and Scovronick 2003, 23). The postsecondary system, complex enough for native-born Americans in its size and stratification, represented another frontier for immigrant parents to negotiate (Louie 2005). The first level of distinction was institutional type by degree, for example, associate's degree, bachelor's degree, or a vocational certificate. Even confining the educational universe to four-year institutions, the distinctions were many and often bewildering—public versus private, large versus small, liberal arts versus specialized (Schneider and Stevenson 1999). Such fine-grained distinctions were not readily apparent to even the parents with higher levels of formal schooling, such as Leonardo's parents, who both completed high school in Colombia and had taken some college classes in the United States. Alegria, Leonardo's mother, noted, "The only thing I know is what I would hear in Colombia

—that the best universities were the ones in New England, in Boston. So that is what I told them."

Verbal Support and Limited Interventions

The children spoke of their parents' involvement with their education largely in terms of ensuring that the children were healthy, went to school, and did not behave badly.[7] The strategies mainly involved monitoring of children's behaviors. Their parents duly bought the children books, pencils, and notebooks for school; took them to and picked them up from school (when the children were younger); and visited the school to sign necessary forms. At home the parents had the children do homework (but did not necessarily actively check the quality of the homework) and tried to restrict the amount and content of their TV viewing. The parents also did their best to make sure that the children were avoiding trouble. They checked to make sure that their children were not coming home late, not failing, not getting in trouble with a teacher, not feeling overly stressed about school, and not hanging out with a bad crowd—the last being especially important to families living in urban neighborhoods, where physical safety was an issue.

Family discipline was a strong theme for the children who grew up in urban settings. They were required to go straight home from school (Portes and Fernandez-Kelly 2008), and if they did not go home after the school day was over, they went to a family business or to a job. Especially as they grew older, the children were likely to head to organized activities both in and out of school, such as sports, literary magazines, student council, music, and church. Their parents approved of these activities because they kept the children safe and under adult supervision. Parents wanted to know who their children's friends were (along with the friends' parents) and to set limits on how much time children spent with friends. Their overall goal was to make sure the children were going to school and doing well in school (Coleman 1988; Dika and Singh 2002; Kim and Schneider 2005).

What most of the parents could not provide was useful guidance for their children's academic development—precisely what schools expect of parents (Zarate 2007). It was the children who realized that this key piece of parental involvement was missing from their lives. They recognized from an early age that their parents were supposed to provide homework support and other kinds of help, such as educational software, even if they did not always know what that support was supposed to look like. The combination of extensive parental verbal and moral support and less direct help with school helps explain why two-thirds of the Dominicans and more than half of the Colombians said that their parents were both involved and not involved with their education

(Auerbach 2006, 2007).[8] The working-class children, who were most in need of multifaceted academic supports, were the least likely to receive them from their family. This is how Julia, the child of working-class Dominican immigrants, put it: "We didn't have that [parental help], the money wasn't there, the know-how wasn't there." Instead, survival was a key memory of childhood for them—parents working twelve-hour days or longer, mainly in factories or as other kinds of laborers; coming home tired; having to cook, clean, and put the children to bed. Sometimes just making sure the children were in school was enough. About 20 percent of the children had spent some time growing up with a largely absent and nonparticipatory father, whether because he was in another country, he had died here, or his whereabouts were unknown, although these children did not usually elaborate on the strains of not having a father around. They commonly and matter-of-factly spoke of the tight fiscal and child-rearing constraints in a household where the mother was the only active parent.

Growing up in a two-parent working-class household was not necessarily easy either. Alexsa grew up in a small house owned by her mother in a hardscrabble and overwhelmingly poor neighborhood in Providence, Rhode Island, where vacant lots and open drug dealing were common. As soon as Alexsa and her brother came home from their organized activities, her mother put a lock and chain on the gate so that they could not go back outside (the house was enclosed by a seven-foot fence). Nor was home a refuge. Arguments were common between her mother and stepfather, both of whom worked in the formal labor market, her mother as an administrative assistant and her stepfather in a factory assembling computers; Alexsa and her stepfather also argued regularly. Daily household maintenance proved to be taxing, and Alexsa felt that the children's needs became too much for the adults to manage. Echoing sentiments expressed by others, Alexsa remembered the lack of strong order in the home:

> [I did my homework] on the kitchen table. You know, with music in the background. Television in the background. It was very, very cluttered in my house. It was just kind of crazy. I couldn't concentrate. A desk is important. Having, like, you know, a clean room. And also having the support of your parents and being able to go to your mother and saying, "Look, can you help me with the homework?"

Homework help was what many of the working-class children, and even some of the middle-class children, wanted but did not get from their parents. This finding is consistent with the lack of direct help in white working-class families (Lareau 2000), but the immigrant experience presented its own distinct set of difficulties. Certainly, without

English-language proficiency, parents could not speak with teachers or understand the assignments given, or even what was required of them (Garcia Coll et al. 2002; Suárez-Orozco, Gaytán, et al. 2010). Furthermore, the parents' own limited schooling in their country of origin and international differences in how content was taught made it hard for most parents to help their children with homework. For instance, long division is done differently in the American curriculum from how it is taught in the Dominican Republic and Colombia. The point at which the children's curriculum became too difficult for the immigrant parents to negotiate varied, but for some it occurred as early as second grade (Zarate 2007). Certainly by the time their children started high school, the working-class parents and even some of the middle-class parents could no longer support their children's school assignments. Lenore remembered how disappointed she was when her mother could not help her with Spanish, the one subject that the child thought would carry over seamlessly from school to home: "I would, like, ask her to correct my papers. And she couldn't do that. I was, like, I do better by myself. I end up correcting her. I guess she forgot a lot of it."

Overall, more than half of the children said that they had participated in an after-school enrichment program, broadly defined, where they found the homework support and other kinds of help they needed. What is interesting is that only a few children reported being referred to these programs by their parents. (I will discuss in the next chapter the other avenues through which children came to participate in such programs.) Alba's description of her working-class mother's strategy shows the use of social capital: her Dominican mother was able to get and then put to use important information about high-quality after-school programs that helped her children succeed in school (Kim and Schneider 2005):

> [My mother] couldn't help us on anything. What could she really help us with? Just putting us in good after-school programs and hooking us up with something like MIT-Wellesley Upward Bound. They would be more qualified to help us. That was her way of doing it.

Dominicans were nearly twice as likely to have participated in a program, which makes sense given that their families were less well-to-do and more likely to have been eligible for programs designed to serve low-income populations. The programs included community-based organizations (Si Puede, the Boys and Girls Club, local athletic leagues), school-based programs, and the federal TRIO programs—notably Upward Bound, which provides additional academic coursework, college visits, financial aid counseling, and cultural enrichment activities. Upward Bound has been shown to have large effects on four-year college enrollments among students with lower educational expectations (Myers et al. 2004; Rab, Carter, and Wagner 2007).

While the purposes of the programs varied, the second-generation respondents generally said that the programs helped them with their social and academic skills from early childhood into early adulthood, from literacy to the college application process and college itself. There were clear benefits to their academic and human development (Eccles and Goodman 2002, Shernoff and Vandell 2007; Vandell et al. 2005; Lemmel and Rothman 2007; Harding, Rimer, and Fredrick 2007; Portes and Fernandez-Kelly 2008).[9] For the children of both native-born and foreign-born parents, these programs fill in crucial gaps. For instance, they can teach children what they are supposed to be doing to prepare for college (Hossler and Gallagher 1987)—including which classes to take, a process that starts as early as the sixth grade (Cabrera, Burkum, and La Nasa 2003)—and the consequences of not taking the needed steps (Lucas 1999).

What these programs could not do was engage with the children's schools, which is what the children wanted but also did not get from their parents. Lenore's comments typify how the children, especially the working-class ones, felt about what they perceived to be their parents' distance from their schools:

> Like, my friends' moms, I saw that they would go to parent-teacher meetings. I had to, like, practically take my mom to the parent-teacher meetings. She never wanted to go on her own. I always had to go and translate. It was just like, oh God. This is such a pain. Why can't you just go on your own like you're supposed to?

The second-generation individuals we interviewed said that their desire to have their parents be more involved stemmed not only from wanting to be like the other children but also from seeing that teachers paid more attention to those students. Natalia, who attended Catholic schools on scholarship, was well aware of this fact: "When parents show interest with school activities, teachers show interest in their kids, and I think in the seventh grade I disliked my mom because she worked so much and she couldn't do those things. I would notice all the time Danny's mom in school."

Some of the working-class children said that their parents stood up for them when it came to curricular placement, such as in ESL or special education, or when they located additional services like summer camps for children with special academic and developmental needs. However, this kind of parental engagement was usually reactive—a response to a school-based situation that had already arisen. Such patterns are consistent with research showing that working-class African American and Latino parents engage with schools when they feel that their children are not receiving equal treatment or that teachers do not care enough about their children's learning (Diamond and Gomez 2004; Pollock 2008b). Francisco's mother went to her son's high school after teachers called her repeatedly about his academic problems. Despite her efforts, she felt that the school officials did not listen to her because they were racist and they were singling out her son: "I felt that they didn't do enough to help my son. They didn't help him to learn more." Interventions by working-class parents in their children's schools were not only infrequent but often unsuccessful, mirroring the experiences of native black and white working-class parents (Lareau and Weininger 2008).

To sum up the findings so far, the mismatch between schools and families occurs because school officials do not see the emotional and verbal support offered by families at home (Carreón, Drake, and Barton 2005), do not always understand that some parents are not capable of providing homework support (Smith, forthcoming[a]), and fail to notice parents' efforts to locate after-school programs to provide homework help for their children. Educators view parents who do not help with homework as not caring about their children's achievement, not as simply unable to do so. This has a familiar ring, as it is similar to how native-born American working-class parents are framed as deficient by schools (Mehan et al. 1996, 173; Lucas 1997; Suárez-Orozco 2001; Tornatzky, Cutler, and Lee 2002).

Twelve of the children we interviewed reported that their parents were involved in their schooling, and their accounts highlight the importance of considering mobility path and social class together. The parents' English facility, of course, proved to be useful. These parents' involvement took several forms: choosing a high-quality school; taking the needed long-term steps for college through daily reading to children (when they were young); closely supervising homework; ensuring that children were in the advanced classes at school; overseeing the college application process; and fostering the children's talents and skills by arranging private tutoring, music lessons, and sports practices. Such forms of engagement are consistent with "concerted cultivation," which, as Annette Lareau (2000, 2003, 2008) argues, is how black and white middle-class parents encourage their children's development. Not surprisingly, the children from middle-class families who had replicated their high status received the most extensive help, although a few also thought that their parents were not able to be involved, for reasons addressed later in the chapter. These children typically had at least two of the following: some homework help from parents, private SAT test preparation classes, private tutors, private music and other kinds of lessons, or family trips to visit colleges. The middle-class families who first attained that status in the United States and a few of the working-class families who were downwardly mobile here were able to offer some of these kinds of supports, but fewer in toto. Again, my findings with the downwardly mobile parents suggest that having once held a middle-class position—in this case, in the home country—is of some benefit to their children; these benefits, however, would not be adequately captured by measures that look only at the immigrant parents' working-class position here.

How Parents Understand Parental Involvement

Nearly all the parents we interviewed were in agreement with their children about their levels of involvement and the reasons for them—lack of time, the language barrier, and lack of comfort engaging with their children's schools (Turney and Kao 2009).[10] The parents with more education were likely to discuss the time factor and the issues involved with getting properly situated in the United States so that survival would not have to define their lives. They spoke of getting recertified for the kind of professional jobs they had held in their home countries; dealing with the precipitous devaluation of their native currencies while trying to pay for graduate school in the United States; and raising children without the services to which they had been accustomed back home, such as drivers, nannies, and cooks.

A few of the parents explicitly linked their reluctance to engage with their children's schools (Auerbach 2006; Gándara 1995) to their feeling of being alone in America as immigrants. Most of the parents had undergone "narrow incorporation" into the United States (Hochschild and Cropper 2010): they made enough to support the family, and they were able to navigate daily life, but in a very bounded sense (for example, not necessarily in mainstream society). Most, however, did not meet the other benchmarks of civic engagement and English proficiency described in the concept of narrow incorporation. Also, feeling excluded from deeper incorporation came at a high cost. Among the working class, the self-described sense of being alone could have multiple sources: the turmoil of a bad marriage; the exigencies of single motherhood in the absence of the extra or familial support that had been readily at hand in the homeland; and the sheer physical and emotional fatigue, even in intact, viable marriages, from the rigors of everyday survival that only seemed to permit parents to go from home to work and back. For varied reasons, venturing from home to be present or engaged with their children's schools did not seem possible to these parents.

Even the more assimilated middle-class families felt themselves to be alone in a powerful way. It was difficult for Ines to see her son and daughter marked for not being able to speak English and marginalized both for that and for being Hispanic, even though they belonged to the elite class in Colombia and lived in great comfort in the United States. In the third grade, her son Jorge was accused by his teacher of stealing a classmate's baseball cards; in fact, the classmate had stolen the cards from Jorge. Ines, already wrestling with her fear of speaking English in public even though she was proficient, waited a while before finally speaking to the teacher.

> So I made a great effort to explain to her that the cards my child had were his, that we had bought them for him. At last, the teacher understood and apologized. For me that was horrible, because my child couldn't express himself clearly. That was at the beginning, for me that was a terrible shock, and I felt discriminated against. I believe they thought he was a thief because he was Hispanic.

Nor was there much help to be had from her white American husband, who advised her to let Jorge stand up for himself. Ines recalled; "I told him, 'No, sometimes you have to make a stand because they are not going to respect him. He is a child, and he is a Hispanic child, and they are going to crush him.'" Despite her best intentions, she often found herself stricken by anxiety and unable to advocate for her child. The thought of even going to the school in this capacity often made her tense and reluctant to go, although she knew that her involvement was necessary.

When she tried to intervene, Ines thought that she was easily dismissed (Ramirez 2003). As she slowly learned about the opportunities available to children who were labeled as gifted, she felt that her efforts to have Jorge placed in those classes (he tested well enough) were stymied. She felt that teachers and administrators always saw her as a foreigner parent who did not have to be taken as seriously and could be put off by excuses, such as lack of time to test her child or to speak with her, or lack of space in the relevant programs. Ines also said that she colluded in her own exclusion by not pushing harder: "I don't know how to fight. I believe I'm a fighter, but I don't know, I get nervous, and I end up fighting with myself because I can't answer back either in Spanish or in English. I cannot answer back." In short, Ines tried to be like any other American suburban, middle-class mother by monitoring the treatment of teachers and other school officials toward her children to make sure their best interests were being served (Lareau and Weininger 2008, 124). Because she was an immigrant, however, Ines felt that she did not have the same right to engage with institutional agents as their equal—and the agents seemed to agree.

Although we could not interview Natalia's mother, a working-class Dominican who had made great gains with migration, she was seen by her daughter as having overcome such barriers in ways that Ines said she could not. Natalia's mother did not, however, overcome the barriers on her own—she had help. According to Natalia, both daughter and mother had long noted that the teachers and leaders at the children's Catholic school did not take the mother seriously owing to her accented and otherwise imperfect English. The mother consistently thought that she could not explain herself properly, and the teachers rarely took the time to get an interpreter, to speak more slowly, or to clarify the points they were trying to get across (Ramirez 2003). Said Natalia:

> I don't think my teachers understood my mom or respected my mother. Then again, these are teachers left over from the 1940s or '50s, and I don't think they were adjusting to the ways of the world, and I really don't think my own elementary school [was] capitalizing on immigrant kids whose parents wanted them to get a better education. [The teachers] were dumb, not us.

The situation never got too tense as long as Natalia and her younger sister did well. In the eighth grade, however, Natalia began to struggle academically. Her mother was concerned enough that she recruited one of Natalia's cousins, a U.S.-born college graduate and an alumna of the Catholic school, to serve as interpreter. With the cousin's assistance, the mother was finally able to communicate with the school's teachers and administrators, and the first point she made was that she and her children should be taken seriously. As Natalia told us, "My mother had to stand up and say, 'Look, my kids are going to school here, just like anybody else's, and you have to respect them like anyone else, and you have to respect me as anyone else.'" The transformation on the part of the teachers was immediate and long-lasting, and Natalia would end her eighth grade year with very good grades.

> They were just a lot friendlier when they noticed somebody could rebut what they were saying, and that just made everything different. My teachers were, like, whenever you need help, just come early in the morning, and I was, like, I'm afraid of you, why are you being nice to me? They literally were, like, this is all you had to do, is just bring this person in.

Eliana, another working-class mother who was upwardly mobile, successfully pushed back against an influential college counselor at the exclusive private school where her son Park was a scholarship student. The fact that Eliana was proficient in English (she had arrived at the age of eighteen with some knowledge of the language) was probably crucial, as she did not need help understanding the college counselor. Both mother and son were quick to point out that many school staff members were ready to help Park get financial aid and other necessities in this rarefied world of privilege, where it was commonplace for students to take the SAT in the seventh grade and for the parents to be wealthy and influential; a few were even U.S. senators. Eliana, who had vocational secondary school training in Colombia, worked two jobs in Miami and was a single mother, and as her son noted, she did not have a lot of time to devote to his everyday academic life. But being determined that her son would have better outcomes, she was proactive with the college application process. The college counselor assigned to Park was known for working only with the top twenty students of each graduating class and for getting only the top five accepted into Ivy League universities; since Park was ranked eleventh, his chances for the Ivy League seemed small —at least to the college counselor.

The initial meeting with Eliana, Park, and the counselor to review Park's list of schools—sorted into ones that were reaches, realistic choices, or backups—was not promising. As Park remembered, his mother was thinking of Princeton, Harvard, and Cornell; it was quickly clear that the counselor had other ideas and was pushing state universities. The counselor, Park said,

> took my reach [list] and said this definitely was not even reachable. She said, "These are your reaches," and moved my realistics over, and she said, "And really, if I were you, I would put the University of Miami and University of Florida and Florida State on that list [of realistics]." ... And I remember we left that meeting, my mom was furious. And she literally was against up that lady—now we're definitely only going to apply to the Ivy Leagues and that's what motivated her. [*Did she get into it with the lady while you were there?*] No, we just kind of sat there. But when I got accepted, my mother made me go back to her and show her. [*Laughs*]

When Eliana spoke with us, she was very measured. She did not bring up any sense of outrage. Eliana merely noted that the counselor did not believe that Park could get into an Ivy League school but accepted their choices when she saw the family's effort and determination and did what she could to support Park. When Eliana was asked why she thought the counselor did not support their choices, however, she briefly but pointedly mentioned ethnic and class bias.

> Personally, I think because she was a lady with some sort of prejudice towards people like us: she thought Park wasn't capable enough—even though he was a very good student—because his father wasn't a lawyer or his mother a senator. She would help out more the son of a prominent person, such as a [former U.S.] president's relative, who was in the same grade as Park.

Park was accepted at and went to Cornell. The accounts of Park's mother and Natalia's mother illustrate that some working-class parents in our study did in fact challenge school officials in ways more typical of native-born middle-class parents. Their accounts, however, show how difficult this process can be—because of the divide that immigrant parents faced, both as members of the working class and as immigrants grappling with language issues and other types of exclusion.

Children on Their Own

In the absence of interventionist support from their parents, the children told us that they took on the task of advocating for themselves in school, with varying degrees of success. In this way, the inherent authority relationship between parent and child was inverted with migration. After Maureen and her mother arrived in Miami in the mid-1980s, life came down to just the two of them. The daughter quickly became the Colombian mother's language and cultural broker in the new land (Tse 1995; Buriel et al. 1998; Orellana 2009). Maureen recalled how this inversion took shape and then continued during their time here:

> So my mother hasn't really been there for me. She hasn't been able to guide me. She really just hasn't been able to do that. It's just not been within her capacity.
>
> With me, I find I'm guiding her. She's going through a lot of health problems. I set up her whole health insurance. She didn't have health insurance. I took four months taking care of her. I'm kind of like raising her!

The transition to the United States, said Maureen, was particularly difficult for her mother, who had gone from a life of comfort as a stay-at-home mom in Bogotá to being a waitress, newspaper delivery person, and clerk in the United States, confined more by language than by choice to the Spanish enclaves of Miami.

Indeed, children spoke of taking the initiative in making all kinds of school-related decisions, from locating gifted and talented programs for themselves and advocating for themselves with teachers and guidance counselors to be mainstreamed out of ESL classes to skipping a grade and getting into more advanced classes. Their accounts suggest the possibly positive effects of children's self-brokering, such as quickened development (Buriel et al. 1998, 293), but their accounts also illustrate the demands that children feel when they have to take on a more parental role and the inadequacy and frustration experienced by their parents (Foner and Dreby 2011). The parents, as the children told the story, developed a trust that their children would make the right decisions for themselves (Auerbach 2006; Smith, forthcoming[a]), but they really had little choice, given their own constrained ability to help. The sense was that the most parents could do was locate a good school and/or a good after-school program for their children. Penny, who came from a very upwardly mobile, working-class Colombian family, knew that she was fortunate because her parents could marshal their salaries as a factory supervisor and line worker to pay the tuition at a K-12 Catholic school for her and her brother. Taking advantage of the Catholic school system became the family's strategy to avoid the struggling public schools of Bridgeport, Connecticut. At the same time, Penny felt the anxiety of being so independent from a young age. Of her parents, she said, "They didn't really believe in, like, teacher-student nights. They wouldn't go. They were never involved in, like, school. It was basically me, like, they pay the tuition and I run the show." Other children would discover a good school, whether at the secondary or postsecondary level—for example, Bronx Science High School, a famed magnet school in New York City, or Brown University—and then have to explain to their parents why it was an honor to gain admittance into such a good school.

A few of the children explicitly connected being on their own in school to family separations and other disruptions from migration. Maureen, for instance, said that her father, a professional in Colombia, tried to help via long-distance calls and during her summer visits with him. Despite his best efforts, however, the fact was that his advice did not apply to the American educational system. Following his advice, she had chosen a business college, only later to realize that, unlike in Colombia, one does not have to specialize in the undergraduate years in an American college. In retrospect, she would have much preferred to pursue a liberal arts undergraduate education and then later obtain a master's degree in business administration. Similarly, a few of the children who were old enough to have gone to school in Latin America recalled that their parents' ability to help with schoolwork changed drastically once the family arrived in the United States.

The longer some parents spent in the United States, the more knowledgeable they became about how to be helpful. Carmel said that her Colombian parents were more involved in her younger brothers' schooling than they had been in hers. The parents went to one brother's school wrestling competitions and tried to help both brothers with their college application essays. Even if the parents' English was not at the highest level of proficiency, Carmel felt that her brothers appreciated the parents' attempts to guide the process. A few respondents assumed the parental role for younger siblings, sharing their own knowledge of what it took to succeed in school. Leonardo, a young Colombian man, started "jumping on" his younger siblings, making sure "they were taking the right classes, studying for the SATs," and he paid for a summer academic enrichment program and SAT study guides for his siblings.

Even the middle-class children whose parents were more involved in their schooling thought they were on their own. These children said that they were fortunate because their parents had been able to identify the better performing schools and send them there. What their parents did not have, according to the children, was the kind of knowledge that native-born white middle-class parents—and sometimes Asian parents—had about the workings of the school system. Since their parents lacked this kind of cultural capital, the children still needed "a cultural broker to help them decipher the way schooling works," such as helping them choose a major or understand the difference between college and university (Martinez-Cosio and Iannacone 2007, 350). This is the kind of information that native-born middle-class families readily give to their children (Lareau and Weininger 2008).

The children's sense was that their middle-class parents could not adequately meet all their educational needs. This impression was highlighted when the children saw what other middle-class parents were doing, and it explains why a few of the children from high replicator families still thought that their parents were both involved and not involved in their education. Rick, who grew up in Princeton, New Jersey, was the son of Colombian professionals who had gone to the United States for college and graduate school. He said that his parents knew that he should take the SAT, suggested a few colleges, and took him on college visits. However, in Rick's eyes, these efforts paled in comparison to those of non-Hispanic parents of the same social class background. The difference was in kind (the other parents gave more assistance) as well as in degree (the other parents were more deeply involved in their children's education, which became a familial enterprise; Lareau and Weininger 2008). It was his (white) ex-girlfriend's idea for him to attend Princeton Review classes to improve his SAT scores (which did indeed rise dramatically). When Rick brought the idea to his parents, they were quick, he acknowledged, to pay for the classes, but nonetheless he stressed that they were neither the source of the idea nor a driving force behind his decision to enroll. When asked whether his parents were familiar with the college application process, Rick responded, "I would say fifty-fifty. I think the average parent knows more than them, but I think among Hispanic parents they probably know more."[11] Although the working-class children in the study would have delighted in having access to this kind of parental knowledge, Rick knew that there was more to be had and felt that he did not have adequate parental supports for his education. He simply said, "I had to do everything on my own."

The children responded to this sense of being on their own mainly with resigned acquiescence, though a few expressed resentment. All were well aware that they were not supposed to be on their own for the educational process and that they might be missing out as a result. Some wanted what they saw as the bonding moments or quality time that can occur between parents and children doing homework together or parents getting to know their teachers and details of their school lives. There was an occasional undercurrent of frustration as the children expressed the feeling that they would have benefited from more attention and help. Lenore remarked, "All the other moms ask their kids how their day went. So can't you be like everybody else's mom and ask me how my day went? She's like, whatever."

Regardless of how involved they were able to be, the parents we interviewed largely agreed with their children's assessment of being on their own in school (Stanton-Salazar and Spina 2003). They used much the same language as their children did—namely, that the children were the primary architects of their educational journeys and, to a certain extent, their destinies. Describing her son as a man "every parent wants to have," Angel's mother did not claim responsibility for his good outcome. Rather, she gave all the credit to her son: "It wasn't because I told him, do this or do that. He has played a determinant role, and the things he has done, he has done them on his own." The mother of Lenore, the young Dominican woman who complained that her mother never took an interest in her school life, was just as matter-of-fact with us as the daughter claimed she was: "Well, you know, I was in my things and she was in hers, and she was the one who won all these merits, and she was the one who chose the schools because she knew which ones were good."

Even when there was disagreement between the parent's and child's accounts, it was not over the lack of parental involvement but rather over what motivated it. The mother of Isabel, a young Dominican woman who wistfully wished for more involved parents, said that her daughter never needed her help. Instead, it was her two sons—one of them diagnosed, at the mother's prompting, with attention deficit disorder (ADD)—who needed, sought, and received her attention. In line with theories around language and cultural brokering, Isabel's mother went on to say that it was she who needed her daughter's guidance as she worked to complete her own undergraduate degree in early childhood education. When asked how often she spoke with Isabel about school, she replied:

> Almost every day, because she has been like my assistant helping me with my schoolwork because I went back to school after too many years. So we discuss schoolwork all the time. She even jokes, saying that she is going to my school to talk to my dean and sue me because my degree should be in her name.

Despite the Colombian and Dominican children's perceptions of low parental involvement, they said that most Latinos have even less involved families. Describing the lack of parental involvement among his Latino neighbors, which he felt hindered the children's education, Julian explained how his family was different:

> Like, my parents weren't on me, but my parents cared. They just didn't really know the language, the material. So they didn't ask me about it. But [for the kids that I knew] their families didn't ask them about it, 'cause they didn't care. I had friends who went to summer school every year because their parents weren't really involved in their educations.

Other Latino families were seen as not valuing their children's education. The working-class Dominicans and Colombians we interviewed confirmed the popular belief that Latinos have "bad cultures" that do not allow them to make use of opportunities in the United States but rather consign them to poverty (Fukuyama 1994; Rumbaut 1997). The key to their own success, said the respondents, was that their families did more and were an exception.

What a Comparison with the Chinese Tells Us About the Ethnic Culture Argument

In confirming the idea that Latino families typically do not value their children's education (and thus are not involved), the working-class Colombians and Dominicans were also confirming a popular explanation for the Latino achievement gap. The Latino-Asian achievement gap is often attributed, for instance, to weak Latino parental involvement compared to the strong involvement of Asian immigrant parents. Yet the Dominican and Colombian children's interpretation of their families' involvement was strikingly similar to the findings of an earlier study I conducted with second-generation Chinese American college students (Louie 2001, 2006a, 2008).[12] There, too, the working-class Chinese spoke of low levels of homework help and school engagement from their parents, for the same reasons found here: low levels of English fluency and formal schooling, limited financial and social resources, and little knowledge about the workings of the American educational system. What the Chinese parents could offer was verbal and moral support—again, in ways similar to the findings here about the involvement of Dominican and Colombian parents. In fact, the comparison reveals a shared *immigrant* working-class cultural model of education that is based on moral and emotional support and that conveys, often in ethnic or folkloric terms, the importance of studying hard and deferring gratification to avoid the parents' lives of manual labor.[13] There is also a shared way of making sense of parents' low involvement. The Chinese respondents believed that most Asian Americans have families who teach them not only to value education *but also* how to do well in school (Louie 2004, 2006a). They, too, believed that their families were the exception.

The working-class second-generation individuals thus endorsed the dominant narratives about their panethnic groups, even though those narratives could not explain their own experiences. They had all successfully transitioned to college, despite not having enough parental supports with school. The Colombians and Dominicans, of course, were not expected to even get to college. Although the children acknowledged the class and migration constraints that factored into their parents' low involvement in their schooling, they subsumed these social structural factors in favor of culture. Their families were just culturally different from their panethnic counterparts. In the process, the children expressed support for the idea that ethnic cultures drive academic performance or that ethnic culture trumps social class.

How can we account for the power of the ethnic culture argument? Certainly there are other possible explanations. The Dominicans and Colombians might have considered that other Latino families face even greater class- and migration-related barriers. The Chinese could have claimed that other Asian families have access to more economic, social, and cultural advantages. It is interesting that the children did neither. Although it seems counterintuitive, this finding makes sense in light of John Jost and Mahzarin Banaji's argument that an individual might be psychologically invested in justifying the existing social system; this tendency to justify the system, paradoxically, can be strongest "among those who are most disadvantaged by the social order" (Jost, Banaji, and Nosek 2004, 912; Jost and Banaji 1994). The children we interviewed still were motivated to legitimize the cultural rationale for the Latino-Asian achievement gap, even when that rationale marginalized the class- and migration-based constraints that they actually experienced.

The Colombian and Dominican parents had to figure out not only who they were in the new American landscape around language, cultural norms, and race but also, as this chapter has documented, where they stood in relation to the inequality structured into the new American system of education, especially as it affected their ability to ensure that the better educational opportunities were available to their children. Further comparative research is needed to determine if and how parental involvement is embedded in the larger context of exclusion perceived and experienced by immigrant parents, a topic I return to in the concluding chapter. In the wake of the mismatched relationship between their schools and families, the children of immigrants, especially the working class, were left on their own with schooling. In the conclusion, I will also discuss how policymakers and practitioners can address this important and largely invisible aspect of immigration and education. Of course, parents are only one in a constellation of influential social actors in their children's lives. In the next chapter, I turn to nonparental supports for immigrant children and the importance of these supports in offsetting children's sense of aloneness in school and helping them see what they need to do to succeed.

Chapter 5

Beyond the Family: Constellations of Support

I WAS in the Blue Room of Faunce House, a graceful early-twentieth-century building at Brown University that counts John D. Rockefeller Jr. as one of its original donors. I was finally meeting José, a thoughtful twenty-year-old Colombian American student who had kept in touch with me as he moved from Washington, D.C., where he had done a summer congressional internship, to a semester abroad in Barcelona, then back to Brown in Providence, Rhode Island. When I asked José how he chose Brown, the young man—the son of a single mother who raised him less than six miles from the university—confessed that he had never even known it existed. He discovered the university—and the possibility that he might be able to attend—through a chance encounter at the local J. C. Penney with a middle school guidance counselor with whom he had kept in touch and who continued to track his academic progress. Since José was then a high school junior, the conversation naturally turned to the college application process. José described the seminal exchange that, in his opinion, set his life on a more expansive course:

> He said, "Oh, have you considered Brown?" I was, like, "Brown? What is that?" He goes, "My kids have fun there, it's a really good school." At that point, I didn't know what Ivy League was. In a way I think if it wasn't for him, I probably never would have applied to Brown, I wouldn't have the confidence. I think the fact that he believed in me and believed that I could get in was really a motivating factor.

José's account captures the key role that nonparental—and indeed, nonfamilial (whether immediate or extended)—individuals can play in the lives of children. After the discussion in the previous chapter of family social capital, this one delves into the other key relations in children's lives—their relationships with teachers, counselors, peers, and other non-school-based persons—and how these contribute to their academic development. Although immigrant parents want the best for their children, the ones with fewer resources often lack the tools to help their children achieve their educational goals (Stanton-Salazar and Spina 2003; Fernandez-Kelly 2008). Thus, social capital is important not just for the parents trying to help their children but for the children trying to help themselves. The stakes are especially high for working-class and poor children, who are most in need of social capital and yet can find it difficult to acquire. The key understanding here is that schools themselves can make this a difficult process, one determined by chance "rather than institutional design" (Suárez-Orozco, Suárez-Orozco, and Todorova 2008; Itzigsohn 2009, 84).

In this chapter, I show that the intervention of nonfamily adults is crucial to understanding how the children we interviewed were able to become academic success stories. It was through teachers, counselors, and other institutional agents that the second-generation respondents tapped into the information and tools they needed to move ahead educationally (Stanton-Salazar 1997). The ways in which nonfamily adults help disadvantaged immigrant children get to and graduate from college as demonstrated by Patricia Fernandez-Kelly (2008, 123) also came out in our interviews:

> A magical sequence of events was set into motion when an admired teacher or counselor took a special interest in a youngster. The child was made socially visible by such concern. Expectations changed and new identities were forged. Previously unknown goals suddenly came within reach.

These non-family-based constellations of support showed children the concrete steps they needed to take to be successful in school. No longer were they on their own in school. Once again, there were ethnic-class differences. Because the Dominicans were more likely to go to struggling public schools, social capital was especially crucial to their success. Although social class was definitely important, the family's social-class status and social mobility path mattered together. The children of working-class parents who had made dramatic gains tended to have both family and nonfamily social capital. The respondents whose working-class parents had made only limited gains or had replicated their status here had to rely more on nonfamily aid. As we would expect, the children who had attended a public magnet high school or a Catholic school—both known for providing a good education, particularly to students from families of lesser means—were less likely to recall such severe challenges. Still, even they noted the difficulties that they or their peers had faced in these contexts where learning conditions were more optimal and the varied sources of nonfamily support they found there.

Neighborhood Urban Public Schools

Challenges

Most of the Dominicans interviewed in our study attended struggling public urban schools, with black and Hispanic student populations in the range of 45 to 90 percent, and the majority of them spoke of a dismal school environment of lowered expectations for students.[1] Learning was seen as secondary to policing (Lopez 2003, 2004; Kasinitz et al. 2008).[2] Students felt that they literally had to "watch their back" and were sometimes advised by teachers not to use the bathrooms alone to avoid being assaulted. Charles, a graduate of Lawrence High School, said, "It was hard to concentrate anywhere. Because they eventually set up video cameras everywhere. They had people like fake security guards, guys with walkie-talkies, just checking up on people and what you were doing." In spite of their reliance on security guards and metal detectors, these public schools, ironically, still did not feel safe to the respondents (Noguera 2003).

The children remembered an underlying disrespect from many teachers (Stanton-Salazar 1997). Some teachers were apathetic, others appeared to be angry, and still others seemed scared and overwhelmed. Charles's description of his high school Spanish class illustrates what has been described as "subtractive schooling": educators viewing students, especially those on the "regular track," as not caring about education, and students believing that the educators do not care about them (Valenzuela 1999). Both Charles's sarcasm and disappointment were evident:

> It was actually hilarious. 'Cause the teacher was like a sports fanatic. And there was at least five students that were, like, doing basketball and football, so she paid a lot of attention to those students. Most of the time, just talking to them, and she'd assign us work, and she'd just leave. It was, you know, it was a joke. And most of the students were Latinos.

For Alexsa, a graduate of Mount Pleasant High School in Providence, the teacher-student relationship was more likely to be adversarial than collaborative: "I saw through the teachers. I knew that they weren't there to help us. They had no control. At least for me, you lose respect for them. Lots of leadership skills weren't shown." When her classmates acted out in class, she said, some teachers responded by yelling at them to "get out and go to the office." In a few instances, the teachers turned inward and just seemed to give up on the task altogether. Alexsa explained, "There was one teacher, in high school, who just totally put his head down on the desk and was just like, 'Oh my God! I'm having a nervous breakdown.' It was bad."

At best, a fraction of students had some of their needs met, and at worst, relatively little content was learned as students advanced to the next grade level regardless of whether they were ready to be there (Espinoza-Herold 2003). Consider two second-generation Dominican men at each end of the academic achievement spectrum. Alfonso, who completed his middle and high school years in the Cambridge, Massachusetts, public school system, met with me on a late December Saturday at his firm's Manhattan headquarters. The firm, a leader in global management consulting and technology service, occupied three floors of a posh high-rise building. Alfonso and I chatted in one of the smaller conference rooms. Although his interactions with his teachers had been largely positive, Alfonso still thought that they had a rather narrow perspective on students' abilities and the appropriate assessment benchmarks. He endorsed the need for and effectiveness of standardized tests; still, he believed that educators should think more broadly about what standardized tests actually measure.[3] He encouraged teachers to think of their students as having multiple intelligences, referencing the theories pioneered by Howard Gardner (1983, 1993, 2006; Chen, Moran, and Gardner 2009).

In sum, Alfonso felt that his teachers had had an incomplete conception of their students' potential. Nor did the responsibility lie entirely with the teachers; he knew that parental involvement was important. Indeed, he saw the inability of his divorced parents to spend enough academically oriented time with him as a great disadvantage: "I know teachers have such a hard job. You can't expect every teacher to analyze every student's background and tailor their teaching just because, you know, this student comes from a disadvantaged background." Alfonso's account was interesting because he was a self-avowed "teacher's pet" in elementary school and valedictorian of his eighth-grade class; in high school, however, Alfonso knew something was not quite right. Although he spent hours studying, somehow he was not getting the highest grades, and he felt that his teachers were not helpful. Instead, they just assigned and received the homework, without inquiring much into how students were processing the material. He came to accept his own leveled aspirations: "I still did well, but no more high hopes, valedictorian, or anything like that." Although he graduated from college on time and landed a consulting job, he felt that this success was the result of finally receiving the attention he needed in college.

Miguel, a graduate of the public schools in Lawrence, Massachusetts, had never been a favorite of his teachers. Completing a bachelor's degree was taking Miguel longer because he had dropped out of the vocational institute he first attended after high school to work for United Parcel

Service (UPS). He continued to work part time there, and an employee program paid his college tuition. Miguel had earned an associate's degree but downplayed that achievement, saying that he did not even attend his own graduation. About to start at the University of Massachusetts at Lowell, Miguel was already looking ahead to a bachelor's degree (which he planned to celebrate). Miguel attributed his winding path to the academic challenges he faced, which, he said, had largely gone unaddressed. His issues dated back to the sixth grade, when he started to struggle with math. His teacher would write a math problem on the board and announce, "Just do it," rather than explain how to approach the problem. Miguel left grade school struggling in math, and the gap kept building through middle school and high school. Admitting that he did not ask for help from his Lawrence High School teachers, Miguel still wondered why they did not take the time to figure out what was wrong, since he clearly was not doing well on tests. Speaking of the relative lack of learning at the school, as well as the fights that took place there, Miguel simply said, "What I went through and my colleagues went through—it wasn't easy." He knew, too, that better schooling options were available even in the city of Lawrence (for example, the local Catholic high school, which his parents could not afford) and certainly in the nearby towns of Methuen, Andover, and Haverhill, all of which had well-funded and better run public high schools.

These accounts evoke the moral contract between students and schools discussed by Theodore R. Sizer and Nancy Faust Sizer in their book *The Students Are Watching: Schools and the Moral Contract* (1999). The Sizers remind us that schools have economic and civic purposes. Schools teach students the labor market skills that they will need but also the skills to be good citizens, including how to respect and take care of one another. Students know when the moral contract is not being maintained—for instance, through under-resourced schools and low academic expectations—even if they do not always say so directly. Students at these schools learn that not much is expected of them, both in school and in life.

The Sizers open their book with a poignant exchange between a middle-class teacher and her working-class student in front of their high school. The student cannot understand why the teacher would choose to be at the school. He has no choice, but surely it must be different for her.

> He has accepted the message that such a high school conveys: You kids deserve to be neglected, to be surrounded by a blatant lack of respect. Besides an ugly, out of date building, you will have inadequate supplies, large classes, and many transient or substitute teachers who have been given the impression that it is their job to babysit rather than to teach. He sees no way out of such a "dump" for himself. But he cannot see why she

would choose even to come to such a place, let alone to work in it. (Sizer and Sizer 1999, xi)

In his prior volumes, Theodore Sizer (1996) shows that students in our schools, across a range of quality, know when they are not being challenged (and when they are) and what their schooling is supposed to signify about them and their potential.

It is within this context that we can understand the reflections of most of the Dominican children who went to urban public schools: all were painfully aware that the moral contract between children and schools was not being maintained, at least not for them. These children understood that they had somehow ended up in the "bad" schools and that teachers did not have to see or even care about them (although some did, as I discuss later). In fact, neglect was normalized. The Dominicans we interviewed were not able to change the overall neglect, but at the same time they realized and expected that children who attended the "better" schools had quite different experiences. In this way, disparities in quality between schools were also normalized.

The Dominicans' schooling experiences must also be understood in the context of post-1960s resegregation along the lines of skin color, poverty, and language (Noguera 2003; Orfield and Lee 2006; Grant 2009; Datnow et al. 2010).[4] Blacks and Latinos tend to be enrolled in public schools that have fewer institutional resources, including highly qualified teachers and lower teacher turnover rates, but whose students are much more likely to come from low-income homes (National Academy of Education 2007; Frankenberg and Siegel-Hawley 2008; Gándara et al. 2003; Gándara and Contreras 2009; Kahlenberg 2009). The result tends to be schools with lower academic expectations and less curricular rigor, higher dropout and violence levels, and little preparation for college (Balfanz and Legters 2004; Diamond, Randolph, and Spillane 2004; Fernandez 2004; Carter 2005; Hill 2008; Kasinitz et al. 2008; Orfield, Frankenberg, and Garces 2008; Suárez-Orozco, Suárez-Orozco, and Todorova 2008; Itzigsohn 2009).

Our comparison of the Dominicans and Colombians points to the importance, however, of looking at the Latino category in the disaggregate. The fourteen Colombian students at public urban schools were more likely to voice concerns about within-school racial and ethnic stratification than about school inequalities. This tendency might have had something to do with different patterns of school segregation. Slightly fewer than half of the Colombians attended schools that were 10 to 20 percent Hispanic and black; the remainder were in schools where this student population ranged from 45 to 80 percent. When the Colombian students spoke of stratification, they typically were referring to the balkanization of Latinos and blacks in less rigorous courses (Fernandez 2004; Conchas

2001, 2006; Hao and Pong 2008). José made the following observation about the racial dynamics at his Providence high school: "The advanced standing group were probably the only white people in the school. I was one of the few minorities in there. I realized that the other [minority] students didn't have the same opportunity, the same access to some of the more, like, college-type teachers." On the whole, the picture of the urban high schools attended by the Colombians was more mixed, with fewer negatives and some positives offsetting the negatives.

Supports

How did the respondents get the supports they needed to successfully navigate these challenging school contexts? Many of the Dominican students in public urban schools and some of the Colombians participated in an enrichment program. As discussed earlier, a key theme was the opportunity these programs gave the children to gain social and academic skills. Just as important was how they gained these skills and from whom, namely, the role of nonfamily adults. Research has shown that assistance from a nonfamily adult, whether through a programmatic intervention or organically within the school, is a key factor in the academic success of poor and working-class immigrant children (Gándara 1999; Stanton-Salazar 2001; Gibson 2003; Harris, Jamison, and Trujillo 2008). Neither authoritative parents nor the presence of a significant nonfamily adult is enough on its own to set the immigrant child on the journey to higher education; however, the combination of the two is "decisive" (Portes and Fernandez-Kelly 2008, 26).[5] However, immigrant youth, especially from such backgrounds, seldom get the kinds of mentoring that they need (Suárez-Orozco, Suárez-Orozco, and Todorova 2008).

Mentoring is a key function provided by nonfamily adults who offer instrumental or psychosocial supports such as role modeling, tutoring, and encouragement (Rhodes, Grossman, and Resch 2000, 1667; Roffman, Suárez-Orozco, and Rhodes 2003; Reddick 2007; Erickson, McDonald, and Elder 2009). In a role typically facilitated by programmatic interventions, a formal mentor is an adult who teaches a mentee how to set goals and how to deal with possible challenges, while also lending moral support and sometimes brokering opportunities. Informal mentors, also adults, provide some of these benefits in an informally based relationship. Although informal mentors have more transitory relationships with their mentees, their role is still valuable; the issue is that there are too few informal mentors available to less advantaged youth (Stanton-Salazar and Spina 2003).

To better understand the importance of such advocacy, consider the accounts of two second-generation Dominican women. Alexsa, the young woman who had negative memories of high school, nonetheless was able to graduate and go directly to a four-year college. In addition to Upward Bound, she also credited the University of Rhode Island's Talent Development Program, which she learned about through the university's recruiting seminars at her high school. Founded in 1968 in response to the assassination of Dr. Martin Luther King, the program provides academic and social supports for students from disadvantaged backgrounds, especially during a summer spent living on campus after their senior year of high school; participants who passed the classes and met the entrance criteria were offered a pipeline into the college, where they were matched with a guidance counselor for further assistance. Alexsa's guidance counselor was a Native American Indian/white man whom she called "an angel" and with whom she still kept in touch three years after college. She framed her relationship with the counselor as one of mutual caring and respect (Noddings 2002). She even described him in familial terms as "fictive kin," a concept that crucially depends on the duration of the relationship (Grossman and Rhodes 2002; Stanton-Salazar and Spina 2003; Smith 2008; Suárez-Orozco, Suárez-Orozco, and Todorova 2008).

> He was like my father. I would meet him every week or every other week. We just have such a great time talking about my classes. I think that's awesome. It's really important to have somebody who listens to you and who really appreciates what you've done for the day. Or what you've done for the week. And your progress. I respected him.

Alexsa's use of a kin term is especially interesting, given that she grew up in a fractious family home in which her stepfather routinely threw out Alexsa and her brother and her mother took his side. She did have the caring relations of her nearby aunt and grandmother, who occasionally took in Alexsa and her brother and who probably served as a model of care that she later employed (Noddings 2002).

Leslie's account highlights the role of a community faith-based organization (Smith 2008). She was a graduate of Greater Lawrence Regional Vocational Technical High School, a newer facility than Lawrence High School, but one criticized by community members for its vocational orientation. Leslie said that her guidance counselor at "the Voc," as the school was commonly known, tended to favor the school's dual-enrollment students, who were also taking college classes for credit. More marginalized were students, like herself, who were not at the top of the class but wanted to pursue college options instead of vocational jobs. It was Tom Meronas,[6] the director of a local branch of the community organization, who proved crucial to Leslie's transition to college. Meronas took a sustained role in the process. He helped her compile a list of three colleges, all in-state, and after she decided on the University of Massachusetts at Lowell, he drove her to register for classes and solicited donations to help her pay fees that her financial aid did not cover and her parents could not afford.

Meronas continued to help Leslie throughout the pivotal first year of college, a time when first-generation college students like Leslie and Alexsa are more likely to leave than other students (Horn 1998; Cushman 2006; Grodsky and Jackson 2009). Although Lowell was only about fifteen miles away, the commute by public transportation—Leslie could not afford a car—took two buses and an hour each way. Because of her class and transportation schedules, Leslie was leaving home before 7:00 AM and returning at seven o'clock in the evening; she would often fall asleep on her books from exhaustion. The first-year curriculum was challenging, and Leslie finished her first semester with only Cs and Ds. Noticing her distress, Meronas raised donations to pay Leslie's boarding fees for the spring semester in the hopes that living on campus would make things easier for her.

The hopeful, focused work of the students and staff was evident during my visit to the small office of Meronas's organization in late January 2002, shortly after I had started the 1.5- and second-generation interviews. One wall displayed college posters that presented schools in picture-perfect settings, and on another were posters of the Christian faith. Leslie was readying her sheet music for rehearsal that evening. Her uncle, who did not look much older than Leslie, was preparing his essay for culinary school, with Meronas's aid. An Asian girl was working on her financial aid forms for private colleges, with the help of a Latina staff member, and a Latina was looking for scholarship materials on the Internet. Periodically, the young adults would use the four computers, the printer, and the college books.

This picture contrasted with what Meronas later said as he drove me to the Lawrence commuter rail station. It was already early evening, and he matter-of-factly noted that a notorious crack house sat down the hill from the organization's office, which was linked to a church. Apparently, the police sometimes used the church's high views to peer in at the crack house. Noting that no one had yet been shot in front of him, Meronas said that the city had an undeserved reputation for violence, an opinion I would later hear from others.

Regardless of the city's reputation, its disadvantages were real. Lawrence's disadvantages were a topic in my informal chats with community members and in the interviews, and they were evident in existing demographic data. Although there was neighborhood variation, overall the city was under duress, especially those communities where poverty, racial and ethnic segregation, schools with poor learning conditions, and violence were concentrated. Such social problems echo those found in other immigrant and native urban enclaves and made obvious the city's need for programmatic interventions like this one (Wilson 1980, 1987, 1997; Stanton-Salazar and Spina 2003, 241).

The federal program Upward Bound was noted by six Dominican respondents as a defining moment in their high school careers. It was through Upward Bound that the students visited college campuses, often for the first time, and boarded at them during the summers. For some, a benefit was having a desk to work at for the first time; for others, it was the chance to learn from adults of minority backgrounds (African American and Latino) and with fellow minority students (rather than being bored with them in public school). For still other participants, a benefit was the additional academic preparation—they took pride in reading and analyzing more challenging material than what was assigned in their high school. For all participants, a key benefit was the step-by-step structure provided for applying to college: learning what the SAT was, taking the SAT, formulating a list of colleges, filling out financial aid forms, getting fee waivers, writing application essays. Students suddenly had a road map that transformed their college aspirations into realistic expectations, and knowledgeable adults were firmly in charge of shepherding them through the process. The immigrant students were on their own no longer.

A closer look at the experiences of sixteen Dominican children who went to especially challenging high schools, nearly all of them working-class, reveals the importance of nonfamily social capital. Almost all of them received at least one form of nonfamily support, and more than half had multiple kinds, including teachers, guidance counselors, peers, and the church. It was common for a teacher or counselor to recommend the student for a particular program or to encourage the student to take classes at a local college as a way of improving his or her college application profile. Peggy and her friends, all graduates of Lawrence High School, frequently asked: Why us? Why did we end up going on to college and graduate school when our classmates, mainly Dominican and Puerto Rican and from similar family backgrounds, did not? Peggy maintained that it was the teachers who made the difference.

> And the only answer that we come up with is that our teachers pushed us. Somebody believed in us, whereas somebody didn't believe in them, in that way. So that's—you know, that's the only thing we could come up with! [*Laughs*]

Again, there is the idea that an adult noticed and believed in the youth's capacity to succeed and offered useful guidance on how to be successful. Through this interaction built on trust, immigrant children with this kind of support realized that they deserved more than the neglect normalized in their high schools, and they found a way to get more.

Peggy's good relations with teachers started in middle school when the staff there selected her to take an exam for Phillips Academy, the renowned boarding school located in Andover, Massachusetts, just south of Lawrence, her hometown. Based on her scores, Peggy was offered the chance to skip the eighth grade and start at Phillips Academy on a scholarship. The only complication was that she had to board at the school, an idea that did not meet with her parents' approval, given her young age. Andover was only three miles away, but the predominantly white, upper-middle-class town and the culture of boarding school life might as well have been worlds apart for her parents. Twelve years later, Peggy said that she was fine with the decision to turn down Phillips Academy, although she did express some wistfulness about the missed opportunity.

> I really wanted to go. So I was a little disappointed about not being able to go, but I also didn't want to skip eighth grade. [*And why did you want to go?*] I knew that the education was going to be invaluable, you know? At that time, I really knew that it was going to make a difference in my education, but, you know, I didn't want to challenge my parents. [*Laughs*]

Although Peggy did not feel academically stimulated at Lawrence High School and quickly mastered most academic subject matter, she had a lot of free time for extracurricular activities, including youth leadership community programs and the school's student council. Her good relations with teachers and counselors continued, proving invaluable when she was applying to college. Even though she was U.S.-born, Peggy had lived in the Dominican Republic between the ages of five and eight, attending private school there. Knowing this, her counselor suggested that Peggy take the TOEFL, which measures the English academic skills of non-native English speakers; using that to replace her relatively low SAT verbal score was a strategy that seemed to work. Peggy was admitted to Wheaton College in Massachusetts.

Even though informal mentoring often came through chance encounters and was sometimes occasional rather than sustained and long-term, it also had lasting effects on immigrant children's decision-making (Stanton-Salazar and Spina 2003). At his part-time job with the Massachusetts Turnpike Authority, Thomas became acquainted with an administrator, a Mexican American college graduate, who became a mentor to him and other young men. When Thomas was thinking of enlisting in the U.S. Army right after high school, the mentor advised him against the idea, telling him, "No, you're a smart kid. You can go to school." Yet, when Thomas was struggling with his college applications, he turned to his friends rather than his mentor or his teachers (Son 2010). He graduated thirty-fourth in his class of two hundred and had good relations with his teachers. Thomas's problem was that he had started a bunch of applications but had sent none of them out because he was stymied by the essays. Finally, he panicked: "And it was kind of that last moment, 'I have to do something! I have to do something!' 'Cause everybody's like, 'College! College! College! College!'" It was at that point that a friend suggested Lasell College in Newton, outside of Boston, because the school did not require an essay. Thomas's teachers looked after him, visiting the campus with him, and he eventually earned a scholarship. However, his mentor was disappointed—he believed that Thomas could have gone somewhere better, although he was pleased that the young man was in college.

Mentors did not necessarily have to be members of one's own ethnic or panethnic group. Alejandro spoke of his godmother, a well-to-do white American woman from Long Island who used to date one of his uncles and stayed friendly with the Dominican family following the breakup. Back then, there was a thriving and violent drug trade in the family's neighborhood of Corona, Queens; when two of Alejandro's family members were ensnared in it, they were deported for their criminal involvement. Aware of the neighborhood's isolation and pitfalls, his godmother sought to show the children other possibilities. For more than a decade, she routinely took Alejandro and his younger brother on outings to privileged institutions and activities in Manhattan that opened the door to important sources of mainstream, elite cultural capital: "She'd take us out to restaurants, to plays, stuff like that, so that we'd get some sense of what it's like to really live." Mentors can help shield young people growing up in troubled neighborhoods from the temptation to engage in criminal and other risky activities and show them life paths of hopeful possibility rather than disaffection and deviance (Stanton-Salazar and Spina 2003; Smith 2008).

Schools with Better Resources

A substantial minority of the children had access to exceptional schooling opportunities beyond what was typically available in an urban neighborhood public school. Consistent with what we would expect, the students' accounts referred to the popularly known hallmarks of such schools—strong leadership, stellar teachers, smaller enrollments and class sizes, high academic standards, excellent academic preparation for college, and help with the complexities of the college application process (Coleman 1981; Coleman and Hoffer 1987; Coleman, Hoffer, and Kilgore 1982; Greeley 1982; Blank 1984; Cookson and Persell 1985; Bryk, Lee, and

Holland 1993; Powell 1996; U.S. Department of Education 2002; Deil-Amen and Turley 2007). These high school students were less likely to draw on a friend's hearsay knowledge about college, and their strategies were more likely to be focused on regional and national searches structured by adult guidance. Finally, the academic environment was sufficiently strong—teachers were strong in their prescribed roles and most students were academically prepared—that there did not appear to be a need for teachers to step beyond their official roles and take on mentoring roles for the students to succeed (Erickson, McDonald, and Elder 2009, 344).

Lest we think that success was a foregone conclusion, the picture was not a uniformly optimistic one. Stratification within the schools, particularly along racial and ethnic lines, was mentioned by nearly half of the children. In the case of Catholic schools, this is surprising. Much of what we know about Catholic schools in the United States has to do with their response to large-scale immigration from southern, central, and eastern Europe into America's cities in the mid-nineteenth and early twentieth centuries, and then their response later to native racial and ethnic minorities who moved into the areas vacated by white ethnics. In the post-1960s era, Catholic schools became known for doing a better job than public schools of educating urban, low-income, native minority students through high expectations, relative lack of tracking, discipline, and an ethos of caring (Coleman 1981; Coleman and Hoffer 1987; Coleman, Hoffer, and Kilgore 1982; Greeley 1982; Bryk, Lee, and Holland 1993).[7]

Relatively little research has been done on the children of post-1960s immigrants and Catholic schools. Jennifer Holdaway and I, drawing on the ISGMNY data set, have found a clear benefit in educational attainment for nearly all native and second-generation groups attending Catholic schools and also a positive impact from the avoidance of certain problems, such as early pregnancy for girls and trouble with police for boys. However, there were important differences across groups; graduating from a Catholic school had a strong positive effect on overall educational attainment for all groups except Dominicans. Looking at arrest rates, we find that Dominican men did not benefit as much from attending Catholic school as young men of South American or West Indian background. We were not able to determine whether this was due to shorter attendance, differences in the quality of the Catholic schools attended, or other factors, such as neighborhood quality or discrimination (Louie and Holdaway 2009). In the present study, however, a few of the Catholic school alumni remembered the teachers as being especially attentive to Irish and Italian Americans, who typically have a family history of attending Catholic schools. Less or even negative attention was directed at the Latino and black students, who often had transferred from public schools and were viewed as more prone to having behavioral issues. Although the respondents did not think that such teacher attitudes were an issue for them personally, they did note that their minority peers may have found them difficult.

The public magnet schools were another distinct experience.[8] Salvador noted that attending the widely recognized Stuyvesant High School in New York City came with both benefits and drawbacks. As he astutely observed, going to such a competitive school, ironically, may have limited his chances of getting into a tier-one university compared with going to a less selective high school (Attewell 2001). Although he fared well at Stuyvesant, he was not in the top 5 percent, the top strata needed to gain admission to the nation's very elite universities. Salvador, who was at Northeastern when we met, had made his peace with the bargain and in hindsight valued what he had learned both academically and socially at Stuyvesant.

Judy's memories of the well-known Boston Latin School are consistent with the racial and ethnic disparities that public exam schools continue to grapple with, notably, the relatively small numbers of Latinos and blacks who enroll (Fernandez 2004). It is estimated that Latino students make up only 12 percent of Boston's exam school enrollments (Uriarte, Chen, and Kala 2008). Judy witnessed rapid attrition among her Latino and black classmates. The possible explanations she advanced intersected with much of what has been discussed and debated in the existing literature, possibly because she graduated magna cum laude with a degree in sociology. She put forth individual, family, and institutional reasons: the lack of Latino teachers; the working-class immigrant families of Latino students being unable to give them much assistance with schooling and allowing them to hang out with friends rather than focus on schoolwork; differences in learning styles across race and ethnicity; and finally, inadequate student preparation without adequate responses from the school. Judy situated herself as an exception because, as we saw in chapter 2, her mother was a university graduate in Colombia who earned an MBA in the United States and was a fluent English speaker; she had been able to afford to send Judy to Catholic schools en route to Boston Latin School.

Although Judy had no academic issues at Boston Latin, she did remember some behavioral ones. She was singled out by teachers for supposedly being defiant. Although she had seen this dynamic before between teachers and Latino students (Espinoza-Herold 2003; Lopez 2004), Judy had rarely been involved, mainly because she "never stepped out of line." Yet, as is clear from the following account, sometimes even this was not enough. The incident reveals how a misunderstanding during the routine changeover between classes could quickly take on a combative tone. The teacher assumed that Judy was challenging her authority and did not give Judy a chance to speak.

> The bell had apparently rung, and I had missed it, honestly, because I had been talking to a friend of mine. It was right before Christmas vacation, and I was wishing her a Merry Christmas. [*Laughs*] And so a teacher came out and said, "You in the ...," and she described what I was wearing. And I honestly didn't hear her. And she thought I was ignoring her, and she didn't know who I was. Like, she didn't know me.

As Judy went on to say, it was aggravating enough that the teacher, who did not know her, made assumptions about her motivations—in effect not seeing her—but it was troubling when her homeroom teacher, someone who did know her, did the same.

> So, she took me back to my homeroom and just chewed me out to the whole class, and said how rude I'd been, and how I'd, on purpose, not listened to her. And when she left, I was about to defend myself to my homeroom teacher, who actually knew me, and then he just chewed me out even more, in front of the rest of the class. And I was so angry, because that was so uncalled for, and so demeaning. I mean—why would you ever do that to a kid?

What makes this incident especially interesting is that it occurred in a highly regarded public school. And yet, Judy's account speaks to a similar kind of dynamic—one of not being seen, or being seen as resistant to authority—voiced by her Dominican counterparts at struggling urban public schools (Sizer 1996). The incident reminded Judy that Latinos are seen in stigmatized ways. In this instance, Judy felt as invisible as some of the Dominicans we interviewed, despite the fact that she came from a more privileged family background and attended a magnet high school.

Still, very few of the students who attended better schools recalled needing extra supports. The few who did were private and Catholic school alumni who received help from nonfamily adults in paying the costs of schooling. The extreme affluence of the lifestyles of his fellow private school students came as a revelation for Park: "Their field trips weren't, 'Oh, we're going to a museum.' They were going two weeks around Florida. You know, you need money for those things. So it was definitely a shock to my system." Park's constellation of nonfamily and non-Latino adult sponsors included guidance counselors who found a scholarship for him to apply for; a coach who bought him sneakers so he could practice and compete with the team; staff members who gave him sports uniforms; and his best friend's father, who paid for his Kaplan SAT test preparatory course.

Unlike the other Catholic school students we interviewed, Wayne needed a lot of help. Some of the teachers were generous in giving him help, while others, he said, gave up on him, thinking that, as a Latino, he would not get far in life anyway (Kasinitz et al. 2008).

> I had some teachers who were really patient for me and really went out of their way to get me to learn the school, and I had a teacher tell me I had a great future as a garbage man or carrying somebody's golf bag. Yeah, so I was, like, thanks [*laughs*], so that's another option.

Wayne's guidance counselor definitely belonged in the helpful category. Admittedly more enthused about his social life than his schoolwork, Wayne graduated from high school with nearly straight Ds, hardly a stellar record for colleges to consider. Thanks to the efforts of his guidance counselor, however, he was able to enter Worcester State College in the fall.

> That was a miracle. But this [high] school was so prestigious that the guidance counselor was able to work out a deal that I graduated in May, and in June I was already at college doing a presummer session on a probationary basis, so my approval was contingent on that summer program. So I ended up taking three classes that summer, and I aced all three, and then I got in. So he had to help me out and get me in. I got rejected by some pretty crappy schools. [*Laughs*]

Antony also received specialized attention from his teachers that he felt encouraged his development. He was a graduate of a predominantly white public high school in Pelham, New Hampshire, which he affectionately referred to as "Small Town, USA." According to Antony, the teachers and administrators took notice of his leadership and academic skills and recommended him for special opportunities, each one of which led to others. He benefited from the cumulative advantages of mentoring (Stanton-Salazar 1997). In ninth grade, he was nominated for a state youth leaders conference. This instilled in Antony a desire to take leadership roles in his school. In eleventh grade, he was nominated by his principal for an international affairs program in Washington, D.C., which led to his interest in the subject. (He later majored in international relations at Tufts University.) Antony was also chosen to participate in a state summer college preparatory program that brought top public school students to the campus of the elite St. Paul's School in Concord, New Hampshire. Finally, he had a close mentoring relationship with the high school librarian, an Ivy League graduate, whom he described as his role model, even though she was a white American woman. The key, as Antony noted, was that he "could talk to her about anything about culture and ethnicity and being different basically." The relationship was a powerful form of cultural connectedness across racial lines (Reddick 2009). The findings so far are consistent with research showing the powerful, life-changing effects that institutional agents can have in the lives of working-class youth by showing them how to actually get to college and believing in their capacity to get there.

Language

For the children of immigrants, a big part of schooling success is acquiring academic English skills (Snow and Freedson-Gonzales 2003; Suárez-Orozco, Suárez-Orozco, and Todorova 2008). That certainly was the case for the respondents we interviewed. What does their success tell us about the controversies over how to educate English-language learners in the United States? Proponents of the "Official English" movement, which originated in the 1980s, have argued that bilingual education is infeasible as an instructional strategy. The passage of Proposition 227 in California in 1998, followed by the Question 2 ballot measure in Massachusetts in 2002, along with other measures around the nation, attests to the widespread public endorsement of this claim.

The respondents' accounts, however, tell the more complex story that language and literacy researchers have long conveyed: it is not that bilingual education per se is flawed as an instructional practice, but rather that there are problems with implementation (Harvard Graduate School of Education 2002; Cazden and Snow 1990; Snow and Freedson-Gonzales 2003). Again, the theme of institutional support was crucial. Depending on how the language programs were implemented, they were experienced as either strong academic nurturance or a way of warehousing students for whom teachers and peers had low expectations (Gutierrez 2002). Eighteen Colombians and sixteen Dominicans had attended bilingual or ESL classes, with the 1.5 generation children about twice as likely to have done so as the second generation.[9] Most attended bilingual or ESL classes for either less than a year or between one and three years before being reclassified as fully English-language-proficient; only a few stayed in ESL five years or longer.

Our respondents' critiques focused on how inadequately the schools facilitated these language programs. Bella, a Colombian, attended ESL classes from grade school through freshman year of high school, all in a Boston suburb. She found herself already falling behind her classmates early on because she had less time to learn the content provided in the regular classroom. She said that the teachers did not help her make up the schoolwork she missed. In high school, Bella clearly felt the stigma associated with being designated as needing language services (McDermott 1987; Stevens 2009). Her classmates would tease her: "You know, 'What's wrong with you? Are you slow?' And it's like, you sit there, and you're going, 'No, I'm not slow. I just know a different language.'" Lucia, a Dominican, received language services for seven years in New York City public schools and liked her teachers. But she, too, felt that the instructional practice did not adequately account for the students' varied levels of English proficiency: "I believe that the theory is great, but the practice—every time a new student comes into the classroom, you're going back. At least in the elementary level, you're going back to ABCs again."

The affirmations of the benefits of language services came from students in *strongly* implemented language programs. José, who was in a bilingual program for two years in a greater Providence junior high school, said, "It's where I pretty much got my language skills. It was very inspiring to me, to see other people in the same situation and to kind of slowly to progress." Like other students who were reclassified, José said the follow-up guidance of teachers and counselors was crucial. Alma, a Dominican who had language supports only in the first and second grades, said that it was a good experience for her; she had since seen her cousins who were "pushed immediately into the English curriculum," without language supports, struggle to keep pace, which only deepened her appreciation for ESL or bilingual instruction.

Peers

Knowing how to avoid the possible downward pull of peers was also key to the success of the respondents.[10] Since many more of the Dominicans spent their youth interacting in contexts with high levels of segregation and poverty and less safety, they were subject to more than their fair share of peer temptations, mostly from panethnics and coethnics. The dangers for young Dominican men were using or selling drugs, dropping out of high school, getting sent to prison or deported, and dying young. A more benign possibility was finishing high school but transitioning into a low-paying job in the formal labor market (Stepick and Dutton-Stepick 2010). For the young women, potential trouble lay in getting pregnant and/or dating someone who used or dealt drugs, went to prison, or died young (Louie and Holdaway 2009). Because the Colombians grew up and went to school in mostly white or more racially and ethnically mixed settings, they were much more likely to speak of a downward pull from peers in other groups as well as from peers in their own. They had different rationales for why whites did not do well in school, depending on context: their peers at exclusive boarding schools knew they were coming into inheritances, while their peers who lived in working-class white neighborhoods were alienated.

Rather than simply avoiding peers who were potentially a bad influence, the children carefully sorted them and thus defined the roles that their peers were permitted to play in their lives: those whom the respondents just knew, friends, and best friends (Son 2010). Their casual acquaintances included classmates they knew by name and sat with at lunch. Their friends were a step closer to the inner circle, and certainly the 1.5- and second-generation individuals we interviewed knew that some of their friends were doing too much partying, hanging out on the street corner, making too much drama about boyfriends, and not paying enough attention to school. Their best friends, they said, were like them in wanting both to have fun and to do well academically. Lenore described her Dominican clique in a specialized public high school in New York City:

> I'm very strict about school. I don't like to be behind. I don't like to get failing grades. I like to read. I like to know about things. I like to discuss things. And everyone I surrounded myself with was always the same. In high school, yeah, we goofed around. We talked about boys. And we would sit down sometimes and have intellectual discussions about religion. About immigration. About, you know, anything that came up. I loved to see that because, it was like, wow! You're educated. You're doing something.

Billy, who went to a struggling public high school in Massachusetts, highlighted the distinctions he made among his peers.

> I'll be honest with you. I had some friends that were really into school, and then I had some friends that hated school. Not friends—I knew people that really didn't like high school, dropped out or left high school, and they're doing other things, but I never considered them my friends, they were just people that I knew.

Children who hung out more often with riskier peers attributed their own success to knowing when to pull back from behaviors that could have very damaging and long-term consequences. How were they able to know when to pull back? The 1.5- and second-generation individuals we interviewed recognized that risky behaviors have different effects for people, depending on their social location. Their perception has an empirical basis. The authors of *Inheriting the City* (Kasinitz et al. 2008) find that native whites in New York City take drugs and break the law just as their second-generation, Puerto Rican, and native black counterparts do, but the whites' families have greater means and the criminal justice system is more tolerant toward them.[11] In other words, the riskiness attached to adversarial behaviors varies by social group (Kasinitz et al. 2008; Snow 2010). Whether they explicitly said this or not, the children at some point realized that they had precious little room for bad behavior since a mistake could have permanent negative consequences. Just as important, they were able to develop an internal metric for gauging when they *absolutely* had to make the right choices—for instance, whether to sell drugs (or continue selling them) or whether to have sex at an early age. For Alexsa, a central part of this internal calibration came from her aunt and grandmother, the sources of her family care:

> My friends in high school, they would become pregnant. And [my aunt and grandmother] would say, "She's not going to be able to go to school. She's not going to be able to travel. She's going to be confined. She's going to be in prison because of the baby, and it's not the baby's fault." They would make things clear. And it hurt, of course. And I would hope it wasn't true, but deep down inside I would say, oh yes, it is true. She's going to have a baby and not be able to go anywhere.

Family discipline and nonfamily adult guidance proved critical to the success of the Colombians and Dominicans we interviewed and to their understanding of why they succeeded and some of their peers did not. They gave credit to family discipline—not necessarily a rigid form but definitely stronger than what their peers had at home—and family organization and functionality. Their parents were working in the formal labor market and were neither wrestling with addictions nor physically violent toward the children. Secondarily, the children mentioned the importance of interventions by nonfamily adults who saw them as "gifted." Their lower-performing peers did not receive such interventions and had no access to enriched academic programs; they were the "regular students" who went to classes but did not really engage with their schoolwork or consider college an option. To borrow from Angela Valenzuela (1999), they were getting schooling, but not an education, and the children we interviewed knew the difference.

Certainly, the respondents acknowledged the institutional barriers faced by Latino youth and the impact of these barriers on outcomes. As Park noted, Latino youth face negative assumptions from others about their potential to achieve, which can make them feel that they are less able to get ahead in life. Right after graduating from Cornell, Park waited tables in Miami for nine months, in part to help his mother financially when she moved to a new apartment. This was right before Park did some traveling in Europe, came back to work in a multinational Internet firm, and finally settled into a book publishing career. He would never forget his experiences waiting on tables, which forcefully reminded him of the negative stereotypes that he and many of his Latino peers had faced since childhood—in institutional contexts, in the media, and in everyday interactions with people (Steele and Aronson 1995; Steele 1999; Valenzuela 1999; Stanton-Salazar 2001).

> And it was amazing how many times I would start speaking to some clients and they'd be, like, "What are you doing? Why are you waiting tables? Where'd you go to college?" And I'd say, "Cornell," and a lot of times they'd be like, "No way." [*The customers?*] Yeah, and it was just amazing how people just assumed, whether because I was wearing an apron or because I was Spanish, that I didn't have a good education. And I feel you

> get those assumptions all the way from when you're young. And my mother would always kind of reassure me.

Asked whether he and his mother talked about such encounters, Park noted that her support was pivotal. Overcoming such challenges and believing in oneself was not an easy process; now that Park was an adult, he did what he could to help young children in similar situations:

> I'd always get so mad, you know? And she'd calm me down, and she'd be, like, "You're smarter than they are, you're going to be fine. You're doing great." And you need that constant affirmation. I try to do that with my little cousins now, you know, or just any really little kid I meet through friends or their kids. It makes a huge difference—at least from my experience.

Analytically speaking, individual agency emerged quite clearly from the respondents' accounts, even if they did not explicitly frame the comparison this way. Although the family could help, the choices were ultimately made by the children, who had to make sense of their options and choose well. The respondents were careful not to judge their less successful peers and were often sympathetic toward them. They acknowledged that their peers had a limited repertoire of choices and might have come from more challenging family situations. Yet individual agency was a strong undercurrent in their own explanations.

Even when peers were beneficial, they were nearly always part of a wider constellation of adults (Erickson, McDonald, and Elder 2009, 359). When Sally's Colombian parents decided that they could not afford to send her to New York University, having put her through Catholic schools, she went to Nassau Community College. The college had been disparaged in her high school circles as the "Thirteenth Grade." Yet it was there that Sally and her friends—all of them bright, motivated, and either lacking the funds to pay full tuitions and/or still trying to figure out their options—banded together. They formed a student club, applied for and received school funding, and hired school vans to transport the club members all over New York State and even to Virginia to look at four-year colleges to which they could transfer. Even more important than these trips was the guidance they received from the Nassau Community College staff, tailored to each student's specific circumstances. The "peer travels" provided a focused way to check into the crucial information provided by the staff.

> They let us know, "Hey, you can go to Cornell, you can go to an Ivy League university, and pay the same that you'd pay at Binghamton, the same that you'd pay at [State University of New York] Geneseo, Stonybrook." And it

was just like, most of us were like, "What are you talking about? We've never heard of this." And so that's how I ended up going to Cornell.

What can we learn from this analysis of the nonfamily constellations of support so crucial to the respondents' schooling success? The public urban school students clearly both needed and received guidance from informal and formal mentors, the latter typically through programmatic interventions. Some teachers also looked after the students at key junctures. It is clear, then, that we need programmatic interventions for low-income and/or minority students and professional development for urban public school teachers to become mentors (Suárez-Orozco, Onaga, and de Lardemelle 2010; Haller, Portes, and Lynch 2011b). Yet not all strategies involve policy intervention. For instance, some individuals are generous enough to serve as informal mentors (Roffman, Suárez-Orozco, and Rhodes 2003).

The experiences of the students who did not go to urban public schools both fit and complicated the prevailing conception of those schools. Overall, the schools were framed and experienced as places conducive to learning. Teacher mentors were not as visible, probably because both the teachers and the students themselves were well matched in expectations, guidance, and outcomes. A few students did benefit from teacher mentors, however, showing that "mentoring is most common among youths who already possess a wealth of social resources" (Erickson, McDonald, and Elder 2009, 360). Still, a number of respondents cited minority peers who were clearly struggling and needed to have someone in a position to help to reach out to them. Although there has been some research on minority and low-income students in these more optimal schooling contexts (Zweigenhaft and Domhoff 1991; Irvine and Foster 1996; Gaztambide-Fernández 2009; Louie and Holdaway 2009; Khan 2011), we need to know more about how and why some students in them succeed (or do not succeed), and what happens to those students who exit. There is particular impetus to pursue this kind of research on magnet schools, which have been seen as a way to improve the quality of urban education and as a desegregation strategy (Blank and Archbald 1992, 81; Frankenberg and Siegel-Hawley 2008). Yet there are many differences among magnet schools, and we do not know which schools have "substantial effects" and which do not (Gamoran 1996, 14).[12] Regardless of the context, peers can be sources of both negative and positive social capital. It is important to look at them alongside adult sources of support and at the ways they work (or do not work) in concert.

To sum up, in this and the previous chapter, we have seen how immigrant families navigate the process of getting their children to college in a land still relatively new to them. The foundation for the children's success rests with both family and nonfamily, or institutional, supports. The children definitely have the care and backing of their families. But they also have the backing of institutional agents who help them decode the rules and languages of their schools and other institutional contexts and show them ways to succeed in them. Some agents also provide emotional and moral sustenance.

Most of the middle-class children went to better schools, and it was easier for them to have a more aligned relationship with their teachers and counselors. Working-class children going to better schools also did not have to work as hard to have advantageous relations with adults. It was working-class children going to inferior schools who had the toughest challenge. Although these were the children who most needed this kind of sponsorship, they attended schools that were the least equipped to provide it. However, the respondents in our study were able to get the guidance and information they needed to finish high school and go to college, mainly from teachers and non-school-based programmatic interventions. Certainly, by transitioning to college (and in some cases completing it), the 1.5- and second-generation individuals we interviewed actualized the hope that their immigrant parents had brought with them to the United States. They had won the immigrant bargain.

Chapter 6

How the Bargain Was Won: Higher Education and Mobility

I met Alejandro, a sophomore at Northeastern University, in the school's student center. Everything looked new at the gleaming student center, a hub of commercial and social activities—the downstairs food court was joined upstairs by a Friendly's and a Starbucks, along with a hair salon, a travel agency, a mini-mart, an art gallery, and a space for quiet. Colorful flags representing the university's student organizations—including the African Club; Hillel; the bisexual, lesbian, and gay association; and students for environmental action—draped the railings of the upper floors, which were visible from below. Alejandro and I sat in an area with two TVs built into the dark wood walls. Northeastern is not too far from Lynn, Massachusetts, where Alejandro grew up after his family moved from Queens, New York, and Alejandro said that he was having a great time there. The advantages of college, he said, were not only the academics (he majored in computer science) but also the opportunity to participate in activities that pushed his thinking and skill sets. He was a member of the Latin American Student Organization (LASO) and would be chairing an upcoming gender forum; he also spoke at special events sponsored by a group of students responding to the events of 9/11, and he mediated for a student judicial affairs group.

Alejandro did feel some pressure to succeed, which he linked to being Latino. He knew that Latinos are stereotyped as academic failures and wondered whether that would affect how others saw him and what they expected of him (Steele and Aronson 1995; Steele 1999). As an immigrant, he also faced the weight of his Dominican parents' expectations for him to do well. He did not think that native white Americans had such strong external or internal pressures: "If we do mess up, it seems more like, 'Oh, look at them. They can't even go through school,' whereas I've seen one of my roommates fail out of college, and he was white, yeah, and it was like, 'Whatever.'"

Park's account of attending Cornell University during the late 1990s also highlighted the barriers of money, race, and ethnicity, along with the remarkable opportunities that college offered him. Because he came from a predominantly Latino area of Miami and felt welcome at the local private day school, where he had been a scholarship student, Park said that he was not prepared for the "racism" and class barriers that greeted him in the university town of Ithaca and at Cornell. He remembered feeling more comfortable in Ithaca "because there were a lot of poor people in town," and yet the residents viewed him as an outsider because he was a student at the elite university. On campus he encountered students making thoughtless comments like, "You can't major in English, you're Spanish, you know," recalled Park with a laugh.

His freshman year was marked by contradictions. He loved the diverse viewpoints expressed in his class on racism in Latin America, and yet he and a few Latino friends got into a big fight with the residents of an entire (largely non-Latino) fraternity house after two of them called Park and his friends "spics" as they walked by. What helped him was the Latino Living Center, one of several cultural houses on campus that allowed anyone in the undergraduate community to join (Museus and Quaye 2009). Yet Park found fissures in the Latino student population. Puerto Rican students from New York City had their own cliques from which he was excluded, and on the weekends and at Thanksgiving they would "go back to the Bronx, and they're just back at home." Park found a home with the Chicano students, who, like him, were from out of state and could not afford to visit family for short breaks. "I almost became honorary Chicano; I was always with them, you know, it was another of my safe havens. And also, very vocal as a group and very strong, so it was nice to hang out with them."

A key assumption of the parents and children we interviewed was that once the children had a college degree, they would have a clear path to material success. The links between a college education and higher earnings, better jobs, and enhanced social status were clear among the families (Barrow and Rouse 2005; Attewell and Lavin 2007; Louie 2007; Grodsky and Jackson 2009). But how did the children experience college and see their trajectories? This question stems from the debates about whether education, and especially higher education, is indeed a great equalizer (Mann 1868) or whether individual and group-based factors, such as family economic status, race, and ethnicity, still matter in higher education and in mobility (Stevens 2007, 2008). In this chapter, I discuss how those debates help us understand the respondents' interpretations of college and their own mobility. I also show how their views are shaped by the multiple frames of reference they drew on as the children of immigrants.

In our study, the child's postsecondary institution was definitely linked to the immigrant parents' class status, ethnicity, and mobility path. Nearly all the respondents from middle-class families went to four-year colleges, compared to three-fourths of the working class. Twenty-four of the four-year college respondents were enrolled in or had graduated from tier-one colleges and universities. Colombians were more than twice as likely as Dominicans to be at tier-one schools. There were also patterns related to family mobility path among the respondents who went to tier-one schools. Three had parents who replicated their high status in the United States; eight had parents who had seen a dramatic rise in their fortunes; and another nine had downwardly mobile parents, many of whom had held in the home country higher-status jobs typically associated with some kind of postsecondary education. In other words, most of the respondents at top schools had parents who were dramatically upwardly or downwardly mobile or had reproduced their high status. By comparison, four had parents who had seen only limited upward mobility. The picture was quite different among the community college and vocational school students; eight of the sixteen respondents had limited riser parents or parents whose low status in the United States was similar to their status in the home country.

That family background was linked to where the children went to college should not surprise us, given the post-1960s story of American higher education. On the one hand, institutional doors have opened up to members of previously excluded groups, including low-income individuals, women, and members of racial and ethnic minorities (Louie 2007). The rapid expansion of enrollments has been concurrent with a rise in the number of postsecondary institutions. On the other hand, owing to a demographic artifact (the coming of age of the baby boom generation's children), the applicant pool has been greater than the number of available slots, especially at the most selective colleges (Alon and Tienda 2007). There continue to be substantial gaps according to income and race and ethnicity (for blacks, Latinos, and Southeast Asians) as well as gender (Teranishi 2010; Lee and Ransom 2011; Uy 2011). Students from more financially advantaged families still tend to go to college at much higher rates and to go to four-year institutions, while their less-well-to-do peers can be found in vocational and technical schools (Ellwood and Kane 2000; Hochschild and Scovronick 2003; Social Science Research Council 2005). Meanwhile, four-year colleges have increasingly become stratified by student family income. Simply put, children from better-off families are going to more selective institutions and thus have better opportunities (Astin and Oseguera 2004; Carnevale and Rose 2004).[1]

That none of the community college students and a number of the students at top-tier colleges had downwardly mobile parents suggests that these parents may have had cultural capital that served them well in negotiating new contexts (Fernandez-Kelly 2008; Zhou et al. 2008). For instance, some of the children's accounts stress access to non-ethnic resources, both those they knew about and those they just stumbled upon. More research needs to be done on whether downwardly mobile immigrant parents do in fact have particular advantages that are not as easily measured but that help both them and their children—including the advantage of being seen as someone whom higher-status individuals wanted to help.

In the rest of this chapter, I turn to how the children themselves understood the intersections of higher education, family origins, and social mobility. I analyze how they saw barriers to social mobility and whether and how they viewed these barriers to be relevant to their own trajectories, both in college and afterward. I also shed light on how the children framed the overall college experience, namely, what they learned about themselves as they navigated their institution.

Views on and Encounters with Discrimination

Most of the children said that they recognized the existence of barriers to getting ahead in the United States. Social mobility, even among the second generation—who were thought to have a more level playing field than the first generation—was not seen as solely a function of individual drive and talent. Rather, the respondents identified complex barriers related to race, ethnicity, and class in access to and completion of college. They saw family class background as having a significant impact on gaining access to better resourced neighborhoods, receiving a high-quality education, and avoiding illnesses related to poverty, which can affect the potential for success in school (Rothstein 2004).[2] They also cited intangible advantages, like the quality of one's connections or social capital. Some also brought up legal permanent resident status and access to citizenship and the important advantages both conferred compared to being undocumented. According to my respondents, social class disadvantages cut across race and ethnicity, although they were strongly correlated; legal status was also thought to cross national origins, although its effects were disproportionately felt by some groups, such as Mexicans (Massey and Sanchez R. 2010).

However, there were differences by ethnicity in actual experiences with discrimination—"not all 'non whites' are alike" (Kasinitz et al. 2008, 326). Philip Kasinitz (2008) and his coauthors argue that discrimination is more than being subject to stereotypes and everyday social distancing, important as those experiences are; discrimination is not the same as unequal treatment, even though the two terms are often conflated. Discrimination refers to those instances when ascribed characteristics, notably race, either alone or combined with other factors, are seen as having a direct bearing on outcomes, like one's treatment by the police and chances of being evaluated fairly in school, getting hired, or being promoted (Kasinitz et al. 2008). Dominicans were much more likely to report physical harassment and the denial of opportunities from people in authority, mainly whites. A few men spoke of being followed in stores and stopped by the police for no reason other than the fact that they were walking in the neighborhood (Itzigsohn 2009). When they ventured into neighborhoods other than their own, women and men alike recalled being spat at and called "spic" and "those damn Puerto Ricans," told to go back to Spain, and denied apartments even though they were qualified renters. They recalled inattention from precollegiate teachers, who seemed to favor the white students, or the wrong kind of attention: one respondent recalled a high school teacher who recommended speech therapy to correct the respondent's "accent." The Colombians were more likely to report social distancing, such as receiving mean looks when they spoke Spanish in their mostly white neighborhoods, being asked by white peers whether they sold drugs—as Colombians are stereotyped as doing (Guarnizo, Sanchez, and Roach 1999)—or being excluded from social activities by their white classmates.

These differences were driven in part by geographic and social incorporation and in part by phenotype. Because Colombians were more likely to live in better-off and more integrated neighborhoods, they did not have to deal as much with negative neighborhood effects. Dominicans were more than twice as likely as Colombians to report being medium- or medium-dark-skinned and having variation in skin color within their families.[3] Thus, it makes sense that they would be more likely to report the kinds of bias and denial of opportunities that darker-skinned individuals, whether native or immigrant, are more likely to face in the United States (Itzigsohn 2009). It is certainly the case that both second-generation and native individuals undergo "stereotyping, peer tensions and fights," often along ethnic lines; however, only blacks and other individuals with dark skin "experience discrimination and unequal treatment from authority figures who have real power over their lives—teachers, police, and employers" (Kasinitz et al. 2008, 325). Indeed, some of the Colombians from families of ranging phenotypes recognized the differential treatment they received as a result.

The College Experience: The Challenge of Being "Poor and Smart"

This relative lack of academic and social preparation and their families' limited financial and cultural resources gave some respondents, mainly Dominicans (although they were joined by a few Colombians), a challenging transition to college (Cushman 2006; Deil-Amen and DeLuca

2010). Some were the first generation to go to college or had missed out on a college-educated parent's guidance owing to divorce or death. Others had parents who were educated in non-American colleges and did not have the requisite cultural capital to help their children. For most of these respondents, college marked their first time interacting in integrated settings, often with middle- and upper-middle-income students who were largely white (Kasinitz et al. 2008). Based on their experiences, some of the respondents were skeptical that anyone with the relevant credentials and skill sets, regardless of social origins, could make it into a selective institution and succeed there (Karabel 2005). Rather, they voiced the idea that colleges and universities operate under market incentives. In such a system, the odds are against "poor and smart" applicants. Lenore said:

> So many kids are so smart and have such a desire to get ahead, and they just can't. No one's willing to give them a chance. College is a business. And that's all they're in for. They don't want to lose money. And why give money out to someone who is poor, when they can make money from somebody that is rich.

Underrepresented minority students, defined by respondents as being from economically disadvantaged backgrounds, were often seen as needing affirmative action and bridge programs to get into college and institutional supports there, like Latino faculty mentors or Latino student centers, to finish. Lourdes, a graduate of the University of Massachusetts at Amherst, was dismayed that the public system was cutting precisely these kinds of programs. She understood where "white Americans are coming from" if they believed that such programs were not fair, but doing away with such programs, she noted, would reduce college access for poor and working-class minority students: "That's the only way that colored people could get any support in the door."

Those respondents who had graduated from lower-performing high schools had to make up for lost ground while adjusting to the new academic climate.[4] For many, the new climate included larger class sizes and a greater expectation of students' self-reliance, especially at bigger universities, where it could be more difficult to get the attention of faculty members (Berger and Braxton 1998; Hearn and Holdsworth 2002). Lourdes, a graduate of Lawrence High School, spoke to this theme:

> Like, I knew my high school did not prepare me at all. 'Cause I was a very bad math student. So I never studied precalculus. So what is it in college? Precalculus. So that affected me a lot because I didn't do well in precalculus in college. Like, I wasn't accustomed to the huge lecture hall, and you know, there's no one-to-one. It's like one-on-three-hundred.

Julia, who graduated from Merrimack College in 1997, described her lack of preparation in using computers for academic purposes: "In my last year of college, that's when I learned about Microsoft Word and Excel, and probably I should have known that in grade school."[5]

Inattention to study skills in their public urban high schools was another common theme (Haveman and Smeeding 2006). As we saw in chapter 5, Alexsa had benefited from the Upward Bound program and the additional supports of the bridge program at the University of Rhode Island. Nonetheless, she still found herself needing to make some key shifts on her own. She had to learn to speak proper everyday English when she was used to speaking slang with her friends back home. In addition to academic vocabulary and other valuable curricular knowledge, she realized that she lacked study skills. Alexsa had to manage all these adjustments while working to pay for school since she received no financial support from her parents.

> I was like, oh my God, what am I going to do? I would see all these people. It was actually making me angry because they would know the answers. I would be, like, here's another challenge. I was just, like, I'll just try harder. I'll study and practice taking notes. I'm going to pay better attention. I'm going to work harder. And you better believe I busted my ass and I started getting better grades.

As with a number of respondents, the study skills sessions at her university proved to be pivotal (Tinto 1987). Alexsa eventually graduated with a 3.8 grade point average in her major, international relations. Study skills were also needed at two-year institutions, where students were relieved to find them (Deil-Amen and Rosenbaum 2003).

Others found it difficult to seek help. As we saw in chapter 5, Thomas, a second-generation Colombian, was thrilled to be accepted into Lasell College, a suburban Boston campus, as his difficulties with writing college application essays had nearly dissuaded him from applying anywhere. During the week Thomas lived the life of a boarder, and on the weekends he brought his laundry back to his parents' East Boston home and went to his part-time job at the nearby airport. Within a few months, however, his new life began to destabilize as Thomas found the freedom at college to be overwhelming and started skipping classes. After Thomas ended up failing out after only one semester, he moved back home. Thomas told us that he had run into academic troubles because he found it hard to manage his time and to seek help from his professors at Lasell. When we met, he was enrolled in a local community college, where he purposefully improved his skills in time management (he continued to work part time) and help-seeking and developed a strong peer network for support (Light 2001).

Even someone like Park, who had gone to an elite private high school thanks to a scholarship, found that he needed guidance in decoding the new rules of college. He mistakenly thought an Ivy League degree would lead him directly to a lucrative job after graduation. "I was like, 'Oh, I'm going to Cornell, I'm going to major in something, and I'm going to come out and make $100,000.' You know? I was going to have the Ivy League automatic job. And that's not true." Park first had to learn how to choose a major. Fortunately, he had institutional supports to help him find his way.

> I didn't know I had to choose a subject. I thought they would be, like, what do you want to be one day? I learned quickly. You know, luckily, people helped me out, but I don't think they were prepared to have somebody as clueless as me, you know, but I think it's pretty common amongst, like, our people, you know? Like, if you never had an uncle or a brother or anyone, then how are you supposed to know what happens?

Park's experience in a freshman math course showed him that he was "not made for a math major." He excelled in his mandatory freshman writing seminars, however, and eventually decided on English, which led him to a career in publishing.

Sometimes institutional supports could be difficult to locate. A few respondents recalled asking for help from college professors who responded by asking whether the students understood English or saying, "I can tell you're Hispanic because of your accent." When the dialogue started off this way, the students felt silenced. Bea reported on her run-ins with a nursing professor at a University of Massachusetts campus. After failing the first exam, Bea approached the professor to see how she could improve. The professor instead referred her to a resource for students with learning disabilities (Bea did not have one). Then the professor suggested that she consult with the local Puerto Rican embassy. (Bea is Dominican, and in any case, Puerto Rico is an unincorporated territory of the United States.) Undeterred, Bea, who was continuing to struggle, kept asking for help. But the professor always seemed to be in a rush: "She used to ignore me, and you know, I just had to ask her the question, 'Why is this the answer?' And then she say, she just said, 'Because it was the best answer out of the four.' And not really specific at all."

Even on a short writing assignment, which might have lent itself to feedback, Bea said that she received only the following: "She put just on the top of the essay, 'You do not follow the outline. 60.' Circled." The professor had little else to say when she saw Bea during office hours. It was not until Bea brought up her problems at the university's Latino student center that she began to get the appropriate referrals. Assisted by sympathetic Latino faculty members, she connected with a woman who was conducting research on how to retain Latinos in the nursing profession, a staff member who offered support in acquiring test-taking skills, and the department chair (Hernández and Jacobs 2004). Bea's scores did get higher; even though her overall course grade remained below the minimum threshold, she passed the final exam with a 78 and won an appeal to stay in the program.

The immigrant children believed that their experience of college as a high-stakes process was different from the experience of white students, who appeared to be more well-to-do. The apparent freedom of whites to do as they wanted was framed by them in decided contrast to the scant margin for error they saw in their own academic lives (Portes and Fernandez-Kelly 2008). The respondents believed that financial constraints limited their options. Sofia, a native of Lowell, Massachusetts, spent the summer after her freshman year at American University working full time in a local factory, inspecting textiles. She was familiar with the job, as her mother was a factory worker. In her view, white students could just "call Mom and Dad" should anything go wrong, a luxury that she did not have. Said Sofia: "I don't have the money to do an extra semester. I don't have time or money to fail a class. They don't care, they'll do whatever, then they'll be like, 'Oh, that's okay, Mommy and Daddy will pay for next semester.' I can't do that." Other respondents compared childhood friends who had ended up pregnant or in jail to their privileged college peers, a comparison that made visible the distinctions in the American opportunity structure. Unable to relate to her college classmates, who cried because they got a bad grade or had a fight with their boyfriend, Alexsa said, "Be real. This is school, and you're here to learn and not here for drama. It was just like, 'You're wasting my time and I don't want to be around you.'"

Scholarships and need- and merit-based financial aid often did not cover all these respondents' costs of attending college; work and loans served as other key sources of funds (Long 2010). More than half of the Dominicans and about two-thirds of the Colombians received family support—not only from parents but also from aunts, grandmothers, cousins, and siblings—to help pay tuition and book costs, rent, or transportation. Some families, however, struggled to help out, even to raise only a few thousand dollars, and relied on tax refunds and careful budgeting. Among those who reported receiving no family assistance, a few said that they felt obligated to help their parents financially; a few others said that their parents had paid for Catholic schools in the hope that the children would be better positioned to earn college scholarships and now could not muster the funds to contribute to college.

In sum, although they shared their families' belief in the American Dream and the capacity of the second generation to avoid the formidable immigrant obstacles of language and culture, most of the children nevertheless identified significant barriers to upward mobility here, especially at the intersection of race, ethnicity, and class. Some experienced these barriers firsthand because they were directly related to their parents' incorporation, such as negative neighborhood effects in the form of underperforming schools and high crime rates. Other firsthand barriers had less to do with the parents' incorporation than with the attitudes and behaviors of people in authority, mainly white Americans; these barriers were experienced as prejudicial treatment in the children's early forays into the labor market, in school, and in encounters with the police (Mollenkopf 1999).

On the face of it, the children's interpretation might seem to challenge the key planks of the immigrant bargain. After all, why continue to strive so hard for something if the path continues to be blocked? How did the children maintain the necessary optimism in the face of rather bleak structural disadvantages that were not readily subject to personal control? As we saw in chapters 2 and 3, the parents themselves maintained a delicate balance between optimism and pessimism about the immigrant journey. The 1.5- and second-generation children had a different challenge. How did they reconcile these two seemingly contradictory ideas—education as the great equalizer and barriers to upward mobility via education—in a way that kept them invested in the process?

The Impact of Discrimination

The children we interviewed had two responses to the barriers they identified. A minority thought that they would face unequal treatment in the labor market and other institutions. These respondents saw higher education as an invaluable tool of upward mobility, but not necessarily adequate by itself. The playing field would still remain uneven for them, owing to race. Others found the African American experience instructive: here was a group whose highly educated members still sometimes did not seem to get a fair chance to advance—being black somehow counted against them as they encountered subtle barriers.[6] These respondents did not expect their experiences to be much different. Penny, a Colombian woman attending Northeastern University who had grown up in a hardscrabble section of Bridgeport, Connecticut, said that the move upward was daunting and would require that she work twice as hard as a white man. As both a minority and a woman, she felt that the bar set by others in authority would be that much higher. Said Penny: "Proving not only to yourself but to, like, the company that you're able to do as much as anybody can. I always feel as if, like, being good isn't good enough. I always have to be, like, on top."

The majority of the respondents, while perceiving barriers in American life and believing that higher education was not necessarily an equalizer, still also believed that discrimination would not limit their social mobility. The dominant theme they expressed was the need for a strong belief in one's own abilities in order to persevere and to defeat any barriers. The respondents were more worried about the power of their own self-defeatism—which they could control—than the power of discrimination in their lives. Dominicans and Colombians alike subscribed to the belief that success depends on the person. Their interpretation is consistent with the immigrant analogy, namely, the idea that immigrants across national-origin groups work harder than native-born minorities and thus do better. Or as Alfonso put it, "My impression is, if I allow myself to be limited by that, then I'm probably just going to be limited, just 'cause I think it."

Many cast a judgmental eye on fellow Latinos and blacks whom they believed succumbed to negative thinking and did not have enough faith in themselves to succeed. The respondents criticized such "negative thinking" with comments like "No excuses," "Stop with the complaining," "You're in withdrawal," and "People are always keeping themselves down." Compare the following two accounts. Lenore was a nineteen-year-old Dominican born in the United States, and twenty-year-old José had arrived in the United States from Colombia at the age of ten. Both had grown up in a mother-headed household with little financial support from their father, and both had gone on to attend a four-year university, Lenore at Northeastern and José at Brown. Lenore said:

> I really hate when they're, like, "Oh, I'm Hispanic, nail me to the cross. I can never make a good grade because I'm Hispanic and the world keeps me down." I hate that! Like, it totally depends on you. And I'm saying this for African Americans too. You're the first one who is against yourself. If you don't bring yourself up, nobody is going to do it for you.

And José said:

> There are mental ceilings that are put on certain groups on what their achievement is and what they are capable of, and that idea is connected to somebody's success. Like the whole inferiority complex—"Oh, I'm Latino and am only able to do this and that"—that limits ourselves.

In both cases, the discussions of what José termed the "inferiority complex" followed and formed counterpoints to their impassioned analyses of the strong obstacles to getting ahead in the United States. Referring to non-Hispanics' perception of her, Lenore matter-of-factly said, "The fact that they think I can't do the job because I'm Hispanic, I speak another language. Because I'm not a rich person, never was and probably never will be. I'm from the ghettos of New York." José, meanwhile, prefaced his comments with a reflection on inequality in public school funding. Such inequalities, he said, derived from racial and social injustices and definitely influenced the kind of education that children received. He pointed to two high schools in his greater Providence hometown as evidence of the variance between schools even within the same district (Hochschild and Scovronick 2003): "Johnson[7] is probably one of the poorest in the entire school system and West is one of the best, and they are a block away from each other. It's very frustrating."

This institutionally inscribed inequality was out of the individual's control, but one's perspective on life—whether to believe in negative societal stereotypes or to work toward dispelling them—was subject to choice. José saw both as being important and thus highlighted the influence of individual "mental handicaps." Indeed, while noting the institutional barriers, respondents emphasized individual agency—or "doing what you had to do." The respondents' underlying optimism about individual agency—the ability to chart one's own destiny even in the face of structural limitations—was very similar to the way some of their parents reacted to racial discrimination in the United States.

For some, affirmative action programs also offered a strong counter to institutionally inscribed barriers. Although Salvador, a young Dominican man, believed that "it is always a lot tougher for Latinos to try to move on up," he also pointed to programs for minorities as equalizing the playing field. Thus, he did not think that he would be limited in the labor market. Diversity, according to this prevailing sentiment, was now valued (Bowen and Bok 1996), and thus, being Hispanic could be an advantage. Similarly, being bicultural and bilingual could be advantages. This viewpoint is consistent with the "diversity rationale for affirmative action," which has a strong empirical basis (Kasinitz 2008, 263). Today the ranks of the upwardly mobile in corporate America and elite colleges include a substantial number of second-generation children who benefited from public policies developed in part to address the legacy of injustices that severely limited life opportunities among African Americans (Massey et al. 2007; Kasinitz 2008; Kasinitz et al. 2008; Waters 2011).

Not everyone was of the mind that Hispanics (or any group) should receive focused attention from these kinds of programs. Wayne, the son of retired factory workers, often found himself arguing against affirmative action, even though he said that his stance did not make him popular, especially in minority student organizations at Emerson College, his alma mater.

> I saw huge problems with "Poor me, oh, I don't get things because I'm this, I'm black, because I'm Latino." And I'm like, "Well, what did you do to distinguish yourself?" And when I asked that question, I become the weirdo, the monster, the unrealistic one, but I'm like, "Answer the question. What did you do to distinguish yourself? Why should you get this and not this other person when they have all this to show?"

Wayne equated affirmative action programs not with promoting diversity as a social good or addressing past injustices but with rewarding people who were not qualified. In his view, employers should hire, fire, and promote on the basis of qualifications: "Look at this application without knowing if I'm female, I'm white, I'm black, I'm old, I'm young. Just look at what is there. Is this the person you want to fill the position? And that is what I want."

Finally, some of the Colombians thought that they were given an opportunity that others did not necessarily get, even with affirmative action. Judy, a Colombian woman whose white colleagues in the field of technology management thus far had responded well to her, still thought that she was an exception rather than the norm.

> It's funny, because I don't think the door is wide open for everybody. Like, a lot of times I just feel like I squeak by. Like a door has been opened, but for a split second, and I happen to be the person at the door. Not because the door's open all the time. It's a real gift.

Some feared that affirmative action would be of less value in coming years as their numbers grew; others were concerned about facing a glass ceiling in the future, although they were hopeful that increased networking among Latinos through organizations like the National Society of Hispanic MBAs would offset any limits on their upward mobility (Vallejo 2009).

The respondents' optimism also derived from their positive college experiences. The children we interviewed generally enjoyed college, especially the opportunity to develop personally and intellectually. As we have seen, some took pride in their ability to figure out the institutional context and to meet the academic challenges they faced. The college experience, however, was not all about academics. Another key theme was the respondents' development through participation in extracurricular activities. As Richard Light (2001) found in his interview-based study of elite university students, students participating in these kinds of activities, which do not have to be related to their academic interests, tend to do better academically and enjoy college more. Indeed, the activities mentioned by the respondents in my study were diverse and included sports, sororities and fraternities, the arts and foreign languages, student government, dispute mediation, debate team, and clubs based on disciplines like business and engineering. There was substantial interest in community service, such as volunteering at local homeless and women's shelters, tutoring local schoolchildren, and working on environmental efforts abroad.

Latino student organizations warrant special mention. Although not everyone participated in them, those who did appreciated the sense of belonging they felt in such a group (Museus and Quaye 2009). Lucia grew up on the Lower East Side of Manhattan, which is close to New York City's Chinatown, Little Italy, and the East Village; living there at a time when it was mostly lower-income Dominican and Puerto Rican, Lucia praised the area for its diversity. Syracuse University came as a "culture shock" because the students tended to be white and higher-income than she was used to. The Latino student organization served as a key resource in helping Lucia adjust. "It was kind of like a home away from home because I was able to discuss the issues that were important to my community that I hadn't noticed beforehand. It was a comfortable place." In contrast, other respondents, like Wayne, felt uncomfortable because they had different viewpoints on political issues or did not understand why Latino students needed a venue in which to identify with other Latinos; some did not feel Latino enough because they did not grow up in ethnic neighborhoods or speak Spanish as well as the students participating in the ethnic clubs.

Regardless of the type of activity, the respondents said that these organizations helped them learn valuable organizational and time management skills—for instance, in organizing conferences, handling budgets of thousands of dollars, or simply interacting with fellow students and faculty. A few students thought that their participation in these activities, in the words of Sammy, a student at the University of Massachusetts at Amherst, "offered a more well-rounded view of college" and taught them more than they learned in some of their courses. The students said that their organizational involvement also brought them into the "outside world" beyond college, giving them entrée to high-status individuals, such as prominent international government officials and corporate leaders. This finding is consistent with the idea that "real learning" for college students "meant learning about oneself, discovering abilities or personal sources of strength, developing pride in one's ability to survive and becoming more independent and self-reliant" (Terenzini et al. 1994, 68). Nor was such participation exclusively found among students at the top-tier colleges and universities; respondents across a range of institutional settings described similar extracurricular experiences. The students who were unable to participate in organized school activities and who also worked—mainly community college students who managed intense work and class schedules and a few four-year students—uniformly said that they missed out on an important part of the college experience.

Overall, then, there was a strong generalized sense of second-generation optimism, despite the acknowledgment of very real barriers. The findings reported here are consistent with those of José Itzigsohn's (2009) surveys and in-depth interviews among first- and second-generation Dominicans in greater Providence, Rhode Island. There, too, widespread criticism of the American social structure and the belief that Dominicans as a group were being discriminated against insofar as they had to work "twice as hard as whites to get as far" (180) were counterbalanced by respondents' equally prevalent hopefulness about their future. In Itzigsohn's research, the working-class respondents were likely to be more optimistic. Our own Dominican and Colombian respondents of diverse class backgrounds shared this kind of optimism. Similar to the working-class Dominicans in Itzigsohn's research, our respondents reported seeing enough upward mobility among coethnics, in either their families or their extended social networks, to reinforce their optimism. Asked about barriers to success in the United States, Frank responded by pointing to his father. The older man had left behind a job as a purchasing agent and salesman in the Dominican Republic; after fourteen years in the United States, he was able to return home as a U.S. citizen with his own business and to rent a swanky apartment for his family in a high-rise building in Santo Domingo with gorgeous views of the ever-changing skyline. Noting that his father had "defeated" racial barriers here, Frank said, "Why can't I do it? Why can't any other Latino do it?" That was why he felt he had the same opportunities as everyone else; he sounded this buoyant note right after telling me that Harvard Business School might reject his application because he was Dominican and his family was not sufficiently elite.

The optimism among the respondents in my study, notably their belief in their own capabilities, can also be explained by the second-generation advantage found by Mary Waters and her colleagues. In their comparative research (Waters 2011; Kasinitz, Mollenkopf, and Waters 2004; Kasinitz et al. 2008), these authors find that second-generation individuals, across varied groups, do better than not only their immigrant parents but also their native "racial" counterparts. Dominicans and South Americans, West Indians, and Russian Jews surpass Puerto Ricans, African Americans, and native whites, respectively, in years of schooling, earnings, and labor market participation. The Chinese, meanwhile, are the outliers in that they do better than everyone on such measures, a finding attributed to both the group's diversity in social class origins and its strong social cohesion in the United States, which facilitates the crucial transfer of social capital across class lines. A counterexample is the South American group, which is also diverse in social class origins; however, South American professionals do not maintain social ties and thus do not share social capital with their less advantaged counterparts.

In accounting for this story of second-generation advantage, which others have found as well (Smith 2003; Portes and Fernandez-Kelly 2008; Rumbaut 2008), Waters and her colleagues emphasize the perception of choice. In contrast to earlier second generations, notably those of the early twentieth century, the post-1960s cohort has not been asked to choose between their parental cultures and mainstream American culture (Kasinitz et al. 2008). Indeed, they believe that they have a choice and can combine elements of both in finding their own way as adults. This is not to deny the reality of family origins and structural constraints, both of which can be barriers to upward mobility and influence intergroup differences along these lines. Yet the belief in choice crosses group lines and can be quite powerful. Mary Waters (2011, 245) writes:

> The advantage lies in having a choice—and the knowledge that one does have that choice. Of course, not everyone chooses well, and different groups clearly have different options, depending on both parents' position and the segment of American society into which they are being incorporated. But, other things being equal, seeing choices where others may see mandates and prescriptions is, in itself, a significant advantage.

Second-Generation Optimism and Pessimism: The Dominican and Chinese Comparison

Not all second-generation individuals have the same degree of optimism about their future social mobility. My findings of second-generation optimism among the Dominican and Colombian respondents are in fact opposite to the pessimism I found in my earlier research among Chinese American college students of diverse social class origins (Louie 2004).[8] In that study, about three out of every four respondents who believed that race mattered in their present lives thought it would bear upon their future mobility, in negative ways. They did not believe that the four-year degree they were working toward would necessarily be sufficient protection against discrimination in the workplace. The Chinese who expressed optimism about their future mobility, despite the racial barriers they identified, had different reasons than the Dominicans and Colombians interviewed for this study. The Chinese were more likely to express faith in the American Dream rather than individual agency as a way to combat self-defeatism (to which they did not really attribute much power anyway). Philip Kasinitz and his coauthors (2008, 327) have found that more Chinese and upwardly mobile Dominicans, among others, perceive workplace discrimination "as a challenge—a need to try harder to succeed." Further comparative research needs to be done to identify whether such perspectives vary according to race, ethnicity, and class.

For second-generation individuals, frame of reference may be important: who do they compare themselves to as they subjectively measure their own outcomes? In a comparison of Dominicans from this study and forty second-generation Chinese college students in New York City (Louie 2006a), I found that the Chinese reported more positive experiences of K-12 schooling, and yet they also expressed more pessimism about their educational trajectories and the future. Overall, their subjective understandings were at odds with census data showing that Chinese and other Asians have higher levels of schooling than Dominicans and other Latinos. Their subjective understandings were also at odds with the high societal expectations imposed by stereotypes of Asian Americans as high achievers and low societal expectations imposed by negative stereotypes of Latinos as underachievers (Fukuyama 1994; Espenshade and Belanger 1997; Rumbaut 1997).

An analysis of whom my respondents were comparing themselves to helped account for this paradoxical variability in optimism and pessimism. As I discuss further in the next chapter, the Dominican children often visited their parental homeland and kept in touch with friends and relatives there; thus, they drew on both Dominican and U.S.-based frames of references. They evaluated their outcomes against those of peers in the Dominican Republic, who had fewer educational opportunities (see chapter 2), and those of coethnic and panethnic members in the United States, who were assumed not to be doing well and in some cases were not. In sum, they were employing both transnational and ethnic orientations.

Even though my Chinese respondents similarly grew up in transnational social spaces (the New York City Chinese enclaves), they felt more disconnected from their parental homelands, which they did not visit as often as the Dominicans did. They were also more disconnected from Chinese language, history, and culture since they were not as emotionally close to their parents as the Dominicans were. Rather than employing a dual-nation frame of reference, they relied on a multilayered ethnic filter. Their first benchmark was the societal stereotype of Asian Americans as model minorities or high achievers (Louie 2004). Additionally, however, segmented immigration by social class among the Chinese and strong social capital ties linking working- and middle-class Chinese translated into many high-achieving suburban and urban individuals, compared to whom my respondents felt less than adequate. Hence, the Chinese wanted to know why they had not done as well (as they felt they should have).[9]

The Dominicans sought to understand why they had done better (than they were expected to do). In addition to individualism, the Dominican respondents emphasized family discipline and organization. As we saw in chapter 4, even though they believed their parents to be relatively uninvolved in their schooling in the ways expected by schools, they still thought that their parents gave them more support than their peers' parents gave their peers, especially Latinos. Despite these explanations, the disparity between their own success and the lack of success of others was often painful. During his adolescence, Alfonso's parents, fearing for his safety, would not permit him to hang out with his cousins, who became involved with drugs and gangs and were getting arrested. When he was at Boston University, Alfonso tried to show his cousins another world, but despite his efforts, they stayed enmeshed in theirs: "I felt like, you know, you *had* to get them out of that environment, and you have to pull them out and let them see something different, but still, I couldn't influence them enough." Julia and her Dominican/white cousin had witnessed the same turbulence in their extended family, and yet it was her cousin who became a drug abuser: "The different roads that were taken—I've seen spousal abuse and drug abuse and overcame that, I came up on top."

In sum, the Dominican and Colombian children we interviewed were notably optimistic. Although many of them had seen and experienced a number of systemic barriers, they mostly resolved those barriers internally by emphasizing individual agency. A comparison of the Dominicans with working-class Chinese from earlier research shows that both their optimism and their sense of agency are not necessarily a second-generation phenomenon. Rather, frame of reference is important. The Chinese were noticeably pessimistic despite the fact that they too had transitioned to college, but they were comparing themselves to coethnic Chinese, a higher-achieving group in the aggregate that is framed as being unusually academically successful. The optimism of the Latinos in our study maintained a key assumption of the immigrant bargain: with educational credentials in hand, members of the next generation will achieve upward mobility.

Chapter 7

Assimilation Processes: Who We Are

THE QUESTION of identity is central to immigration. In popular debates about assimilation, the question has typically been framed as follows: will the new immigrants become American, or will they challenge what it means to be American? The reality, of course, has been more complex. Both the concept of assimilation and the American mainstream have been subject to change over time. "Mainstream" America once meant being white and Protestant, but Judaism and Catholicism have both been incorporated into today's American mainstream. This transformation happened gradually and contrasts with the suspicion and hostility that greeted Jews and Catholics arriving in the United States from southern, central, and eastern Europe during the mid-nineteenth into the early twentieth centuries. The white racial category also has displayed elasticity, as it was expanded to include these Europeans and their descendants (Alba and Nee 2003; Gold 2009).

The process of becoming American, however, can be more challenging for the first generation than the second generation. As we saw in chapters 2 and 3, the immigrant parents in our study adopted key American norms, such as a belief in the American Dream, but claiming the American identity was complicated for them, not because they viewed it as contradictory to being Colombian or Dominican, but because they viewed the American national identity as excluding the foreign-born like themselves. Identity work for the first-generation parents also involved the cultural adjustment of the immigrant journey as they tried to figure out the new terms being used to describe them, such as "Latino" and "Hispanic," and where they belonged, if anywhere, in the dichotomous American black-white racial classification system (Mahalingam 2006). Situating themselves in this landscape was often confusing and clearly challenging for the immigrant parents, who often believed that they did not fit into it too easily. However, the parents had different expectations for their children who were born or raised in the United States and assumed that they would experience fewer constraints on who they could be here.

The children indeed were a different story. When asked if she thought of herself as American, twenty-year-old Bea, who had been in the United States for eleven years, assented, but with a wry laugh: "Well, I have learned that, yes, I am—I cannot deny it. I have been here half of my life, and right now I say that I am Dominican and I am Hispanic, so I guess I am American! You know?" As we shall see, the 1.5- and second-generation respondents had grown up inhabiting a distinctly Latino social and cultural milieu and continued to do so as adults. But as many moved into more integrated settings in school and at work, partly in response to the immigrant bargain with their parents, the children's worlds also became increasingly diverse. They developed contacts with middle-class whites who served as a cultural frame of reference (as did the parents of those contacts, often in a more abstract sense). Their experiences also ran counter to the theorization that affinity with African Americans among the second generation would pull them downward, through an affinity with a purportedly oppositional culture (Portes and Zhou 1993; Ogbu 1995; Portes and Rumbaut 2001). Overlooked in such theories are the existence and cultures of African American *strivers* (Neckerman, Carter, and Lee 1999; Carter 2005; Kasinitz et al. 2008; Warikoo and Carter 2009). Indeed, many of the 1.5- and second-generation respondents knew and drew on the resources of African American strivers. And while they understood the exclusionary aspects of the American identity, most of the respondents still viewed it as more inclusionary, at least for them. Like their parents, many were aware of the complex racial histories of Colombia and the Dominican Republic and the different racial definitions in the home countries. But the children did not have to grapple with the dual frame of reference in the same way their parents did. Certainly, the 1.5- and second-generation respondents believed that they were included in America. In the rest of this chapter, I show the multiplicity of their identities, highlighting the generational nuances and what this tells us about racialization and second-generation assimilation.

Both Ethnic and Panethnic

The 1.5- and second-generation respondents were first asked to respond to open-ended items on race and ethnicity in a demographic survey, and later they were asked to elaborate on their choices in the interview. As table 7.1 shows, about half of the Colombians wrote "Hispanic" as their race on the survey, and about one-fifth wrote "Latino." Five said that their race was white. Dominicans were somewhat more likely to say they were Latino. None of the Dominicans said that they were white,

Table 7.1 Most Frequent Answers to the Open-Ended Racial Question

	Latino	Hispanic	White
Colombians (N = 37)	7	18	5
Dominicans (N = 39)	18	10	0
Total (N = 76)	25	28	5

Source: Author's compilation based on children's surveys from the Dominican and Colombian Immigrant Family Study (2009).

and one wrote down "Black Latino." Twenty-two of the Colombians self-identified ethnically; another twelve either reported mixed ethnicity or answered with "Latino" or "Hispanic." Just as with race, Dominicans were slightly more consistent in their ethnicity answers. For both, the most frequent answers were a variant of ethnicity (for example, Colombian or Colombian American) or panethnicity (Latino, Hispanic).

The interview data showed that race did not necessarily mean skin color to the respondents. As table 7.2 indicates, only four Dominicans described themselves as phenotypically white, and twelve described themselves as between white and light. Like their parents, the 1.5- and second-generation Dominicans used intermediate skin color labels to describe themselves. Twelve said that they were in the medium range, and eight said that they were a mixture of black and white or dark-skinned. The 1.5- and second-generation Colombians were more likely to say that they were white or light-skinned, although some also used "medium" as a descriptor.

By and large, the interview data revealed that the children had accepted the identities ascribed to them by mainstream society. They had learned to give the "appropriate" response, especially on closed-ended, "check the appropriate box" surveys. In their case, the "appropriate" response was either "Latino" or "Hispanic," especially because "Dominican" or "Colombian" was typically not an available choice. To borrow from José Itzigsohn (2009, 189), "becoming American means becoming Latino." Similar to Itzigsohn's findings in his study of first- and second-generation Dominicans, our respondents interpreted panethnicity in both ethnic and racial terms.

The processes of racialization of panethnicity were different for the second generation compared to the first (Itzigsohn and Dore-Cabral 2000; Jensen et al. 2006). In chapter 3, we saw that some of the parents used the terms "Latino," "Hispanic," and even "Colombian," "Dominican," and "Spanish," as intermediate racial categories for themselves. They were neither black nor white but rather Latino. For the children,

Table 7.2 Children's Self-Reported Phenotypic Classification

Phenotype	Frequency
Dominicans	
White	4
White/light	3
Light	9
Light/medium	4
Medium	3
Medium/dark	3
Black/white/medium	2
Black/white	3
Dark	5
Missing	3
Colombians	
White	20
White/light	2
White/medium	2
Light	2
Light/medium	3
Medium	4
Dark	1
Missing	3

Source: Author's compilation based on children's interviews from the Dominican and Colombian Immigrant Family Study (2009).

however, it was common sense that they were racially Latino or Hispanic—that was the categorization they had known for most, if not all, of their lives. Many felt little tension about being (or not being) black or white because they had never really thought of themselves in that way. Furthermore, there was perceived advantage to claiming a Latino or Hispanic identity. According to the children, it was common knowledge that checking off "Latino" or "Hispanic" (whichever term was being used on the form) might translate into greater financial aid for school or perhaps even an admissions advantage. As one Dominican woman said, "Everyone knows [this]," even though she believed that such an advantage was not fair. That said, just because the children tended to converge on choosing ethnic and panethnic labels does not mean that they attributed the same meanings to them.

A minority of the children—eight of the Dominicans and six of the Colombians—expressed confusion about race and ethnicity. Unlike the parents we interviewed, however, the confusion signaled a conceptual tension rooted in the U.S. context. The children asked questions like: What does ethnicity mean? What does race mean—is it skin color? What is the difference between race and ethnicity? Are race and ethnicity conflated concepts? If so, why and how? These more philosophical questions were no less important than the more pragmatic challenges faced by the first generation as they sorted and slotted their "old" identities into a new system of classification.

The experiences of Jorge and his mother, Ines, whom we heard from in chapter 3, illustrate these kinds of generational nuances. Jorge, who arrived in the United States at age seven, was one of the few children who keenly remembered an identity shift with migration. He went from being white in Colombia to Hispanic in the United States. This was clear to him when a few of his new American (white) classmates consistently called him "spic" to signal that he was not like them. Even his white teachers seemed to treat him with suspicion because he was Hispanic, an identity that he was only just learning about. Nevertheless, Jorge grew to accept the classification, although he also saw himself as white. His mother's experience was very different. Ines, an adult when she arrived, was incredulous that in the United States she could not be included in the white category, which she also knew to be the dominant group. It was especially difficult for Ines because she had come from the dominant (white) group in Colombia. She believed that the "Hispanic" label referred to people sharing a common language and could not understand why speaking Spanish precluded her from being seen as white in the United States. The crucial issue for Ines had to do with the American racial classification system, particularly as personified by native whites. This system denied her the privilege of being white.

Jorge had different issues with that system. He grew to accept that American institutions and natives would not view him as white, and he neither debated whites about this contradiction, as his mother did, nor engaged in the internal struggles of other immigrant parents about how they were neither white nor black here. Because he came at a young age, Jorge eventually accepted that he was Latino here. However, he still had issues with the identity. Like his mother, he viewed Latino as a cultural identity rather than a racial one (Rodriguez 2000). He, too, had long arguments with people about the idea that Latino is not a race. It was *with whom* he engaged in these arguments that was different. Jorge's conversations about the meaning of being Latino were with fellow 1.5- and second-generation panethnics, who, like him, accepted that they were Latino. He believed that some of his peers were overly separatist in reacting to being excluded by non-Latinos (much as he had been excluded) by associating only with Latinos; in contrast, Jorge believed that he was open to all groups—blacks, Asians, whites—along with Latinos. Jorge attributed this "separatist" tendency to the U.S.-born seeking to connect with their ancestral roots. The 1.5ers and the international students, according to him, did not have to do this since they already had a connection and so had less to prove.

Table 7.3 Children's Self-Reported Abilities in Spanish

	Fluent	Functional	Minimal	No Response
Speaking and understanding Spanish				
Colombians	31	5	—	1
Dominicans	30	9	—	—
Subtotal	61	14	—	1
Reading and writing Spanish				
Colombians	24	12	—	1
Dominicans	20	16	3	—
Subtotal	44	28	3	1

Source: Author's compilation based on children's surveys from the Dominican and Colombian Immigrant Family Study (2009).
Note: N = 76.

Ethnic Lives

Home Language

Identity begins in the family home with the language, stories, and cultural traditions of parents being transmitted to their children. In this way, the immigrant family home serves as a symbolic connection to the family's country of origin. The Colombian and Dominican 1.5- and second-generation individuals we interviewed were deeply familiar with and shared their parents' understandings of the family home culture. Language was, of course, crucial. As indicated by table 7.3, most of the Colombians and Dominicans said that they were fluent in speaking and understanding Spanish, and close to two-thirds of the Colombians and about half of the Dominicans said the same for writing and reading Spanish. Such patterns are consistent with large-scale survey data revealing higher levels of Spanish-language retention between generations and fluent bilingualism among the children of immigrants from Spanish-speaking countries compared with children of immigrants from Asian nations (Portes and Rumbaut 2001; Rumbaut 2002; Bean and Stevens 2003; Tran 2010). As table 7.4 shows, most of the Colombian and Dominican children reported using Spanish a lot of the time in speaking with their parents, who, as we might expect, were reported as even more likely to speak to their children in Spanish. Table 7.5 gives us a sense of the Spanish language as a key part of the cultural landscape inhabited by the children, both growing up and as adults. Most of the children said that they both had grown up with and continued to listen to Latin music—for instance, on the radio. And while fewer 1.5- and second-generation respondents watched Latin television programs (the news, sports,

Table 7.4 Self-Reported Language Use Between Children and Parents

	Children Use Spanish with Parents	Parents Use Spanish with Children
Colombians (N = 37)		
Yes	28	31
Sometimes	9	6
Dominicans (N = 39)		
Yes	32	36
Sometimes	7	3

Source: Author's compilation based on children's interviews from the Dominican and Colombian Immigrant Family Study (2009).

novellas), a sizable proportion still did. Reading Spanish-language materials (newspapers, magazines, and books) was also a common activity for many of the children.

According to the children's interviews, speaking Spanish was a feature of shared family activities (Tran 2010). Parents read in Spanish to their young children, and as the children grew older, the parents borrowed library books to have them read for themselves; when the second generation became adults, parents and other family members shared their own Spanish-language books with them. Writing letters and, later, emailing in Spanish to extended family also maintained knowledge of the language. In addition, family members were on hand to answer questions about grammar and accent marks. Sara, an American-born Colombian, remembered that she earned a 5, the highest score, on the advanced placement exam in Spanish even though she had never taken a formal Spanish class. Growing up in a home where her parents were learning English but also speaking Spanish, Sara said that she developed

Table 7.5 Children's Ethnic Activities

	Regularly Listened to Latin Music	Regularly Watched Latin TV Programs	Regularly Read Spanish-Language Materials (Newspapers, Magazines, Books)
Colombian (N = 37)	31	20	26
Dominican (N = 39)	35	25	26

Source: Author's compilation based on children's interviews from the Dominican and Colombian Immigrant Family Study (2009).

an ear for the language that carried over seamlessly to writing and reading it. (Her facility was admittedly on the higher end of the spectrum.) The transition was much easier for her than for her parents, who wrestled, for instance, with the silent letters in English, which are known to be difficult for second-language learners.

Two additional points about language are important. We should not overestimate the full bilingualism of the children, since these are self-reported data. Even children who said that they were fluent in Spanish did not necessarily mean that they could have a conversation in either Spanish or English with the same depth and complexity. Maureen had attended international school in Colombia before moving here at the age of nine. Although she was very comfortable speaking Spanish, she was still careful about the domains in which she used it:

> Like, let's say we were discussing vouchers being used for public schools in the United States. I could have that conversation in Spanish, but it's going to take a lot of effort on my part. Because all my academic training has been in English, even when I lived in Colombia. I feel more ownership of the language of English when I am speaking about serious terms.

Even José, who had six years of formal schooling in Colombia and was in a bilingual program here for a few years, was starting to "second-guess" his Spanish abilities: "The distinction between speaking Spanish and English is kind of getting very blurry. Sometimes I speak Spanish with an English mentality, like the verbs, sentences, trying to say an English word in Spanish." Another interesting artifact noted by a few of the respondents was what scholars have called the "museumization" of cultural practices with migration (Gupta 1997). In short, migrants retain and pass on to their children the linguistic practices with which they left, even as those are changing back home. This became clear when the children paid homeland visits. Said Sally, who was born here and had visited Colombia four times, each time staying a month:

> They say my Spanish is fine, it's just, you know, over thirty years old, because my Spanish is my parents' Spanish. You'd notice. 'Cause you don't know a lot of the new language, you don't know the new slangs. . . . And so one of my things is, when I've been going, is to try to contemporize my Spanish to make it more to date. . . . I'm constantly writing down, like, all the new slang, and, you know, asking how to use it properly.

Family and Parental Homeland Histories

The relative openness of communication between generations, in both style and substance, also made it easy for children to learn about the history of their family and of the homeland. Most of the Colombians and Dominicans knew what their grandparents had done for a living in the homeland and were also knowledgeable about the factors that had pushed their kin to migrate. The children often could name the specific town or city their parents were from and discuss its cultural uniqueness (such as Medellin's famed August Flower Fair). With the same ease, many discussed current and historical events in the homeland (for example, the Trujillo dictatorship in the Dominican Republic, La Violencia in Colombia, the economic crises), the workings of the higher education systems (for instance, Colombians knew that students are expected to undertake professional specialties as undergraduates), and long-standing skin color and social hierarchies and gender distinctions.

Charles, a U.S.-born Dominican whose surname was northern European, learned from his father that the northeast region of Samana and Las Terranas in the Dominican Republic had been settled by freed American slaves in the 1800s; today some of the residents, whom Charles said are known as the "U.S.-ers," continue to speak English, and many have European last names. Nor was African ancestry, which Charles also had (he was the only respondent to identify racially as black combined with Latino in the survey), limited to people from that region. Charles pointed out that Dominicans with Spanish surnames can also have African ancestry, as he saw in his three visits to the Dominican Republic. "They could look just like me and just have a Spanish last name, but they're also mixed. It's the same. Everybody's very mixed. There's no, like, pure person who has this or this, you know?" As Charles learned from his father, this mixing was reflected in the skin color variation of their own family. "Like, my grandmother's grandfather was white, so my grandmother had really light skin. My father was light-skinned. Basically, you know, he told me she was white, had, like, blue eyes and blond hair."

The Dominican children also realized from their visits to the homeland why their families and fellow Dominicans in the United States held the views they did on skin color. The children cited the efforts of the Dominican Republic to disavow its history of blackness, which, as noted in chapter 3, is associated with Haiti, its neighbor and rival (Duany 1998; Bailey 2002). As active members of a transnational field, the Dominican children had learned the underpinnings of the combination of skin color, facial characteristics, hair color, eye color, and hair texture so stressed in their families and communities (Candelario 2007). Alexsa put it this way:

> Many Dominicans are very racist towards blacks. And so, they like to exclude that part from their Dominican side, and like, if you have black kinky hair, you know, if you have really curly hair, then you must be, like, from a bad race or bad blood. It's like you're not black, you're Dominican. And don't hang around black people, because they are of a lower class. This is still in the Dominican Republic. It still goes on now.

In counterpoint to this ideology, both Alexsa and her brother acknowledged their African ancestry. Calling her own long, black, wavy hair something between "bad" and "good"—because she could wear it curly or straight (with the help of a blow-dryer)—Alexsa knew that her mother felt otherwise. "But for my mother, if I wear curly hair, it's like, 'Oh no, it looks like black, or bad hair. You should wear it straight.'"

Mary, a second-generation Dominican, had less family support. Although her father was a black Dominican, he did not like American blacks and discouraged his children from hanging out with them, an exhortation that Mary did not heed. Her brother and sister were "light Dominicans" with "straight hair." Mary said that she had a medium-dark complexion and coarser hair; was frequently mistaken as a mix of black and white or Cape Verdean; and was criticized in her family for having a "wide, flat nose," which her mother encouraged her to change through plastic surgery. When the family moved from Cambridge, Massachusetts, to Miami, Mary saw similar dynamics separating the black Cubans from the white Cubans. It was during her visits to the Dominican Republic that she realized her family came from a nation with a strong color hierarchy in which being lighter was seen as better and often translated into more material privilege.

Audrey and Pilar were interesting examples because neither had visited Colombia yet both spoke quite knowledgeably about it.[1] Pilar spoke of racial mixing in much the same way that Charles did, only in the Colombian context (Wade 1993; Green 2000; Erlick 2010): "There's so many types of people in Colombia, there's mulatto, there's black, African black, Indian people, white with blue-eyed people who came directly from Europe." I was curious about how she knew this, given that she had left at the age of five, been raised in the Boston area, and had never been back to Colombia. She answered:

> Oh, Colombians here. And my family knows Colombians from other cities. And like, a friend who comes by sometimes, she's white with blue eyes, she's Colombian. And then I know black people, totally black. And then I know Indian-looking people who are Colombian. My father's family migrated from Europe, my great-grandfathers. And I think there is a little Indian descent in my mother.

Audrey's grandparents and mother had gone back, and between their accounts and what she learned from keeping in touch with her cousins there, she had an idea of the nation's challenges and rewards. From her family in America, Audrey heard the stories about the inequalities in Colombia, the political corruption, and the armed conflicts. A cousin who worked with the United Nations office in Bogotá had made her well aware of the present-day threat of bombs and the web of security put in place to protect against them (Erlick 2010). And yet, from her grandmother, who had been here thirty years and occasionally went back, Audrey also grew to love and to miss a place she had never seen firsthand.

> But then, it's just not all about the war and drugs. So, I mean, I would love to go see it, because I know how beautiful it is. I mean, it's just really beautiful. My grandmother is always telling me. She misses it. The landscape and the city, and just the culture. I think I've really missed out on that.

In short, the Dominican and Colombian respondents did not view their parents' native language or representations of the ancestral homeland as a mediated phenomenon that held little meaning for them. Rather, it was a part of them. This is how Alma described Dominican culture in the home her parents created here:

> It was just around all the time. Like, my mom cooks the same thing that they cook over there. My father's a very big history buff, Dominican history buff. So he has tons of books, and he just likes to talk a lot. [*Laughs*] So he'll sit there, and he'll tell you about all the dictatorships from 1933 to 1962, and he has videotapes and everything. It's just that type of environment. So you can't really get away from it.

Often furthering this sensibility was the children's use of ethnic and national-origin media, such as reading *El Tiempo*, a Colombian newspaper; watching the Spanish-language news; visiting ethnic neighborhoods (if they did not already live in one) and festivals; and doing their own research for school papers. One young man joined the Colombian Colloquium, an academic forum on issues related to the nation, jointly sponsored by MIT and Harvard.

Homeland Visits

The frequent back-and-forth movements between the parental homelands and the United States also fostered a strong sense of ethnic identity, one built on the foundation laid here. The stays were often for long stretches of time, from two weeks to a month or more; when one young man added up the time he had spent visiting Colombia, his estimated total came to three years. Table 7.6 shows the frequency of trips made by children to the home country.

Through these visits, the respondents found that ethnic traditions and gender and social norms acquired deeper inflections. Some women gained deeper insight into the sources of the gender distinctions in their families and ethnic communities in the United States, including stricter parental supervision of daughters, who were expected to live at home until they got married, and standards for how women should look. Alma, who had been to the Dominican Republic four or five times, com-

Table 7.6 Frequency of Children's Trips to Family Country of Origin

	Never	One to Four Trips	Five or More Trips
Colombians	8	17	9
Dominicans	0	15	18

Source: Author's compilation based on children's interviews from the Dominican and Colombian Immigrant Family Study (2009).

pared her life of greater freedom from such strictures to the lives of her female cousins still living in San Pedro de Macoris, Dominican Republic. She especially contrasted their aspirations with her drive to get an education and have a career. Alma had just graduated from Boston University and worked as a coordinator with a risk prevention program for families. Her cousins seemed to have different ambitions:

> And it's more like, "I'm going to go to high school, I'm going to graduate, and then I might do a secretary job, but I'm only going to do that until I find a husband. And only then will I move out of my house." And I'm like [*respondent and interviewer laugh*], "I'm not waiting around to get married before I leave my house."

Remembering her one visit to Colombia, Carmel said that she left with a better understanding of her mother. Unlike her mother, Carmel loved doing her errands in sneakers, a T-shirt, and sweatpants and had always wondered why her mother "never left the house without makeup on" and never wore sweatpants or even running pants outside the home. Even when her mother stayed at home, she always would do her hair. The reason Carmel's mother gave was that Carmel's father worked all day, and it was nice for him "to see his wife looking pretty." (Carmel's mother also worked all day.) Carmel accepted her mother's explanations, although it was not until her visit to Colombia that they really resonated.

> And then when I went to Colombia, nobody leaves their house looking uncomfortable. They are always dressed to the nines. They always have makeup that is perfect. Their face is perfect. Even when they go jogging, my aunt would put all her makeup on and her face would be all nicely done. Then I understood why they are the way they are.

The visits also gave women the chance to situate the overprotectiveness of girls, both here and there, in light of homeland gender inequalities. The prevailing understanding was that in the Dominican Republic and Colombia girls and women had to have strong family protection;

otherwise, they were likely to be exploited. Said Pilar: "In Colombia, if you're married and have children, you won't get a job 'cause it's just a dirty way of thinking, but I don't know if you heard but many people hire young women because they want to have affairs with them. It's very sad." Judy, who used to spend her winter breaks and summers in Colombia, was also disturbed by what she saw as systemic gender inequity in the labor market. It was widely accepted that beauty and youth were important to women's employability. Employers, she said, routinely asked applicants to submit a photo with their résumés.

A final word on the relationships between identity, language, and the family home: What I found among the Colombian and Dominican immigrant families contrasted with my previous findings among the Chinese. Only 15 percent of the Chinese whom I interviewed in 1998 and 1999 reported being fluent speakers and listeners of the language, and only 2 percent said that they were fluent in writing and reading. Owing to this generational language gap and an authoritarian parent-child relationship, the ethnic language, history, and domestic cultural practices of working-class Chinese immigrant parents were not necessarily understood by their children and thus not really shared (Louie 2003, 2004; Qin 2006). Although Chinese parents expected their children to celebrate ethnic holidays and engage in ethnic practices such as ancestor worship, the children rarely knew what the holidays were called, why the holidays were being celebrated, and what exactly they were doing to celebrate them. Nor did they know the names (in Chinese or English) of the various objects used in the rituals, beyond incense. Rather, the holidays became markers of ethnic food and foreignness (Louie 2003, 2004). Nor did the children often visit the parents' home country or know much about the history of the home country or about their parents' lives there. Although the children nonetheless still felt themselves to be very Chinese, the key parts of that identity were Chinglish and popular youth culture from Asia, not the more traditional culture of their parents (Louie 2003, 2004; Qin 2006).

Being Latino/Hispanic

How did the Colombian and Dominican children understand a Latino or Hispanic identity to be relevant to their lives outside the family? In the interviews, it was clear that the children were friendly not only with coethnics but with a mix of Latinos. As the children moved into more integrated settings, their friendship patterns diversified. Thus, the Dominicans' friendship patterns changed from a Latino mix growing up to a mix of black, white, Latino, and Asian (Itzigsohn 2009). The Colombians' childhood friendships tended to be more mixed overall, and this pattern continued into adulthood.

As with the parents we interviewed, the children viewed a Latino or Hispanic identity as a meaningful one that refers to people with a shared language (Spanish), religion (Catholicism), culture (food, music), and history of oppression by colonial powers in their native country. Similarly, although some respondents thought of Latino/Hispanic as a "made in the USA" identity (Portes and Rumbaut 2001, 154), they still viewed it as conveying a shared sense of being minorities and striving to make use of the opportunities here. In most of these accounts, "Dominican" and "Colombian" were viewed as subgroups of the Latino/Hispanic category characterized by specific areas of origin in Latin America and cultural particularities.

For a minority of the 1.5- and second-generation respondents, this sense of shared language, history, and culture translated into greater comfort around Latinos than other people. They used words like "connectedness," "comfort," and "familiarity" to describe how they felt with panethnics. For some, that comfort level had to do with how they had been raised by their parents. Non-Latinos were not as likely to understand practices like having a curfew, but such rules never had to be explained to Latinos. Said Nora, an American-born Dominican:

> So, I'll be with my Latino friends, and I'll say, "You know, it's getting late, I'm going to go home." And I mean, they totally understand. But, I mean, it's like the white American race, where if I'm to say, "Okay, it's getting late, I need to go home," they're going to say, "No, wait! Stay some more." And if I'm like, "No, my parents," they're going to be like, "Your *parents*! Girl, what is *wrong* with you?" [*Laughs*] And I think that's something where it's *totally* different.

These respondents believed that this shared way of looking at the world extended to ways to have fun. Instead of hanging out at a bar and drinking, they were more likely to want to dance or just listen to Latin music. Patricia, born in the United States to Colombian and Ecuadorean parents, said, "I just feel more at ease, like I can be myself. If I go to a Spanish party, like, I know there'll be music that, like, I want to dance to. So I think it's just more what we have in common, and what I've been used to." It was not necessarily meaningful that these children spoke Spanish when they went out with panethnics, although some did (along with English), but rather that they shared the experience of growing up in a Spanish-speaking household. Even more than language, that shared experience meant that Spanish was a key part of their lives.

Like the parents, the children spoke of the differences among Latinos, although typically they discussed them not with the same heat and more matter-of-factly as something that was diminishing in effect, particularly with intermarriage. They criticized Puerto Ricans, again, for having the freedom of movement and access to social subsidies that other Latinos did not. Some Dominicans and Colombians saw Colombians as well deserving of their reputation for being a bit more formal, disciplined, culturally developed, and snobby. The children also framed the Spanish language, which was seen as a key comfort and source of commonality, as a possible flash point of difference. The dropping of the *r* sound and the quick pacing of Dominican Spanish were consistently brought up and contrasted with "purer" forms of Spanish (like the Colombian version; Bailey 2002). Park, a Colombian, had had a difficult time understanding his Dominican ex-girlfriend's family when they spoke Spanish. Initially, his girlfriend had been hurt by his confusion, which she took to mean that he thought her family belonged to a lower-status cultural group. Park said:

> Yeah, Dominicans speak really fast and really different. And I think she took it as, "We don't know how to speak Spanish, and we're ignorant, and. . . ." I was like, "No, it's just different." And she was like, "Well, we understand you." And I was like, "That's great! But you know, I'm sorry—I just have a hard time." And to this day, I'll call her, and her mom will be on the phone, and she'll crack a joke or something, and I'll be like, "I totally didn't get that, you know."

Alba was part-Dominican and identified strongly with that side of her heritage. Even though her Ecuadorean mother raised her in Cambridge, Massachusetts, their neighbors tended to be Caribbean, and Alba grew to love the music and what she saw as the more easygoing ways of that region. The exception was language. She still described Dominican Spanish as a "bad trait." She said:

> Sometimes I'm like, "You guys ruin the Spanish language." Which is why a lot of people have, like, resentment I guess towards them. They chop up the Spanish language, and it's not as beautiful because they're too harsh on their tone. But it's true. You know, if you go into Washington Heights [in New York City], or if you go uptown, it's just like oh, like the Spanish, it just sounds so different.

And yet Alba exhorted Latinos to be more unified than divisive, believing that a unified Latino identity would serve the best interests of all ethnicities.

Stereotypes highlight the social construction of the Latino/Hispanic identity in the American context. Colombians and Dominicans alike pointed to similar negatives and positives in Americans' largely one-dimensional views of Latinos as low academic achievers and generally unintelligent; as troublemakers in school; as uniformly lower-class or poor, unskilled, uneducated laborers well suited to working as housecleaners, janitors, cooks, busboys, gardeners, and farm workers; as speakers of poor or accented English; and as the parents of lots of children (Fukuyama 1994; Espenshade and Belanger 1997; Rumbaut 1997; Falicov 2002; Massey and Sanchez R. 2010). These stereotypes paradoxically frame Latinos as both lazy and hardworking, and they are especially hard on men, who are characterized as both macho and criminal (Rodriguez 2008). More positively, Latinos are stereotyped as friendly partiers, good dancers, and part of a great culinary tradition of spicy foods. They are also thought of as brown or dark-skinned and short—a view that denies the skin colors, not to mention the physical characteristics, of the population. The respondents spoke of the particular stereotypes attached to being Colombian (global drug trafficking, kidnappings, guerrillas, coffee) or Dominican (domestic drug trade, baseball), even though most Americans, they believed, could not tell the difference between the two groups. Some respondents pointed to the more neutral aspects of being Latino/Hispanic—namely, that it is an umbrella category of racialization created by institutions to contrast them with other groups (blacks, whites, Asians).

Pan-Minority Identity

For a substantial number of the children, affinity to African American cultures was a big part of their lives. Dominicans reported being close to African Americans mostly as both friends and dating partners, while Colombians were more friends than mates with African Americans. We might expect the Dominican pattern given how that group, especially its darker-skinned members, have often been racialized as black (Bailey 2002). In New York City, for instance, many Dominicans settle in Puerto Rican and African American neighborhoods and face racial barriers in the labor market similar to those faced by African Americans (Newman 1999; Waters, Mollenkopf, and Kasinitz 1999). The Colombian finding was unexpected, since the group has not been racialized as black here; however, nearly all of the Colombians expressing an affinity with African American cultures grew up in racially and ethnically mixed neighborhoods.

In both groups, the reasons for the perceived closeness with African Americans were similar. One was cultural diffusion: Dominicans and Colombians alike had a clear affinity for the musical genres associated with African Americans and with foreign-born blacks and their children, such as hip-hop and reggae (Neckerman, Carter, and Lee 1999; Carter 2005; Smith, forthcoming[a]). Another reason was the common ground of being racialized as nonwhite and often lower-income and sharing the perceived struggles that accompany that status—namely, a strong sense of marginalization and the need to strive harder to be successful. It is worth noting, too, that some of the 1.5 and second generation's positive images of blackness were part of the counternarrative of black self-definition and pride that arose out of the civil rights movement (*Time* 1967). The respondents' identification with a pan-minority identity, strongly situated in the African American experience, came from living with or near blacks and going to school with blacks. Alba, who grew up in a public housing project in Cambridge, Massachusetts, that was majority-black (African American, Haitian, and West Indian), described this closeness:

> I have always had a nice mix of friends, but my closest friends have always been African American girls. Growing up in the city, you kind of fit into the same category anyway. It's funny, because a lot of African American people will say that Spanish people and Latino people, they'll say, "You're black. Because if you're not part of the white group, then you are." You know, I can be three shades lighter than a black person, but I'll still be viewed the same way, because everyone else is actually still considered minority.

Being identified and self-identified with blacks and black culture, however, did not negate her Dominican/Ecuadorean and Latino sensibilities; rather, they were complementary. Alba noted that she always knew the difference between the two identities—she and her close friends just never saw them as one versus the other. Their identities were inclusionary, and the friends accepted one another.

> And because I grew up in their house too, so I know about the foods and the culture. As well as when they come to my house, they know that they're going to eat Spanish food. So it works together. That's how it is. Living in the city and being raised in the city, and African Americans and Latinos would grow up close together, and it's common ground.[2]

Similarly, Park said that even though he felt comfortable with different groups of people, it was still "a very hard thing to pull off." Yet growing up in a mostly African American neighborhood in North Philadelphia had made African Americans his first primary nonfamily reference group, even more so than Latinos, and Park never lost that deep connection. Wherever he went afterwards, whether it was private school or an elite university, he "tacked onto the black population." As he met more whites, he also grew comfortable with them, but getting to know whites was an additive rather than subtractive process.

Common goals and experiences were also voiced by Amalia, who had always been seen and saw herself as a striver. On the basis of guidance counselors' references, Amalia gained admittance to Mott Hall, a small magnet junior high school near her home in Manhattan's Hamilton Heights. Having been raised among and gone to school with Dominicans, Amalia, who was of Colombian and Cuban descent, did come in for a fair amount of teasing: she was pale and had very fine dark hair. Amalia said that her wish to join "the professional world dominated by white people" set her apart as well; she realized that to meet her goal she would need to know "how to interact with other people." She was not alone, however: she was close to two Dominican girls from the neighborhood who shared her college-going ambitions. Amalia's own journey was facilitated by bridge programs. From Mott Hall, she was referred to and accepted into two programs designed to increase the presence of underrepresented students in top high schools. Through Prep for Prep, a program for independent day schools in the city and in boarding schools in the Northeast, Amalia enrolled in Deerfield Academy, an elite New England boarding school.[3]

At Deerfield, Amalia found that the route to the predominantly white world of professionals lay with like-minded black strivers, many of whom she had met at Prep for Prep. "When I joined Prep, I saw the difference—everyone there wanted to be something. Everyone there had that ambition of, you know, working for a huge firm one day. And I was just like, 'I like this. That's what I want.'" At Deerfield, she was copresident of the Latin American Society, but her circle of close friends was both Latino and black. Although whites were the school's majority, at the end of four years there she was close to only four of them—in large part, she said, because of social exclusion along socioeconomic lines. Distinctions were made on the basis of speech (slang) and dress (certainly Gucci and even nondesigner labels like J. Crew and Abercrombie and Fitch were outside of her budget). She found that most of the white students were not as likely to accept her, especially in the company of other whites.

> Like, I would walk down a path at Deerfield, and a girl who I just spoke to twenty minutes ago was with her friend—she wouldn't even acknowledge my presence. But when she's alone, she does. And I was like, "I don't need fake people like that! I want people who just accept me for who I am." And that's what the black community did, or the Latino community. They never denied my existence.

Although none of this kind of experience with white students diminished her love for Deerfield and her appreciation for being a part of the community, Amalia's comfort with the school may have also been a function of small numbers, given how relatively few blacks and Latinos were enrolled in the boarding school and their tendency to be marked as not wealthy. Indeed, to Amalia's surprise when she went on to Brown University, blacks and Latinos there were not close. The two groups were not only separate from each other there but even distrustful of each other. Amalia attributed this distancing to the lack of experience among many of the minority students with integrated settings, not only with whites but with members of other minority groups. Instead of openness, there was "miscommunication and ignorance."

Friendships with African American strivers helped the children make sense of some of their own challenges with meeting the immigrant bargain—and indeed, with being strivers themselves. As they tried to meet their parents' expectations for academic success, the children were also moving away from their parents' social and cultural norms around race. As mentioned earlier, there are skin color hierarchies in both Colombia and the Dominican Republic: whiteness and lightness are seen as superior to blackness (Wade 1993; Streicker 1995; Duany 1998; Bailey 2002; Roth 2008). The parents occasionally mentioned to their children that they were "acting too black," as one young woman in her midtwenties put it, or they asked their children why they did not have more white friends. The children did not hesitate to tell their parents that they were "old school" and "a little racist." These parent-child exchanges were not necessarily adversarial, as the children were not deliberately setting out to challenge their parents; rather, they acknowledged that their parents came from a different world and that their own friendships with African Americans were unintentionally testing that mindset. Julian recalled his Colombian mother's initial suspicion of his black friends, all of whom had attended the prestigious Boston Latin School alongside her son: "I remember my mom being like, 'Where you going? You're always hanging around with all those black people. What are you doing?'" To his amusement, rather than doing the "bad stuff" she was afraid of, his "super smart" friends were going on to Boston University and Wesleyan.

Thomas, another Colombian, related two examples. In the first, he was driving his cousins and an African American friend home from Massachusetts Bay Community College when they were stopped by the police in the affluent and mostly white town of Wellesley, Massachusetts. The police searched their book bags and the car trunk, telling the young men that they fit the profile of some suspects in a local bank robbery, especially Thomas: "You're dark-skinned, and you've got a crew—you know, you've got short hair." Framing the stop as racial profiling on the part of the police, his cousins and friend joked with him afterwards: "Hey, Thomas, they finally saw that you were dark!" The punch line was twofold—Thomas was known to have African American friends, and he was also known to be quite pale and did not even tan, although he did have dark brown hair. In the second instance, he was walking with his cousins and aunt on 125th Street in Harlem during a visit to New York City. The rest of the family wanted to move rapidly along, intimidated by the many blacks on the street. Thomas, thinking their nervousness was funny, made a point of saying that he wanted to visit a few of the stores. When they refused, he said, "I was like, 'What are you talking about? They're just regular people.' I was like, 'That's the bad rap that people get.'"

In sum, then, for these children there was a clear sense of being a racialized minority, but more specifically as a pan-minority situated in the black experience. The children we interviewed viewed themselves as striving to join a pan-minority middle class, one not necessarily oppositional to white middle-class culture but existing alongside it and even intersecting with it. Their experiences were consistent with the factors that, as Kathryn Neckerman, Prudence Carter, and Jennifer Lee (1999) propose, are salient to the emergence of a minority culture of mobility among immigrants and their descendants. These factors include the respondents' perception of a racialized identity, their incorporation into the mainstream economy, and their sense of being distinct from their less well-to-do coethnics. Consistent with another key piece of this hypothesis, the children met striving and upwardly mobile blacks in school and adopted their culture of mobility via education. Furthermore, they often engaged in a repertoire of symbolic expressive practices developed by African Americans, as transmitted in personal interactions with blacks and the media (Neckerman, Carter, and Lee 1999). Robert C. Smith (2008, forthcoming[a]) also provides empirical evidence of this formulation of a minority culture of mobility in his research on "black Mexicans"—for example, youth who look phenotypically Mexican but who identify as black during adolescence and deploy blackness as a strategy for upward mobility. Taken together, our findings complicate segmented assimilation theory, which does not consider the presence of upwardly mobile, urban, native minorities and their interactions with the second generation. Not only do these minorities exist (Carter 2005), but they serve as key connections for some 1.5- and second-generation Dominicans and Colombians.

It is worth noting that while the children's social networks and identities diversified as they got older, the process was generally additive rather than subtractive. The closeness of some respondents to African Americans was not an artifact of adolescence; it continued to have meaning for them into early adulthood. This prolonged affinity with African American cultures contrasts with Smith's (forthcoming[a]) finding that the identification with blackness among his Mexican subjects did not persist into early adulthood. He argues that the black minority culture of mobility serves as a "strategic social action promoting success, an adolescent identity experiment, and a conjunctural event emerging from particular stages and contexts of Mexican settlement in a new destination." Although instrumentality may have been part of the reason for the Dominican and Colombian children's identification with blackness, the ease or acceptance that many expressed cannot be discounted. The meaning of the concept of a minority culture of mobility, the strength of its link to blackness, and the ways in which 1.5- and second-generation individuals engage with it, both at a perceived intrinsic level and as extrinsic instrumentality, are fascinating topics for further research.[4]

Dating

In addition to having friendships and strong identifications outside the panethnic group, the respondents were likely to date non-Latinos. Twenty-four Dominicans and twenty-two Colombians had dated someone who was not Latino. Patterns differed, however, by ethnicity. Dominicans were only a bit more likely to have dated whites than blacks (both native and immigrant).[5] In contrast, only three Colombians had gone out with blacks, while more than half had dated whites. Colombians were also less likely to say that dating outside the panethnic group proved to be an issue in the relationship owing to different cultural norms, including different views about the closeness of family ties, the partner's inability to speak Spanish, and the partner's discomfort at the Colombian child's family gatherings. Some parents preferred that their children date Latinos (for linguistic and other cultural reasons) and whites (since they were the dominant group). It would be inaccurate to say, however, that the Colombians were more likely to identify as white. Certainly, the Colombian respondents who had grown up in mostly white, mainly suburban neighborhoods felt comfortable with native white Americans. But they continued to identify in panethnic and ethnic terms and tended to believe that race, ethnicity, and national origins, sometimes in combination with social class, influence the lives of individuals. Although they may have felt at home around whites, especially middle-class whites, they did not necessarily think that whites or others had the same privileges as them. Rather, they saw the less flexible and less voluntary aspects of racial and ethnic identities in the United States (Waters 1990).

Being American

How did the children understand the meanings attached to an American identity and their ability to claim it? One could argue that children growing up in ethnic homes and leading panethnic lives might not think that being American could include them. Certainly, their parents saw being American as a restrictive identity, one that excluded them on the basis of not having been born here, not having grown up here, not being a native English speaker, and being seen as Latino. Four themes can be gleaned from the most common responses given by the 1.5- and second-generation Colombians and Dominicans in regard to what it means to be an American (respondents often gave more than one answer): (1) rights, such as the pursuit of happiness, freedom, and democracy; (2) diversity, tolerance, and multiculturalism; (3) opportunity, whether material (to get a decent education, to own a house), individual (to achieve, to be yourself), or fundamental (to have running water); and (4) loyalty to, respect for, and knowledge of the United States. Probably because of the turbulence in Colombia that had pushed many parents out, these children were more likely to speak of a rights-based model of being American. Overall, these themes are consistent with the fundamentals of American national identity, which are based on non-exclusionary, "egalitarian abstract principles" (Devos and Banaji 2005, 451) that, in theory, neither belong to nor exclude particular racial or ethnic groups (Jiménez 2011). Under these principles, *anyone* can be American.

Indeed, according to the children, being American includes many different home cultures, and so they themselves, having grown up in a panethnic culture and retaining many of its elements as adults, could also be American. Being American, in this view, does not refer only to whites, although the children acknowledged that this aspect of Americanness still needs work. Moreover, in our conversations many of the respondents themselves used the term "American" to refer to whites (Kasinitz et al. 2008; Itzigsohn 2009). Finally, even for all the positives, the respondents also widely acknowledged that America could still be even better. They pointed out that more progress could be made in eliminating poverty, reducing violence, and providing free health care in the world's richest nation, one with so many freedoms.

In decided contrast to the immigrant parents we interviewed, most of the Colombian and Dominican children said that they considered themselves to be American. They said that they did not hesitate to exercise the rights that come with being American. Betty talked about being detained in customs as she was leaving the Dominican Republic. She and her young son had just visited a part of the country with a thriving black market in adoptions of local (light-skinned, fair-haired) children by Americans. Apparently, the authorities stopped Betty because they thought that she was trying to steal a child (her own son) for that purpose. Betty was livid. "I was like, you can't do that. I'm an American. You know, that's the first thing I said. I'm an American citizen, and you cannot do this to me. I was, like, very offended, because I was an American citizen. I consider myself an American." Ana, the U.S.-born child of Dominican and Colombian parents in New York City, volunteered for three summers tutoring the children of mainly Mexican and Central American migrant farm workers in North Carolina, then a new destination for immigrants (Griffith 2005). According to Ana, she was confusing to the residents. The longtime native white and black members of the community could not understand how she could be Hispanic, since she was light-skinned, spoke English, interacted easily with authority figures and did not hesitate to express her views. Ana also knew that the migrant farm workers and their children welcomed her assertiveness and that of the Latino staff and volunteers in the outreach program, even if they did not seem entirely sure that they could ever have the same right themselves to speak and to be heard (Dicker 2006).

> I went as a city girl, basically, [*laughs*] who spoke English and who was not going to be afraid of the police or anything, because I had nothing to fear, because I consider myself, I guess, American. [*So, did the migrant farm workers see you as a role model?*] Yes, oh, they did, yes. But I also noticed they saw us as something that they couldn't be? And it seemed to them like a dream, like, "Wow, you know, you're going to college!" So, yeah.

There were differences between the Colombians and Dominicans in their understandings of being American. Certainly, the Dominicans acknowledged their Americanness in the rights they enjoyed, the tolerance and opportunities they valued, the loyalty they felt to the United States, and their cultural adaptation to the country. However, the Dominican respondents were more likely to see a possible tension between being American and being ethnic. They were more likely to highlight the racialized (native white) dimension of being seen as American, which made it difficult for them to feel American. Compared to the Colombians, a greater number of Dominicans framed their American identity as situational—for example, they felt American when they were in the Dominican Republic. They were also more ambivalent about being American because they did not believe that others, especially non-Latinos, accepted them as American. This tension identified by the 1.5- and second-generation Dominicans is consistent with the findings of Itzigsohn's (2009) study. A key difference is that nearly all the Dominicans we interviewed still viewed themselves as American, in contrast to Itzigsohn's Dominican respondents, who believed that "the American label" belongs "only to white Americans" (138).

For these Dominicans in our study, being American was framed not as an either-or proposition but rather along a scale. These Dominican perspectives on the racialized dimensions of Americanness are consistent with the important interplay between panethnicity and national identity shown by other researchers. Thierry Devos and Mahzarin Banaji (2005) find that, while individuals explicitly endorsed equality as core to the American identity (very much as my respondents did), their implicit responses revealed a clear sorting by ethnicity. Through the use of "assessments that cannot be consciously controlled" (448), which the authors argue are better suited for investigating such subtle distinctions, they find that respondents expressed the view "that some ethnic groups are simply less American than others—not in rights and liberties but in the degree to which they embody the concept 'American'" (451). Indeed, their findings point to a "very consistent and robust American = White association" (463) and are consistent with social dominance theory (Sidanius and Pratto 1999), which links whites, sitting as they do at the top of the American racial and ethnic hierarchy, to being seen as quintessentially American.

According to these Dominicans, the combination of language and racial and ethnic minority status was crucial to this implicit hierarchy of Americanness. While the first-generation parents expressed social anxiety about not speaking English at all, or not speaking "correct" or "good" English, the second generation was anxious about not speaking *perfect* English and about speaking with an accent even though they had been born in the United States or raised here. Nora, a U.S.-born Dominican, described how she felt in everyday interactions, especially with non-Latinos:

> And I don't know if you noticed, I stutter, sometimes, like, these words come out with the little twists where, like, a little Spanish accent comes out—I don't know if you noticed. So I feel like they're looking at the way I talk, like, "Okay, I thought she was American. What is she? I guess she's not American." I think that's when I feel like I'm not an American.

Feeling invisible in the workplace was another theme. Within this context, Alba explained how she was able to believe in both an inclusive definition of Americanness and a definition based on racial exclusion.

> We're all American. I'm American. Even though, honestly, when I think of being an American, the first thing I think of is being white. And that's wrong, but I think because for so long you are raised and every day you're reminded of your color. You're reminded of your race, or whatever. That even to be an American, you have to be Latino-American, or Chinese-American, or African-American. It's like, God! There's always another label attached to being an American. So when I think of American, I automatically think of you're just white.

In most of the jobs that Alba held (her university curriculum was partly based on an extensive job internship program), she was the only native Spanish speaker and the only Latino; the rest of her coworkers were white. It was not that the whites tried to remind her that she was not like them, but rather, "just the lack of people who look like you will then remind you of exactly where you are."

Alba acknowledged that some whites have class-based challenges similar to hers because they, too, grew up in a poor or low-income household. In a college class discussion about affirmative action, Alba saw parallels in how she grew up—the daughter of a single mother who worked in a university office and a father who was a retired pot scrubber in a university kitchen—to how several white, working-class students had been raised. Yet Alba still believed that poor and low-income racial minorities faced distinctive challenges that might limit their upward mobility.

> One [white] student was saying, like, "I'm not rich. My parents have struggled too." And I was like, you know what? That's very true. But you will never, ever, ever, go into a job interview and say, "I don't think I got the job because I was white." You will never experience that. You know, you'll think you didn't get it because maybe you weren't smart enough. You didn't get good enough grades. Or you weren't as good as the other person. But race will never be the reason why you did not get something in this world. When other people, we go through that, it's an everyday struggle. And it's hard to explain.

Although the students in her class initially did not want to talk about race (Pollock 2004, 2008a), Alba believed that their discussion gave them a space to reflect, to hear one another, and to respond (Gutmann 1994; Light 2001). For Alba, the classroom discussion was a chance to consider evidence counter to her belief in a white-nonwhite divide in the United States that keeps blacks, Latinos, and Asians "[working] twice as hard as the next person and [getting] less in the end."

Alba's reflections are consistent with those of Catalina, a first-generation immigrant who had replicated her high status in the United States. For all her credentials, including an MBA earned here, Catalina said that she understood that she, along with fellow "people of color," were coming from the "outside" of the power structure. It was her sentiment that they would always be limited in some way and never reach the top—at least not in banking, her industry. The comments of these two women—one a first-generation immigrant at the capstone of her career and the other a U.S.-born child of working-class immigrants just beginning to explore hers—recall the minority striver analogy. Upwardly mobile nonwhite immigrants and their children, after encountering the isolation and subtle racism that middle-class blacks have encountered here, including a feeling of marginalization as one of the few minorities in mostly white settings (Zweigenhaft and Domhoff 1991; Lawrence-Lightfoot 1994), identify with the struggles of upwardly mobile blacks (Neckerman, Carter, and Lee 1999).

In sum, unlike their parents, the children believed that being seen and seeing themselves as Latino did not automatically preclude them from being American. And unlike their parents, but true to their parents' hopes, the children were more likely to believe that they simply belonged in America. Overall, the children laid claim to the voice, agency, and sense of inclusion that the immigrant parents did not believe could be theirs—at least not to the same extent as the American-born and/or -raised. The children's experiences confirmed the families' assumptions that the 1.5 and second generations would be more fully accepted into the American mainstream than the first.

Chapter 8

Conclusion: Institutions and Individual Agency

A KEY debate in contemporary immigration research centers on how the children of immigrants are faring educationally, the extent to which they are upwardly mobile in relation to their parents, and the reasons for variation in their outcomes. Segmented assimilation has been a foundational theory to describe and explain the diversity in these outcomes (Haller, Portes, and Lynch 2011a). A core contribution of this theory is the idea that second-generation individuals are assimilating into different segments of American life. Upward mobility characterizes two pathways of assimilation, the first being classic assimilation into the white, middle-class segment; the second includes children who are able to draw upon cohesive ethnic communities and develop strong ethnic attachments along with positive outlooks on schooling. The coethnic model still allows for the possibility of the children's later assimilation into the white middle class. Downward mobility is the predicted scenario for children who experience discrimination and settle near native-born minority groups in struggling city neighborhoods; these children tend to adopt negative outlooks on schooling, do worse than their parents, and assimilate into urban minority poverty.

Empirical studies have revealed where segmented assimilation has done a good job of capturing outcomes and the reasons for them and where more theorizing is needed. Consistent with the theory's tenets, the highly educated among the second generation typically have parents of high socioeconomic status or are embedded in coethnic communities that facilitate the crucial transfer of social capital about education across class lines. However, segmented assimilation does less well with capturing the outcomes for children who grow up in low-income, native minority areas and go to struggling public schools. The majority do not do well educationally but are nonetheless in the labor force, in low-skilled jobs, having "a marginal working-class status" similar to their parents' status. Only a minority drop out of school and engage in risky behaviors such as teenage pregnancy and trouble with the police or incarceration, as predicted by segmented assimilation; it is interesting that a smaller minor-ity manage to overcome these substantial obstacles and become highly educated (Fernandez-Kelly and Portes 2008; Stepick and Dutton-Stepick 2010). Across these pathways, most second-generation individuals still have better educational outcomes than their parents (if only because their parents' outcomes are so low) and native-born minority groups (Zhou and Lee 2007; Kasinitz et al. 2008; Rumbaut 2008; Park and Myers 2010). That said, there are well-warranted concerns about the slower rate of progress among some Mexican Americans (Bean and Stevens 2003; Perlmann 2005; Telles and Ortiz 2008).

In this book, I focus on social contexts and social processes, an approach that extends the existing typology in three critical ways. First, I provide a fine-grained analysis of how success actually happens among the small number of working-class children who beat the odds. I trace how second-generation individuals whose parents have neither the financial and human capital nor the ethnic community social capital typically associated with children getting ahead still end up doing so well. While the educational attainment of some of these respondents (for example, community college) might seem modest by conventional norms, earning an associate's degree or even having attended community college tends to translate into higher wages for individuals (Attewell and Lavin 2007). The respondents attending a four-year college, and certainly the ones who had graduated, were definitely successful compared to their ethnic counterparts (Kasinitz et al. 2008; Portes and Fernandez-Kelly 2008).

What were the mechanisms of success for the working-class children we interviewed? How did they get ahead compared to the unsuccessful cases documented by other researchers (Lopez 2003; Smith 2008; Nicholas, Stepick, and Dutton-Stepick 2008; Stepick and Dutton-Stepick 2010)? The working-class children in our study had several things in their favor. First, there was the optimism they shared with their immigrant parents that, as the U.S.-born or -raised, they could really make use of the opportunities available here and be successful in school and in life (Kao and Tienda 1995; Fernandez-Kelly 2008). Second, they benefited from strong parental supervision (even if it seemed weak to them at times); despite struggling here, their parents, on the whole, were able to adequately care for the children. While there was some absenteeism on the part of fathers, the mothers were able to manage, and the children did not feel unsupervised. Moreover, virtually all the children we interviewed had siblings who also finished high school or earned a GED in the United States (although the picture of educational attainment, criminal behavior, and addictions was decidedly less rosy for some extended family members, in both the first and second generations). Strong parental supervision included discipline of the children to ensure that they complied with the parents' rules about doing homework and not getting into trouble, although there was a range on this measure—the parents were not all strict in the same ways and to the same degree. Third, the children were close to their parents and wanted to please them by behaving well and doing well in school. Fourth, some of the working-class parents were able to offer some useful supports for their children's schooling. They leveraged any contacts they had to find good schools and after-school programs for their children. Both proved to be crucial because strong parental supervision in working-class households did not necessarily translate into strong oversight of the children's school assignments or even much knowledge of what went on in their children's school lives.

Although all of these family-based factors were important, they acted in concert with an especially crucial element—institutional networks of support provided by nonfamily members, especially adults. Such supporters guided the children through the educational system and believed in their ability to succeed. This element was particularly key for the working-class families, especially the Dominicans, but even the middle-class families benefited from it (although not the high replicators, who were the most privileged economically). Let me be clear: this book does not tell the story of the so-called "good" Latino immigrant families—the families whose children succeed because the families are so optimistic and strive so hard (similar to the oft-told story of the "good" Asian immigrant families). The danger with such a story line is that we are left thinking that all anyone has to do to succeed in this country is to channel the pluck, enthusiasm, and perseverance of those individuals who seem to be striving. While pluck, enthusiasm, and perseverance are certainly important, we would be telling an incomplete story and doing a disservice if we left out the institutions that engage immigrant families and are engaged by them. It is that crucial interplay between institutions and immigrant families that we need to learn more about (Kasinitz et al. 2008; Crul and Holdaway 2009; Holdaway and Alba 2009).

Certainly, our findings show that immigrant parents work hard at the task of getting their children a good education. Working-class immigrant parents are involved in their children's education even when schools see them as uninvolved. Across social class, the immigrant parents scrambled first to learn about how schooling in America works and then to do what they could to get the best opportunities for their children. The language and cultural exclusion that comes from being an immigrant powerfully came into play, along with social class, as the parents, feeling alone, took it upon themselves to decode the education system. Working-class immigrant parents felt constrained, believing as they did that no one in authority (such as school officials) would listen to them because of their class status and because they were foreigners. This decoding task was easier, of course, for the more economically privileged parents in the sample: after putting their children in good schools with highly qualified teachers and getting the children other sources of help, they did not have to work as hard. But even the dramatic riser middle-class families struggled to help their children navigate the schools, and they often could not do so as effectively as they or the children would have liked.

In the working-class families, however, the parents' hard work was not enough to ensure the children's success. The working-class children were able to succeed because they encountered people who were willing to give them the information and strategies about education that their parents could not. The children met these people in schools (teachers and guidance counselors) and through community-based after-school and other kinds of enrichment services, including the federal TRIO programs like Upward Bound. Most of these encounters were happenstance rather than intentional; all of them were transformational, opening doors to opportunities that the children did not know even existed and showing them how to walk through those doors. In sum, the working-class children were able to beat the odds in their transition to college by having family and peers who facilitated their development, sometimes pointing them to useful social capital, and having good relationships with institutional agents who could help them decipher the educational system and reach their goals (Stanton-Salazar 1997; Portes and Fernandez-Kelly 2008; Smith 2008; Stepick and Dutton-Stepick 2010). Their experiences were similar to those of non-immigrant working-class youth, but there are also differences. The latter have parents who, having been educated here, bring their own complicated past relationships with schools to how they rear their children and interact with schools (Luttrell 1997; Lawrence-Lightfoot 2003). There may also be advantages: native minority working-class youth can get useful information from their parents about how to deal with whites in authority that immigrant children cannot get from their parents (Carter 2005).

Second, I show that a key immigrant demographic is missing from our second-generation typology, namely, working-class parents who were middle-class in their country of origin. In some of the unexpected success stories, downwardly mobile working-class parents were able to get helpful advice for their children from higher-status persons outside their ethnic group. Apparently, having once held a middle-class position and attained a higher level of education continues to have a positive effect on outcomes for one's children, even in those families where the immigrant parents are unable to use those "middle-class credentials" to better their own position in the new country. New immigrants often end up taking jobs that have lower status and require less education than the ones they held in their home country, so our existing typology needs to find a way to include and understand their experiences.

Third, I show that native minority strivers can play a strong positive role in the upward mobility of second-generation children. This positive finding contrasts with the alienated role assigned to native, minority, urban youth by segmented assimilation theories. Across social class, some of the children believed that they and their high-achieving black friends were similarly striving against the odds, even if only to defy society's expectations for them by being successful. The working-class respondents especially found their kinship with native minority strivers to be helpful as they tried to make sense of the unease they felt entering white, middle-class worlds. Social closeness with blacks was far more common than social distancing from blacks, which historically has been the experience of second-generation individuals.

Different from the Past

Much of the story told in this book is contemporary, and that is certainly the case with the optimism we found among the immigrant parents. Although they had their fair share of pessimism, the parents in my study were not alienated and believed themselves to be part of the American Dream. The parents' cultural adjustment, while difficult, might have been eased by the fact that they came from nations whose institutions had been considerably influenced by American military intervention, dealings with American businesses, and American mass media (Min 1999, 85; Jaret 1999; Hernández 2002; Menjívar and Rodríguez 2005; Palacios 2006; Hoffnung-Garskof 2008). The worldwide dissemination of American "life standards" through global diffusion (Portes and Rumbaut 1990, 12) has also prompted the more advantaged individuals of various class strata to migrate as a way to satisfy their perceived "relative deprivation"; thanks to technological advances, migrants maintain ties more easily with people in their home countries and are also able to retain institutional ties through dual citizenship (Min 1999). In sum, exposure to American culture before migration and transnational ties may have buffered the parents from some of the challenges of adjusting to a new country.

The picture was considerably different for the European immigrants who arrived in the nineteenth and early twentieth centuries; they had a tougher time adjusting to American life and were slower to learn English (Jiménez 2011). Although immigrants engaged in copious written correspondence with relatives back in the home country (Morawska 1990), they did not arrive with the kinds of preexisting exposure to American culture made available by contemporary technology. This disjuncture between the Old and New Worlds was only amplified by the European immigrants' harsh reception in the United States. In language, dress, celebration of holidays, religious practices, and political ideologies, the immigrants were seen and treated as quite different—indeed, as perhaps not even capable of joining the American mainstream (Hartmann 1948). The decidedly unwelcoming reception was evident in the rise of nativism (Ralph and Rubinson 1980; Dinnerstein and Reimers 1999). Through public schools that sought to Americanize their children and other systemic efforts to assimilate them, immigrants found the state intruding into their lives (Bodnar 1976, 1985; Gerstle 2000; Olneck 1989, 2008). A notable example was the early-twentieth-century Americanization class at the Ford Motor Company, designed to erase national differences; the company inspected the homes of immigrant workers to ensure that only American foods, not ethnic varieties, were being consumed (Waters 2011). Their work lives were unlikely to have been a great comfort to the immigrants. Absent social insurance policies, immigrants were subject to their ability to work, the availability of jobs, and the will of employers, all of which made for a rather grim daily existence.[1]

It took some time before the children of immigrants became as likely as their native white counterparts to go on to high school. The (correct) parental assumption that public schools were seeking to Americanize immigrant children and in the process disparage family cultures certainly did not make them seem inviting. Nor was a child's education beyond the first few years of schooling seen as bringing a sizable enough payoff to the immigrant household. Daily life for immigrant families, on average, was so economically marginal that the decision to allow a child to attend school, especially secondary school, rather than work in the paid labor force and contribute to the household economy in the short term had to be seen as making financial sense. Not until the 1930s, well after large-scale immigration from southern, eastern, and central Europe had been restricted, did immigrant children in American cities, across national origins, choose extended schooling over work, thus becoming more similar to their peers with U.S.-born parents (Bodnar 1985, 193).[2] The reasons for this transformation were not simply cultural; by this time, immigrant families had discerned the labor market payoff associated with more schooling for their children (Hogan 1978; Cohen 1982; Bodnar 1976, 1985; Perlmann 1990; Fuligni 2006; Olneck 2008).

In sum, the European immigrants of yesteryear fled conditions of "absolute deprivation," such as famine in their home countries (Portes and Rumbaut 1990, 14), and were more likely to be culturally alienated in America and to draw on a dual frame of reference in which the United States was viewed "as a lesser evil" (Morawska 1993, 258). Because most of the descendants of the pre-1924 period did eventually assimilate and were upwardly mobile in the post–World War II period, we tend to forget how difficult the process was and how long it took. In contrast, the immigrant parents we interviewed came to this country owing to "relative deprivation" in their home countries and were able to balance their pessimism with some optimism about their opportunities in the United States, which they perceived as offering a better future. Characteristic of today's immigrants, the parents interacted much more quickly with mainstream institutions (to both their advantage and disadvantage). Furthermore, they did not see schools as culturally alienating places that would force their children to assimilate and abandon their home cultures. This finding makes sense given the emphasis on multiculturalism, or the value placed on diversity, in contemporary schooling (Banks 1994, 2007). Rather, the parents knew that higher education was important to their children's success in America. It was the question of how to make this happen that they saw as the difficult task.

Noting the relative optimism of immigrant families, of course, is not the same as saying that their children in the contemporary era will actually do well educationally. The educational gap between today's second-generation Mexican Americans and native whites exceeds that of American-born children of European immigrants arriving between 1890 and 1914 and their native white peers (Perlmann 2005). Such educational gaps arguably have even greater importance today, given how important the bachelor's degree has become to upward social mobility in the postindustrial economy (Wilson 1980, 1987; Murnane and Levy 1996; Furstenberg, Rumbaut, and Settersten 2005). Yet we should not overstate the importance of that degree as a benchmark of success. Certainly, the children of native-born Americans, including whites, are not all going to and graduating from a four-year college (Alba, Kasinitz, and Waters 2011). There is not even agreement that the bachelor's degree should be a universal goal. The fastest-growing segments of the labor market are jobs for computer and health technicians, which pay decent wages but require only certificates or associate's degrees. Some have argued that we need more work-linked learning, with greater input from employers, and stronger linkages between secondary schools and community colleges and the needs of the labor market (Deil-Amen and DeLuca 2010; Symonds, Schwartz, and Ferguson 2011). Regardless of where exactly we define the benchmarks of educational success, there are lines of further research and recommendations for policy and practice that will help us increase the numbers of second-generation individuals transitioning to at least some form of postsecondary education.

Directions for Further Research

Immigrant Exclusion and Second-Generation Success

In this book, I have shown that the other part of the immigrant parents' bifurcated incorporation was their pessimism about their own assimilation. This pessimism was derived from the social exclusion perceived by the parents. They felt a lack of competency in English, were unaware of American cultural norms even if they were proficient in English, and believed themselves to be out of sync with the American racial and ethnic classification system. The one thing they felt sure about was that, as foreigners, they were perceived as inferior and not American. Being a Latino foreigner was seen as especially stigmatizing. This perceived exclusion informed the parents' hesitation to engage with their children's schools. Immigrant parents felt strong barriers in their interactions with school officials, and even middle-class parents, whom we would think would feel more entitled owing to their class status, experienced those barriers as well.

Given the racial diversity among post-1965 immigrants, we need to consider whether race trumps immigrant status in some groups, giving rise to a type of exclusion that functions as more of a barrier for second-generation success. Scholars have found, for example, that race assumes a central place in the lives of Afro-Caribbean immigrants (Waters 1999; Foner 1985; Kasinitz 1992; Deaux 2006, 184). While Afro-Caribbean immigrants might have advantages as native English speakers, albeit in the Caribbean context, and familiarity with British cultural norms owing to the history of colonization, they also confront the daunting obstacle of racism. Their experiences and perspectives are likely to differ in some aspects from those of the Dominican and Colombian parents we interviewed. Given the diversity in the Latino category, further research should also explore possible in-group differences related to phenotype.

Given the disproportionate number of undocumented immigrants who hail from Latin America, documentation status is also crucial to consider. If we compare our findings to those of Douglas Massey and Magaly Sanchez R. (2010), we see that documentation status interacts with ethnicity to shape different patterns of perceived exclusion. The parents we interviewed, who were virtually all documented, were able to balance their belief in the American Dream and their perception of exclusion and discrimination in the United States; the respondents interviewed in the Northeast study largely went from optimism to pessimism (Massey and Sanchez R. 2010). This difference is not surprising if we consider that more than one-third of the respondents in the Northeast sample were Mexican and undocumented. Contemporary Mexican immigrants face an especially negative context of reception (Portes and Rumbaut 2001; Telles and Ortiz 2008), and because of ongoing Mexican immigration in large numbers, they also continue to be seen by Americans as foreigners rather than as an ethnic group in the process of assimilating (Jiménez 2010). Undocumented immigrants, of course, have a very negative context of reception. In the absence of legal status, they tend to experience higher economic disadvantages and incur greater psychological costs (Mahler 1995; Yoshikawa, Godfrey, and Rivera 2008).

Hirokazu Yoshikawa (2011) finds that undocumented parents of young U.S.-born (and thus citizen) children are less likely to access institutional resources, including those to which the children are legally entitled. A longitudinal approach would help us understand whether the experiences of undocumented immigrants and their children shift over time—for instance, with a change in the parents' legal status (Singer and Willett 2003). This approach would allow us to see whether their social exclusion assumes a different form, along with its possible effects on second-generation success.

It is interesting that some of the immigrant parents and children we interviewed justified the social exclusion of Latinos that they themselves criticized. They paradoxically pointed to real obstacles faced by Latinos and yet expressed the idea that some Latinos deserved their place at the bottom of the American social hierarchy. The parents and children had contradictory motives—they both criticized the existing system that kept their group at the bottom and legitimized the system and the low status of Latinos within it (Jost, Banaji, and Nosek 2004). With migration, however, individuals have to negotiate two different systems of inequality: the one in the home country and the one in the receiving nation. They are also likely to have different positions within those systems and rationales for why they belong there. How do immigrants make sense of these two systems and understand their own outcomes within them, along with their children's in the United States? Again, with answers to this question, a better picture might emerge of the messages that immigrant parents give to their second-generation children about whether success is possible in the United States, and if so, how to achieve it.

An Educational Profile of the Second Generation

Our findings carefully parsed out where the second-generation children went to school and how they actually experienced schooling. The children of the residentially segregated Dominican working-class families went to urban public schools that were inferior compared to those of their Colombian counterparts. The availability of more detailed macro-level data would help us identify such neighborhood and school effects and their impact on outcomes. This demographic information on immigrant children should be collected by public schools, which currently do not identify students by immigrant status (Clewell, Cosentino de Cohen, and Murray 2007), and by national surveys (Hernandez, Denton, and Macartney 2008; Takanishi 2008).[3] With this information, studies of large representative samples can make generalizations about the impact of segregation, for instance, on the quality of schools attended by second-generation children. It would also allow for nuanced comparisons of second-generation children with their native black and white counterparts. We would have an idea of how second-generation children fit into the achievement gap data, which is presently told mainly along racial-ethnic lines (Clarkson 2008).

A look at what we have gained with the mandates of No Child Left Behind (NCLB) to collect these kinds of data for English-language learners (ELLs) is instructive. We now have a more detailed educational profile of ELLs, who are more than 10 percent of American public school students, and relatedly, we now have a clearer picture of how school-based linguistic isolation and practices influence their outcomes (Bataloval and McHugh 2010, 1). In states with high immigration, a portion of in-state math achievement gaps between ELLs and white students can be explained by the fact that they were not attending the same public schools (Fry 2008).[4] Most ELLs attend schools that are largely composed of ELLs and have higher percentages of working-class and poor students. There is also wide variability between schools in how ELLs are assessed as needing services (Ragan and Lesaux 2006) and between school districts with high numbers of ELL students in the tests they use to determine students' subject knowledge and English-language proficiency, as required by NCLB (Clewell, Cosentino de Cohen, and Murray 2007).

Recommendations for Policy and Practice

Immigrant Integration

We know enough about certain concerns that we can take the appropriate steps toward better outcomes. Our findings of immigrant exclusion—the parents' sense of being alone in America—highlight the gap in our integration policies. While there have been vibrant efforts at the local and state levels to help newcomers with learning English and learning about life in the United States, few national policies have been put in place to link up with them (Progressive States Network 2009; Jiménez 2011). National policies have tended to focus on control of immigrant flows rather than the actual integration of immigrants and their children (Tienda 2002; Uriarte and Granberry 2005; Suárez-Orozco, Suárez-Orozco, and Todorova 2008; Kerwin, Meissner, and McHugh 2011). This gap exists despite the fact that local and state initiatives would benefit from more guidance and collaboration and an overarching vision rather than the current piecemeal approach.

A federal office on immigrant integration, ideally located in the White House, could take a leadership role in managing many of the issues we have identified as crucial to immigrants' adaptation (Galston, Pickus, and Skerry 2009; Kerwin, Meissner, and McHugh 2011). These include adult English-language education, adult basic education, and civic education. This office could facilitate relationships with state and local actors and other relevant federal agencies to create a shared database of which programs work (or do not work), who they serve, and how much they cost. This office could also help organize efforts to increase dialogue, knowledge sharing, and, possibly, joint efforts among community-based organizations that provide similar services to different immigrant populations in the same city or region that might not otherwise know of one another.[5]

Parental Involvement

Our findings on parental involvement reveal that schools and immigrant families, especially working-class ones, are not in sync. There are ways, however, to reduce the parents' sense of social exclusion. One is through a culture of care that is respectful of parents and inclusive of them from the outset through home visits, regardless of how often (or not) they engage with the school (Mapp 2003; Comer 2005a), and through interpreters for parents who need them (Lucas 1997; Ramirez 2003). Listening to the parents to learn what they need and want to know and having some parents serve as role models and sources of information for other parents are further useful practical strategies (Larrota and Ramirez 2009; Crosnoe 2010). Certainly, these kinds of parental needs should at least be taken into account by larger-scale districtwide efforts involving school parent liaisons, notably in New York City and San Diego (Martinez-Cosio and Iannacone 2007, 351).[6]

Community-based organizations serving immigrant families should also be included in parental involvement efforts (Suárez-Orozco, Onaga, and Lardemelle 2010). These organizations have a rich history of engaging with families in urban, low-income areas, offering valuable information about the communities in which they live; fostering their civic participation; and providing services in health care, housing, and job training. Thus, they should be better deployed in strategies to increase parental involvement, as defined by not only traditional measures but also the more expansive ones discussed here, for example, ensuring that parents feel that they are part of the process (Warren 2005; Warren et al. 2009). At one end of the spectrum are community schools that actively partner with community-based organizations, but other kinds of public schools would benefit from at least some kind of relationship with these organizations.

Our findings revealed that the second-generation children were largely on their own with schooling because of the out-of-sync relationship between the families and schools. This finding not only highlights the pressing need for mentoring and enrichment programs geared for youth but also has implications for parental involvement programs for immigrants. Such programs need to be aware that the children are already attending to crucial processes on their own and consider the possibility that some conventional forms of engagement, intended to dramatically increase the capacity of homework help from parents and their knowledge of the American higher education system, might not be feasible, given how long such processes could take. This is especially the case if parents have not been here long, do not know much English, have little time, or have children who are older and thus have less time to adjust before facing the transition to college or the labor force. Thus, parental involvement programs should collaborate closely with mentoring and enrichment programs geared for youth to ensure that as many of the children's needs are met as possible, if not through the parental involvement channel, then through another. Indeed, increased collaboration between these two kinds of programs is a worthy goal in and of itself.

Public Schools and Programmatic Interventions

Most of the children we interviewed went to public schools, which are a key stakeholder for many children in the United States. The children, especially those from working-class families, benefited from teachers who respected their ability to learn, took an interest in them as individuals, and referred them to key learning opportunities—in essence, "vouching" for them. Such vouching supports the idea that students do best when teachers know about their students' social and emotional domains as well as their cognitive ones. In other words, teachers "knowing the children—individually, culturally, and developmentally[—]is as important as knowing the content being taught" (National Council for Accreditation of Teacher Education 2010, 5). This knowledge should include the commonalities in how all children learn and behave, in addition to the particularities of certain populations, such as immigrant children (UCLA Center for Mental Health in Schools 2011). Teachers also need to know themselves individually, culturally, and developmentally. For instance, teachers would benefit from awareness of how their own social bias and perspectives in handling conflict influence their pedagogy (Adalbjarnardottir and Selman 1997) and from insights into the ways they can teach about inequalities without feeling overwhelmed by the task (Pollock et al. 2010) or leaving their students fearful that social change is a futile project (Seider 2009; Seider and Hugeley 2009). To better implement these nuanced kinds of approaches, we should address a key gap in our teacher training programs by paying more attention to developmental science theories that focus on both teachers and students as learners and the best practices that employ such theories (Comer 2005b; National Council for Accreditation of Teacher Education 2010).[7]

Our findings also support the idea that teachers can connect with and mentor their students in meaningful ways, even if they do not belong to the same racial and ethnic group, as the respondents' precollegiate teachers, both good and bad, were mainly white (Carter 2005; Pollock 2008a; Reddick 2009). To be sure, we must diversify the teaching profession to reflect the students' changing demographics (Graham 1987; Carter 2005; U.S. Department of Education 2007), but we also need to ensure that our current (and future) teachers have the necessary tools to build trust with their students across different backgrounds. Certainly, teachers can use "wise strategies" to provide critical feedback to minority students along with explicit attention to high standards and their belief in the students' ability to meet that benchmark. Such strategies can mitigate the distrust that minority students might feel owing to negative stereotypes about their group's ability to succeed academically (Cohen, Steele, and Ross 1999). Teachers can also develop expectations of students' present performance that are not overly informed by their past benchmarks (Carter 2005, 169; Ferguson 2003; Dee 2005; Son 2010) and diminished for non-white, low-income children (Anyon 1995).

That being said, the burden of change should not fall exclusively on teachers. We need to be aware that teachers do their work in complex institutions where they are one of several key stakeholders (Lawrence-Lightfoot 1978). Policies should take into account findings from research on how principals can facilitate programs to support teachers of varying needs and preferences (Drago-Severson 2004) and the contexts in which teachers work (Johnson 1990). For institutional change to succeed, it must proceed "from the inside out," drawing on the voices and expertise of teachers and school leaders and staff (Elmore 2004).

A final point cannot be overstated. The respondents in our study had one more key advantage: the largely non-school-based resources that helped them with schooling. Schools are important, but they cannot do the job of educating children alone. We should prioritize and invest in after-school programs, broadly defined, that perform a vital service by helping children meet their academic and developmental needs. These programs have been shown to make a significant difference with academic achievement for both non-immigrant and immigrant children, especially those from low-income and poor families (Eccles and Goodman 2002; Shernoff and Vandell 2007; Vandell et al. 2005; Lemmel and Rothman 2007; Harding, Rimer, and Fredrick 2007). They include the better-known federal TRIO programs, notably Upward Bound, along with the less well-known but nonetheless very valuable services provided by community-based organizations.

Institutions and Immigrants Revisited

Our findings, told from a comparative frame and over the course of two generations, tell an important story about institutions and immigrants' mobility and assimilation. There is a tendency in the United States to view success as a function of individual effort, one made easier by coming from particular groups that encourage the cultural dispositions supposedly needed for success. This tendency is inscribed in American mythology, popular discourse, and scholarly work. While the pioneering immigrant community studies of the Chicago school of sociology highlighted institutions, such as schools, businesses, the press, and politics (Thomas and Znaniecki 1918; Wirth 1928), institutions have assumed a less significant place in more recent writings. Indeed, American research on immigration has tended to focus on ethnic group differences rather than educational and other institutions. In contrast, European researchers have been more likely to address the effects on outcomes of institutional arrangements, whether for all individuals or particularly for immigrants (Crul and Schneider 2009, 1509). With its emphasis on national origins and ethnicity, even segmented assimilation, a bold theory that has changed how we study second-generation educational and economic outcomes, can inadvertently take us back to group-based and especially cultural explanations. That is why this book's analysis of the social processes giving rise to outcomes is so crucial.

Let us revisit the popular analogies with which this book began. The immigrant analogy is meant to explain why immigrants are doing so well and doing so well in comparison with native racial minorities. The ethnic cultures analogy seeks to account for why all immigrants are not doing well. In this book, I have added another—the minority analogy—to account for why some native urban minorities are doing so well and what immigrants have learned and continue to learn from them. These group-based accounts are useful because they can illuminate immigrant selectivity and native minority selectivity, the cultural histories specific to groups, and the powerful ways in which society views people as group members and the meaningful consequences of this dynamic for members of those groups (Kasinitz et al. 2008). Even so, group-based accounts are incomplete by themselves because they shield from view the critical process-based factors that influence differences. In the words of Roberto Suro (2011, 14):

> All the emphasis has been on drawing comparisons between the major groups, Latinos and Asians, whites and blacks. Meanwhile, less attention has gone to characteristics like English-ability, time in country and parents' education which could help explain outcomes across groups. All the focus has been on the columns when the rows deserved greater attention.

In this vein, we should pay more attention to how these and other characteristics actually influence the social processes underlying the interactions of immigrants and institutions and how these processes influence differences in group outcomes.

In this book, I have adopted this approach to analyze how academic success happens. The children we interviewed were able to win the immigrant bargain—making up for their parents' sacrifices with the immigrant journey by going on to college—but at considerable cost to themselves and their families. Their success should not blind us to the real costs they incurred. A great many of those costs have to do with the reluctance of American institutions to facilitate the integration of newcomers and their children. The parents believed that they were alone in America, and the children believed that they were on their own in schools. The story of success told here is one of individual agency, family agency, and institutional supports *combined*. The combination was especially relevant to the working-class 1.5- and second-generation respondents. Again, the story told here is *not* about how the children of immigrants succeeded—many despite great odds—with pluck and perseverance and how institutions therefore do not matter. The story is quite the opposite: the success of these 1.5- and second-generation individuals reveals that institutions matter a great deal (Fernandez-Kelly and Portes 2008; Kasinitz et al. 2008; Haller, Portes, and Lynch 2011b).

This book's analysis of the role of institutions in incorporating immigrants and their children changes the ways in which we think about why the second generation has done better than some native minorities. A number of the immigrant families faced challenges similar to those that low-income and poor native racial minorities have long confronted: living in segregated, urban, low-income neighborhoods with few institutional resources and going to de facto segregated, struggling, urban public schools. How were they able to move up and out of these conditions? The answer has to do with the programmatic interventions and diversity policies that grew out of the civil rights movement and were designed to provide equal opportunities for native minorities. Some also benefited from a minority culture of mobility situated in the African American experience—for example, from close ties to native minorities who were successfully deploying those very same opportunities. The success of the respondents in our study highlights the importance of such institutional mechanisms for themselves and for their native minority peers.

This book's comparison of the Dominicans and Colombians with the Chinese working-class respondents from my earlier research reveals how access to different kinds of institutions can make the journey to success more difficult or easier. That the second-generation story for both the Latinos and the Chinese was one of success—despite the obstacles—is certainly cause for optimism. But it was not optimism that made for this success. Their success was striking given how the children spoke of similar kinds of verbal and moral guidance from parents but not interventionist support like help with homework or the college application process. The reasons were the same—the immigrant parents were not fluent or even proficient in English, did not have much formal schooling, and did not know the workings of the American educational system. Far more crucial than whether the children inhabited their parents' ethnic cultural milieu was the fact that they shared their parents' belief about the importance of education and valued their parents' care. But these ingredients were not enough for success. The key for all three groups was access to an infrastructure that provided assistance at critical junctures, especially to the children, often unsolicited. This included referrals to gifted classes or better middle schools, after-school programs, and high-quality college counseling.

From the outset, residential segregation shaped different starting points, and the gap was only compounded by the groups' different kinds of access to that crucial infrastructure. To start with, the Chinese were less residentially segregated; furthering this advantage, they quickly learned from middle-class kin and coethnic friends about the availability of better public schools elsewhere and how to get one's children into them. The Chinese also benefited from an ethnic infrastructure—from ethnic media that publicized information about how American schooling worked to ethnically owned and run academic preparatory schools, such as cram schools—that provided this kind of information. This ethnic infrastructure not only reflected the value attached to education in their communities but was shaped by complex material forces, including the availability of educational information derived from cross-class ties and of domestic and transnational wealth—the latter in the form of capital flows from East Asian economies to start ethnic capitalist enterprises (such as schools and media) that helped make the information readily available (Louie 2011). Both poverty and class inequalities existed in these ethnic enclaves (Kwong 1987), but even families that could not afford to send their children to the cram schools gained from the information circulated in the ethnic media and in informal conversations. In other words, even the families on the economic margins managed to profit from the community's intertwined material and cultural currency with education.

The picture for the Latinos was quite different. The Dominican parents, already finding themselves in poorer, more socially isolated communities with little ethnic or transnational wealth, confronted a double bind. First, they lived in areas with inferior schools, and then, they were left to figure out on their own that there were better public school options and how to access them. This knowledge was typically scarce. Their coethnic kin and friends told them about Catholic schools as an exit option, but these schools required tuitions that the families often could not afford. For the Dominicans, non-ethnic institutional supports, such as teachers, Upward Bound, or community-based organizations, were vital to their children's success. That was where the children got the facts and mentoring they needed to succeed. The working-class Colombian families were somewhere in between. Like the Chinese, they were less residentially segregated than the Dominicans and belonged to a group with middle-class coethnics. However, owing to mistrust born of divisions back in Colombia, including the drug stigma, racism, and regional factionalism, the working- and middle-class Colombians in the United States did not have close ties (Guarnizo, Sanchez, and Roach 1999; Guarnizo and Diaz 1999). The working-class Colombian immigrants thus did not benefit from the information and experiences of higher-status coethnics.

But these nuances can be easily missed. In New York City, for instance, the communities of Chinatown, Washington Heights (where many Dominicans live), and Jackson Heights (home to a sizable Colombian population) are all vibrant places with ethnic businesses, ethnic languages, and ethnic cultures. These communities seem so similar that an observer might think that the key difference behind the varying patterns of academic achievement among the second-generation people living in them is that the Chinese emphasize education more. But as I have argued, less visible social forces make educational success a more difficult proposition for Latinos. The family and nonfamily mechanisms of success certainly operate in similar ways, but the Latinos have a tougher road toward accessing the latter.

Something different may also be happening in the schools attended by the second-generation Latinos and Chinese that adds to the former's relative disadvantage. In both this study and my earlier one, the respondents spoke of their teachers and peers being well aware of the stereotype of the Latino underachiever and the Asian overachiever and of the potentially powerful impact of such stereotypes on expectations. Knowledge about where second-generation children are going to school—which, as we noted, we need to know more about—would help us understand this dynamic as well.

These are the differences in social processes and social contexts that we should be looking at more closely. Yet it is precisely these kinds of inquiries that can be obscured if we focus too much on the group optimism model, whether the overall immigrant group or a particular ethnic group. Ethnic group membership definitely matters in the lives of the second generation, as shown here and in other studies (see Kasinitz et al. 2008, 22–24). But because Americans have typically thought about group differences in success as having so much to do with the groups themselves, we need to be careful that we also tell the story of institutions and their impact on the social processes experienced by the second generation—in this case, on how they actually achieve success. The role of institutions has been less resonant, even though they have been and continue to be a critical dimension in the story of second-generation mobility and assimilation in the United States. We need to recognize the merits of this dimension and learn from it to build an America where success is not as readily framed as a function of group membership—and where success is more easily achieved regardless of the group to which one belongs.

Appendix

Methodological Notes

Research Design

Recruitment

From its inception, this study was designed as a qualitative analysis of two generations in one family, namely, grown children and their immigrant parents. I chose the dual-generation approach to explore the connections and disconnections between the children's and parents' perspectives and experiences around the immigrant journey, specifically, education, mobility, and assimilation. Because we tend to organize our experiences through the prism of narrative (Bruner 1991), I decided to use life story interviews. This method is particularly useful for investigating how individuals make sense of new contexts and for charting connections between such concepts as social status and an immigrant identity (Atkinson 2001; Jensen 2008).[1] About one-fifth of the questions asked of the children had to do with their parents—who their friends and coworkers were, why they came to the United States, why they sent the children to particular schools, and how involved they were with their children's schooling. By the same token, about one-third of the questions asked of the parents had to do with their children.

The first stage of the study involved in-person interviews with the grown children, who had to have transitioned to college and been born in the United States or arrived by the age of twelve.[2] The second stage of the study involved interviewing a subset of the parents, some in person and others over the phone. All the interviews were tape-recorded, and thirty-six of the thirty-seven parent interviews were translated from Spanish into English. The average length of the children's interviews was two hours, and the parental interviews ranged from one to several hours.

The challenges came with actually implementing the research design. In the fall of 2001, I thought that I could quite easily replicate the research strategy that had been the foundation of my first book, *Compelled to Excel: Immigration, Education, and Opportunity Among Chinese Americans*

(Louie 2004), an analysis of how the second-generation Chinese Americans at Hunter (City University of New York [CUNY]) and Columbia Colleges in New York City viewed their paths to college and incorporation into American life, based on interviews with the children and a small number of immigrant parents. However, after spending six months unsuccessfully trying to gain access to Boston-area postsecondary institutions, public and private, I realized that this strategy was not feasible. From 2001 to 2005, I contacted nine postsecondary institutions; four granted me access to their students. Of those four, only one, Northern Essex Community College (NECCO), had a relatively high proportion of second-generation Dominican and Colombian students. At the time of the study, NECCO was designated a Hispanic-serving institution by the Hispanic Association of Colleges and Universities (HACU), a national educational association. According to the 2008 HACU website, postsecondary institutions qualify for this designation with a Hispanic student enrollment of at least 25 percent of the entire student body.

As any researcher can tell you, the key is to stay flexible when the unexpected happens. I realized that I had to find other avenues to recruit subjects. In the early summer of 2002, I made two key decisions: First, I decided to expand the sample from currently enrolled students to alumni who had gone to or completed postsecondary school in the five to seven years prior to participating in the study. I reasoned that recent alumni would be easier to access and would still be close enough to the time when they graduated to have insights into their transition to college and perhaps also their transition to adulthood. Second, since I was already conducting informational interviews with community-based organizations to get to know the immigrant Dominican and Colombian communities in greater Boston, I decided to actively recruit through them. In the end, I contacted thirty-one community-based organizations and other local and regional ethnic/panethnic, largely non-school-based organizations (see table A.1 for the list) and spoke with more than fifty individuals, some linked to organizations and others not.

In the process of conducting the interviews, I became aware of another recruitment strategy that did not directly involve me—the project information had been forwarded to a number of personal and professional email lists, including the Congressional Hispanic Caucus Institute (CHCI). For example, Cindy Rodriguez, then a reporter at the *Boston Globe*, referred me to Hector Bina, owner of a popular restaurant in Jamaica Plain. Mr. Bina suggested that I touch base with Digna Abreu, who sent out electronic word of my project through her numerous personal and professional networks. From all these efforts, there ended up being three major sampling chains: Northeastern University (twelve respondents), thanks to Prof. Luis Falcon and Elena M. Quiroz, then director of the Latino/a Student Cultural Center; NECCO (ten respondents), thanks to Katharine Rodger, then dean of the college; and the CUNY

Table A.1 List of Organizations Contacted for the Study

List of Organizations Contacted for the Study
Amigos School
Bajucol
Charlestown High School
Chelsea Human Services Collaborative
College of New Rochelle
Colombo-American Alliance (Boston)
Colombian Colloquium/Harvard-MIT Colombian Society
Colombian Consulate (Boston)
Concilio Hispano (Cambridge, Massachusetts)
Congressional Hispanic Caucus Institute
David Rockefeller Center for Latin American Studies at Harvard University
Dominican Consulate (Boston)
Dominican Studies Institute at City University of New York (CUNY)
East Boston Area Planning Action Council (APAC)
East Boston Ecumenical Community Council
East Boston Social Centers Inc.
El Centro Hispano (White Plains, New York)
Gaston Institute at the University of Massachusetts (Boston)
Graduate/Professional Hermana of Sigma Lambda Upsilon/Señoritas Latinas Unidas Sorority, Inc.
Higher Education Resource Center in Boston (Roxbury) and Lawrence
Hispanic Association of Colleges and Universities (HACU)
La Alianza Hispana
La Comunidad
LASPAU Academic and Professional Programs for the Americas at Harvard University
Latino Professional Network
National Society of Hispanic MBAs (New England chapter)
New English Resource Center for Higher Education at the University of Massachusetts at Boston
Society of Hispanic Engineers
Society of Latin American Alumni
Somerville Youth Commission
Voices of Action

Dominican Studies Institute (DSI; six respondents), thanks to Dr. Ramona Hernandez, the director.[3] About 54 percent of the children's sample was recruited through these three channels, along with additional organizations, each of which yielded two to three respondents. The remaining thirty-five individuals in the sample were recruited in one of two ways: when they reported having heard of my project but not remembering the source, and when I or a research assistant recruited them by canvassing immigrant neighborhoods with local institutions that served substantial numbers of Dominicans and Colombians and sponsored local events that drew this population.

Table A.2 Children's Educational Attainment

	Colombians (N = 37)	Dominicans (N = 39)
Graduated from vocational school	1	0
Enrolled in two-year college	3	8
Graduated from two-year college	0	1
Previously enrolled in two-year college, no degree	0	3
Enrolled in four-year college	23	12
Graduated from four-year college	10	15

Source: Author's compilation based on data from the Dominican and Colombian Immigrant Family Study (2009).

Children's Sample Characteristics

Despite my best efforts, there were enrollment patterns that were probably nonrandom and nonrepresentative sampling artifacts. As table A.2 shows, Dominicans made up the bulk of the community college students (twelve of the fifteen respondents), which is likely to have been an artifact of my having gained access to a community college located in a predominantly Dominican and Puerto Rican town in Massachusetts. Meanwhile, most of the Colombians had been in four-year colleges. Table A.3 provides a full listing of the schools by type and selectivity. Overall, about one-fifth of the respondents went to public institutions.

Table A.4 sorts the sample by four-year college selectivity. Ethnicity was relevant here too. More than half of the Colombian four-year college students were found at tier-one (top fifty) institutions. By contrast, about one-quarter of the Dominicans were at such places.

Although I recognized that my sample would be neither random nor representative, I tried to obtain variation along key indicators. After about a year in the field, I saw two emergent sampling patterns that needed to be addressed. The first had to do with gender. I found that Dominican women were volunteering to participate at much higher rates than their male counterparts. (This was not the case for the Colombians.) In January 2004, I closed the Dominican women portion of the sample and focused on recruiting Dominican men to the study. I was fortunate to be able to rely on the indefatigable Silvia Covelli, whom I initially thought I would need only to help with recruitment. However, it became clear that my professional schedule was not flexible enough to conduct on-the-spot interviews (for example, being contacted at 1:00 PM about meeting at 2:00 PM in Lawrence, a good forty-minute drive from Cambridge with no traffic and assuming I had nothing else scheduled). Silvia conducted interviews with six Dominican male respondents in ad-

Table A.3 Postsecondary Institutions Attended by Respondents, by Type

Type of Four-Year Institution	Top Fifty	Second Tier	Third Tier	Fourth Tier
Best national universities (PhD-granting)	Brown, Cornell, Harvard, Massachusetts Institute of Technology, New York University, State University of New York at Binghamton, Tufts	American University, Boston University, Fordham, University of Massachusetts at Amherst, Syracuse University	Northeastern, University of Massachusetts at Lowell, University of Rhode Island	University of Massachusetts at Boston
Best liberal arts colleges	Amherst, Middlebury, Smith, Wellesley	Wheaton	—	—
Best universities, master's, by region	Bentley, Emerson, Simmons	—	Buffalo State College, Fitchburg State College, Long Island State University	College of New Rochelle
Best comprehensive colleges, bachelor's, by region	Merrimack College (North Region)	—	—	—

Source: Author's compilation based on data from *U.S. News & World Report* (2001).
Note: In addition to these four-year institutions, respondents also attended four community colleges (Massachusetts Bay, Middlesex, Northern Essex, and Northshore) and one vocational school (one-year program).

Table A.4 Selectivity of Children's Four-Year Colleges

Selectivity of College	Frequency	Percentage
Top fifty	24	39
Second tier	9	15
Third tier	20	33
Fourth tier	5	8
Missing[a]	3	5

Source: Author's compilation based on data from *U.S. News & World Report* (2001).
Note: N = 61.
[a]There was no available information in *U.S. News & World Report*, "Best College Rankings," for Miami International University of Art and Design in Miami, Florida; Hesser College in Manchester, New Hampshire; and Newbury College in Boston, Massachusetts.

dition to two Colombian male respondents whom she helped recruit to the study. In the end, sixteen of the thirty-nine Dominican respondents and sixteen of the thirty-seven Colombian respondents were men.

In the spring of 2004, I noticed the second pattern, namely, that middle- to upper-middle-class Colombians were becoming the bulk of my sample. While greater Boston has a strong working-class Colombian representation in East Boston, Lowell, and Chelsea, which I tapped into through Spanish-language recruitment posters and meetings with local community leaders, it was still proving difficult to reach them effectively. From my conversations with people familiar with the East Boston community, I learned that the nature of my sampling criteria was again proving to be problematic. There tended to be fewer second-generation children among the Colombians, who were arriving in greater Boston later than the Dominicans did; moreover, of the ones who fell into my age-at-arrival category, a significant number were financially unable to transition to college from high school because of their documentation status. (Lacking papers, they did not qualify for financial aid.) In January 2005, I decided to spend an additional six months recruiting working-class Colombians with the stellar assistance of Dr. Claudia Pineda, then a doctoral student, who conducted interviews with five Colombian respondents. The result was more social class diversity. About 30 percent of the Colombian mothers had gone as far as middle school or high school, and 16 percent of the fathers had completed grade school or middle school, with another 21 percent having finished high school.

Overall, the children's reports revealed that they came from families doing better than foreign-born Colombians and Dominicans on average. As table A.5 shows, this is clear in the higher rates of high school completion among the children's mothers in my sample; the disparity between the Colombian and Dominican mothers was also smaller compared to the census data. The exception was female-headed households with children under the age of eighteen—substantially more of the re-

Table A.5 Selected Indicators of Foreign-Born Dominicans and Colombians in the United States, Census 2000, Compared to Parents in the Sample, 2001 to 2005

	Census		Sample			
	Colombians	Dominicans	Colombians		Dominicans	
			Mother	Father	Mother	Father
High school graduate or higher	72.1%	47.8%	81%	70%	72%	44%
Bachelor's degree or higher	21.6	9.4	22	24	8	18
Female-headed household with children under eighteen	10.2	23.9	35		36	
Families living below poverty level	14.6	28.3	—		—	
Living in owner-occupied unit	41	20	70		49	

Source: Author's compilation based on data from U.S. Census Bureau (2000) and the Dominican and Colombian Immigrant Family Study (2009).

Table A.6 Current Occupations of Foreign-Born Colombians and Dominicans in the United States, Census 2000, Compared to Parents in the Sample, 2001 to 2005

Census Occupational Category	Census: All Colombians	Sample: Colombian Mothers	Sample: Colombian Fathers	Census: All Dominicans	Sample: Dominican Mothers	Sample: Dominican Fathers
Management and professional	24%	39%	13%	15.3%	34%	32%
Service	24.2	45	20	26.4	31	36
Sales and office	23.2	6	3	24.4	7	5
Construction, extraction, and maintenance	8.5	6	23	7.8	24	18
Production, transportation, and material moving	19.8	3	7	25.8	3	8

Source: Author's compilation based on data from U.S. Census Bureau (2000) and the Dominican and Colombian Immigrant Family Study (2009).

spondents, particularly among the Colombians, had spent some time growing up in one.[4] However, a look at the kinds of jobs the immigrant parents held further reveals their relative advantage. As seen in table A.6, most of the working Colombian mothers in my sample were in management, professional, or service occupations, compared to only about 48 percent nationally.[5] The occupational advantage of the mothers was offset by the relative disadvantage of the fathers, who were less likely to be in these fields compared to both the mothers in the sample and the national figures. The results were somewhat similar for the Dominican parents, with both mothers and fathers more likely to be in a management, professional, or service field: around two-thirds held this type of job, compared to 41.7 percent on average.

For a more detailed look at the jobs held by the children's parents, both before and after migration, please consult table A.7. The parents who experienced a downward occupational slide with migration are highlighted in bold.

Parental Sample Characteristics

I encountered fewer issues with recruiting the parental subsample, although the Dominican families proved more of a challenge, which was surprising given the enthusiasm of the children. Across the parental subsample, however, scheduling was an issue, especially for the working-class families, whose schedules tended to be in flux. Owing to the voluntary nature of participation in the study, the parental subsample did not entirely mirror the demographic characteristics of the families in the overall sample. We interviewed parents who tended to have been in the United States longer: about 77 percent had been here between sixteen and thirty or more years (compared to 87 percent in the overall sample). The overall bifurcation between parents with a grade school education and those with some postsecondary schooling was maintained among the Dominicans. However, the Dominican mothers we spoke with were somewhat less likely to have gone to a postsecondary school, and the fathers were more likely to have done so. Both the Colombian fathers and mothers were more likely to have a postsecondary education than the overall sample. The thirteen Dominican family interviews tended to underrepresent the dramatically upwardly mobile and the limited risers, while overrepresenting the low replicators and downwardly mobile. The mobility paths of the eighteen Colombian families also varied from the overall sample, but by smaller margins. Table A.8 provides a more detailed comparison. Middle-class families tended to be underrepresented among both the Colombian and Dominican subsamples.

In the parental subsample, there was also a substantial overrepresentation of Dominican families whose focal children were in community

Table A.7 Parents' Jobs Pre- and Post-Migration, Overall Sample

Pseudonym of 1.5- or Second-Generation Respondent	Father's Job in Native Country	Father's Present Job in the United States	Mother's Job in Native Country	Mother's Present Job in the United States
Dominicans				
Alfonso	student	real estate entrepreneur	student	secretary/legal assistant
Paul	unknown	unknown	unknown	nurse's assistant
Leslie	tailor	tailor	housewife	housewife
Nora	unknown	superintendent	bank teller	clerical assistant
Natalia	agriculturist	restaurant owner	none	hospital worker
Alejandro	own business (sports complex)	did not migrate	**housewife**	**mailroom clerk, previously on welfare**
Alba	unknown	retired	travel agent	buyer
Lenore	merchant	merchant	lab technician	lab technician
Alexsa	unknown	unknown	unknown	administrative assistant
Mary	unknown	housekeeping	unknown	supervisor
Lourdes	mixed mauual labor	construction	maid	housekeeper
Alma	**electrical engineer**	**self-employed electrical contractor**	**clerk**	**machine operator**
Peggy	**government agency director**	**security guard**	housewife	housewife

Lucia	agriculture	chef	housewife	housewife
Paula	unknown	unknown	owned sewing school	sales
Laura	farmer	unemployed	housewife	hotel income auditor
Carolina	**businessman**	**taxi driver**	**teacher**	**home attendant**
Elisa	unemployed	delivery person	unemployed	factory worker
Andrea	unknown	unknown	housewife	school bus matron
Bea	**engineer**	**unknown**	**secretary**	**maintenance worker**
Elias	**military officer**	**retired superintendent**	teacher/principal	retired teacher
Angel	**mechanic**	**janitor**	student	dry cleaning clerk
Julia	N/A—too young	machine operator	N/A—too young	legal assistant
Betty	unknown	deceased	farm worker	disabled
Marissa	mechanic	janitor	unknown	health aide
Charles	unknown	deceased	teacher	retired secretary
Michelle	business owner	retired	housewife	factory worker
Miguel	unknown	grocery store owner	unknown	factory worker
Ana	student	unknown	cleaner	factory worker
Isabel	student	airplane engine inspector	student	assistant teacher

(Table continues on p. 188.)

Table A.7 *(continued)*

Pseudonym of 1.5- or Second-Generation Respondent	Father's Job in Native Country	Father's Present Job in the United States	Mother's Job in Native Country	Mother's Present Job in the United States
Carlos	unknown	taxi driver	unknown	factory worker
Raymond	shoeshiner	factory worker	housewife	seamstress
Rafael	unknown	van driver	unknown	floral arranger
Salvador	mixed	unemployed	housewife	home attendant
Frank	salesman	businessman	flight attendant	housewife
Francisco	ticket seller	small business manager	housewife	nurse's assistant
Cliff	unknown	unknown	unknown	unemployed
Wayne	grocery store worker	retired factory worker	**teacher**	**retired factory worker**
Billy	businessman	returned to the Dominican Republic	**housewife**	**home day-care provider**
Colombians				
Eduardo	**architect**	**gardener**	administrative assistant	none
Sally	technology repair worker	retired technology repair worker	keypunch operator	executive assistant
Maureen	business owner	did not migrate	**housewife**	**waitress, newspaper delivery, clerk**
Julian	painter	factory worker	**secretary**	**hotel maid**
Bella	N/A—too young	subway conductor	ticket agent	home day-care

Aurora	unknown	did not migrate	**administrative assistant**	**nanny/security guard**
Patricia	N/A—too young	taxi driver	nutritionist	mail carrier
Leonardo	student	deceased	student	bank teller manager
Judy	business owner	did not migrate	teacher/college professor/corporate controller	bank vice president
Audrey	N/A—too young	unknown	N/A—too young	unemployed
Claudia	student	U.S. Postal Sserviee clerk	student	bank worker
Carmel	student	FedEx courier	student	medical office biller
Thomas	unknown	cook	unemployed	airport security
Amalia	movie theater worker	construction worker	N/A—too young	social worker
Natasha	chemist	deceased	**accounting secretary**	**hospital housekeeping**
José	attorney	did not migrate	**secretary**	**factory worker/housecleaner**
Shirley	unknown	unknown	secretary	paralegal
Pilar	unknown	unknown	accountant	unemployed
Javier	**business owner**	**car salesman**	**business owner**	**school bus driver**
Pedro	business owner	did not migrate	**real estate agent**	**college housekeeping**
Sarabeth	bank teller	self-employed T-shirt silk screener	unknown	supervisor for state agency
Jorge	dentist	deceased	housewife	computer engineer
Calida	varied	plumber	housewife	hospital worker

(Table continues on p. 190.)

Table A.7 *(continued)*

Pseudonym of 1.5- or Second-Generation Respondent	Father's Job in Native Country	Father's Present Job in the United States	Mother's Job in Native Country	Mother's Present Job in the United States
Penny	shop worker	factory supervisor	housecleaner	unemployed
Elena	architect	architect	student	interior designer
Sammy	public relations	did not migrate	public sector official	family-owned business
Rick	student	chemical engineer	student	personal trainer
Nelson	**industrial engineer**	**kitchen staff**	unknown	maintenance head
Antony	**exports-imports**	**cleaning company supervisor**	real estate agent	housewife
Sara	N/A—too young	city agency worker	student	tax preparer
Park	unknown	restaurant manager	executive secretary	real estate agent
Jeffrey	factory worker	technician	factory worker	home day-care provider
Herman	textiles	retired	textile worker	retired
Sergio	unknown	unknown	student	pastry chef
Violeta	N/A—too young	carpenter	N/A—too young	cashier
Cristina	unknown	unknown	**secretary**	**textile machine operator**
Sofia	mechanic	factory worker	factory worker	factory worker

Source: Author's compilation based on data from the Dominican and Colombian Immigrant Family Study (2009).
Note: Boldface text indicates parents' downward occupational slide with migration.

Table A.8 Mobility Paths of Immigrant Parents in Subsample, Compared to Overall Sample

	Dramatic Risers		High Replicators		Low Replicators		Limited Risers		Downwardly Mobile	
	Overall Sample	Sub-sample	Overall Sample	Sub-sample	Overall Sample	Sub-sample	Overall Sample	Sub-sample	Overall Sample	Sub-sample
Colombians	12	7	5	3	2	0	7	3	11	5
Dominicans	12	2	1	0	5	4	12	3	9	4
Total	24	9	6	3	7	4	19	6	20	9
	(32%)	(29%)	(8%)	(10%)	(9%)	(13%)	(25%)	(19%)	(27%)	(29%)

Source: Author's compilation based on data from the Dominican and Colombian Immigrant Family Study (2009).

Table A.9 Highest Level of Education Among Focal Children in Parents' Subsample, Compared to Overall Sample

	Four-Year College	Tier-One School	Community College	Vocational School	Total
Dominican					
Overall	27	7 of 27	12	—	39
Subsample	7	3 of 7	6	—	13
Colombian					
Overall	33	17 of 33	3	1	37
Subsample	16	6 of 16	2	—	18

Source: Author's compilation based on data from the Dominican and Colombian Immigrant Family Study (2009).

colleges, compared to the overall Dominican sample; to a lesser extent, this was true with tier-one institutions as well. As table A.9 indicates, there was less representation of children who had gone to a four-year college. Among the Colombian families, the proportions of focal children who had gone to a four-year college or a community college approximated those in the overall Colombian sample. Such caveats must be kept in mind when interpreting the findings from the parental subsample.

Table A.10 lists the pairs of 1.5- and second-generation children and their parents who were both quoted in the book, along with relevant characteristics, such as where the child grew up in the United States and the educational levels of both the child and parent.

In analyzing the children's and parents' characteristics, I benefited enormously from the expertise of Vidya Sampath and Galo Falchettore of the Russell Sage Foundation; they made great efforts to further organize and sort my copious data, which were in both paper form (the surveys) and electronic form (some surveys, field notes, transcripts), en route to winnowing the relevant characteristics of the sample. They also leafed through back issues of *U.S. News & World Report* and U.S. census data. Finally, to obtain descriptive data on the racial and ethnic compositions of the public high schools attended by my respondents (chapter 5), they drew on the Common Core of Data (CCD); collected by the U.S. Department of Education's National Center for Education Statistics (NCES), these data are not easy to work with. Thanks to their considerable efforts, I was able to get a much clearer and more detailed picture of my overall and parental subsamples and, when relevant, to situate both against Dominicans and Colombians nationally—a view that afforded me greater analytical purchase.

Table A.10 Referenced Pairs of Children and Their Parents and Their Characteristics

Pseudonym of 1.5- or Second-Generation Respondent	Parent Referenced	Location in the United States Where Child Grew Up	Educational Attainment of Parent Referenced	Educational Attainment of Child
Dominicans				
Lenore	Mother	Greenpoint, Brooklyn, in New York City	3.5 years of post-secondary education (in the Dominican Republic and the United States)	Enrolled at Northeastern University
Andrea	Mother	Washington Heights, Manhattan, in New York City	General equivalency diploma and two months of college in the United States	Graduated from Cornell University
Angel	Mother	Jamaica Plain, Boston	Completed secondary schooling in the Dominican Republic, vocational certificates in the United States	Graduated from Bentley College
Rafael	Mother and father	Lawrence, Massachusetts	Mother: Two years of secondary school in the Dominican Republic Father: Nearly four years of secondary school in the Dominican Republic	Previously enrolled at Hesser College (two-year program)
Billy	Mother	Lawrence, Massachusetts	Graduated from secondary school in the Dominican Republic	Enrolled at Northern Essex Community College

(*Table continues on p. 194.*)

Table A.10 *(continued)*

Pseudonym of 1.5- or Second-Generation Respondent	Parent Referenced	Location in the United States Where Child Grew Up	Educational Attainment of Parent Referenced	Educational Attainment of Child
Colombians				
Julian	Mother and father	East Boston	Postsecondary vocational schools in Colombia	Enrolled at University of Massachusetts at Boston
Leonardo	Mother	Brighton, Massachusetts; and Nashua, New Hampshire	Graduated from secondary school in Colombia	PhD student at University of California at Berkeley
Judy	Mother	Chelsea, Massachusetts; and Jamaica Plain, Boston	Graduated from university in Colombia, business school in the United States	Graduated from Harvard University
Carmel	Mother and father	Londonderry, New Hampshire; and North Andover, Massachusetts	Mother: Graduated from secondary school in Colombia Father: One year of university in Colombia, some college classes in the United States	Enrolled at Northern Essex Community College

Thomas	Mother	Chelsea, Massachusetts; and East Boston	Six months of university in Colombia	Enrolled at Massachusetts Bay Community College
Jorge	Mother	Croton, New York; and Jupiter, Florida	University in Colombia and in the United States, from which she graduated	Enrolled at Northeastern University
Penny	Father	Bridgeport, Connecticut	Graduated from secondary school in Colombia, took some college classes in the United States	Enrolled at Northeastern University
Park	Mother	Philadelphia, Pennsylvania; and Miami Florida	Completed secondary vocational certificate in Colombia	Graduated from Cornell University
Herman	Mother and father	Lowell, Massachusetts	Mother: Two years of secondary school in Colombia Father: Nearly two years of secondary school in Colombia	Graduated from University of Massachusetts at Lowell

Source: Author's compilation based on data from the Dominican and Colombian Immigrant Family Study (2009).

Coding

During the data collection process itself, I wrote detailed field notes of my impressions of the interview, the interviewee, and the themes that struck me as I conducted the interview; I then grouped them into categories, such as neighborhood, migration, and education. I also read through the transcripts many times. When the children's sample was nearly complete, I sought the assistance of my very capable doctoral advisee at the time, Dr. Yeon-Jeong Son, who is skilled in ATLAS.ti, a qualitative data analysis software program, which I also knew. She and I discussed how to organize the data within ATLAS and relevant subgroupings—for example, Dominicans and Colombians. We also went over the kinds of codes that I thought would be useful—for example, descriptive codes (such as neighborhood, migration, and child-rearing) and analytical codes (such as "guidance counselor/school pushed for public university") that both emerged from the data and were from the relevant literatures. While the coding was under way, Dr. Son and Dr. Sheila Casey, another very capable then-doctoral student who worked on the project, and I shared our coded transcripts as a way of tapping into intercoder reliability.

Once I started to wade into the completed data set on ATLAS, I started to merge certain codes into a super code of sorts that tapped into my analytical strategy, whether for a journal article or for this book. As an example, *Colombia print* pulled outtakes from all the Colombians' responses in the identity section of the interview—for example, whether the respondent participated in ethnic festivals, listened to Spanish-language music, or read Spanish-language newspapers. As another example, the comparative argument for chapter 2 was based on output from seven codes: four involved transnationalism (framing the homeland as having a poor economy, instability, class stratification, and fewer opportunities and the United States as consequently more stable and open), and three were based on the United States and had to do with definitions of being American around freedom/democracy, opportunity, and other conceptions (which contrasted favorably with the country of origin and other nations). Sometimes I further parsed out ATLAS output by coding the old-fashioned way, using pen and paper. For the parental subsample, I cut into the data in several different ways, using Microsoft Word, both in thematic analysis and in the development of relevant charts to see the sample. Finally, throughout the process I kept several journals—for instance, to track preliminary themes emerging from the interviews, to keep field notes and transcriptions, to make comparisons to the second-generation Chinese working-class sample of my earlier research, and to make notes on my role as a researcher.

My Role as a Researcher

As a non-Spanish-speaker (beyond a few fundamentals acquired in middle school and then, decades later, an adult education course) and a non-Latino, I was prepared for the issue of being an out-group member. No one explicitly asked me why I, a Chinese American woman, was studying Dominicans and Colombians and education. A few asked why I was not studying Chinese Americans, and they seemed satisfied when I said that my first book was about Chinese Americans. Most expressed curiosity about why I was interested in the topic, generally speaking. My response would be to highlight the comparative frame in immigration research, and in my own research in particular. I did try to defer such conversations until the end of the interview so as not to influence the interviewee's responses. I would spend as much time as the respondent had to spare discussing this subject (with the recorder turned off) and write up my field notes afterward. I can remember only one case in which a graduate of an elite university seemed to be distant though polite. Responses toward me tended to be positive and warm, and both respondents and community leaders appeared to be equally curious about why I was studying Dominicans and Colombians rather than, for example, all Latinos, or Cubans or Puerto Ricans.

Although there are disadvantages to being an outsider, such as not having firsthand knowledge of the ethnic cultural norms brought up by the respondents and having to make more of an effort to build rapport with them, there are also benefits. I believe that my outsider status gave the respondents an unspoken permission to speak freely about Latinos, especially about class differences and in-group differences, such as those between Puerto Ricans and Dominicans or between Dominicans and South Americans. In other words, my being an outsider gave respondents a space in which to discuss some potentially uncomfortable subjects without feeling disloyal or fearing that I would be insulted, as they might have felt if I had been an in-group member. I also believe that my outsider status allowed the female respondents to speak very freely about gender, for similar reasons.

Indeed, what consistently struck me was how many of the respondents were open with me and the study itself. On the whole, they generously accepted my genuine curiosity and enthusiasm about their lives and thoughts; many took their participation as an opportunity to piece together for themselves why and how they had overcome obstacles around the transition to college—or at least why they were the exceptions to the popular discourse about Latinos and education in the United States. Some of the respondents seemed to see the interview as a chance to negotiate the sense of aloneness they had felt while they were becoming academically successful. Their willingness to speak with us made me think of the trust many had developed with institutional agents, as I discuss in chapter 6, and I wondered whether those prior experiences made them more comfortable with speaking to us. In many of the interviews, the respondents underscored the commonalities between us as the children of immigrants and/or as racial-ethnic minorities. In part, they may have drawn these parallels precisely because I was not Latino. Yet their attitudes were consistent with the ways in which they framed their friendships and their worldview, as I discuss in chapter 7 and as Kasinitz et al. (2008) have found.

Language, meaning Spanish, was not a problem in the interviews I conducted. I asked the 1.5- and second-generation respondents to translate, spell out, and explain Spanish phrases when they came up. All were by that time English-language-dominant, or strongly English-language-conversant.[6] Moreover, my research assistants were second-generation Dominican or natives of Colombia and had considerable experience researching Colombians and Dominicans in the greater Boston area. We had lengthy conversations at multiple points during data collection to discuss what I was finding and also what they were finding through their own recruitment efforts and interviews with some of the children and parents.

Notes

Chapter 1

1. We interviewed the parents of thirty-one respondents. In six cases, we spoke with both parents but one served as the focal respondent in the interview.
2. All names of respondents reported in this book, both children and parents, are pseudonyms.
3. Unless otherwise noted, references to the second generation include the 1.5 generation.
4. In July 2008, the U.S. Census estimated that close to 47 million Hispanics lived in the United States, representing about 15.4 percent of the overall population (Passel and Taylor 2009). I use the terms "Latino" and "Hispanic" interchangeably, unless otherwise specified. Please see chapter 3 for further discussion of the genealogy of these terms in the United States and how immigrant parents in this study understood them, and chapter 7 for an elaboration of how the children understood them.
5. The Telles and Ortiz (2008) study involved reinterviewing 684 Mexican Americans who had originally been surveyed in 1965 and 1966 in Los Angeles and San Antonio, interviewing 758 of their adult children, and analyzing the results of the 1965 survey.
6. My argument builds on previous studies of the post-1965 second and 1.5 generations that have analyzed their outcomes in light of how their immigrant parents fared socioeconomically, based on large-scale surveys of and interviews with the adult children (Rumbaut et al. 2003; Kasinitz et al. 2008); and on several longitudinal studies of young and adolescent children that have included subsamples of immigrant parents as additional tools to situate the children's journeys (Portes and Rumbaut 2001; Suárez-Orozco and Suárez-Orozco 2001; Suárez-Orozco, Suárez-Orozco, and Todorova 2008; Smith 2008).
7. It is estimated that more than 23 million immigrants arrived in the United States between 1880 and the mid-1920s, when large-scale immigration was restricted; foreign-born individuals made up nearly 15 percent of the overall population in 1910 (Foner 2006).
8. In 1916 there were only 272 evening schools in the ten states with the largest number of immigrants. According to the 1910 U.S. Census, there were 13 million foreign-born individuals living in the United States, 3 million of

whom could not speak English; of this fraction, only 1.3 percent of the adults age twenty-one or older attended school (Gaus 1918).

9. The entry of Asians was restricted starting with the Chinese Exclusion Act (1882) and the Gentlemen's Agreement (1907) between Japan and the United States (Hing 2004).
10. Such tensions were evident in the discussions surrounding then President-Elect Barack Obama's selection of an education secretary (he chose Arne Duncan, former chief executive officer of the Chicago Public Schools), notably, what his choice would signal about his strategy for school reform (Brooks 2008; see also Tyack 1974; Angus and Mirel 1999; Graham 2005; Reese 2005; Louie 2005, 73–76).
11. The Longitudinal Immigrant Student Adaptation Project is a study of foreign-born schoolchildren in the Boston and San Francisco areas whose origins are in Mexico, Central America, China, the Dominican Republic, and Haiti. The data have been the basis of numerous books, articles, and chapters in edited volumes. Please see Suárez-Orozco and Suárez-Orozco (2001), Suárez-Orozco, Suárez-Orozco, and Todorova (2008), Suárez-Orozco and Qin (2006), Qin (2003), Doucet and Suárez-Orozco (2006), and Song (2009).
12. In both the greater Boston area and New York City, Dominicans are the second-largest Latino national-origin group and Colombians the fifth (Shea and Jones 2006; Limonic 2008). Overall, however, Dominicans tend to be more geographically concentrated in the United States. My sample was consistent with this pattern: 59 percent of the Dominicans had grown up in the greater Boston area and one-third in the greater New York City area. The Colombians were relatively more geographically dispersed (Guarnizo, Sanchez, and Roach 1999). About 57 percent had grown up in either the greater Boston area or the New York City area. The rest, however, came from Florida (Palm Beach, Tampa, and Miami), southern California (Orange County), northern New England (New Hampshire and the Providence, Rhode Island, area), Texas, southern New England (Bridgeport, Connecticut), and New Jersey.
13. While state-sponsored violence is a common concern in Latin America (Inter-American Development Bank 2000; Menjívar and Rodríguez 2005), Colombia has had a particularly complex history of past and present violence arising from an "internal armed conflict" that has spanned more than four decades (Suarez 2000, 580). The central actors are both state (for example, the police and the military) and nonstate (guerrilla groups, paramilitary groups, and organized crime; Dugas 2005).
14. Colombians have also migrated to Venezuela, Ecuador, other Latin American and Caribbean nations, Spain, and the United Kingdom (Castano 1984; Bushnell 1993).
15. These responses were drawn from the following write-in question on the demographic survey: "Why did they [mother and father] immigrate to the United States?"
16. Adapting the risk factors identified by Watson Swail, Alberto Cabrera, and Chul Lee (2004), I asked my respondents whether they had grown up in a single-parent family, received welfare growing up, one parent with less than a high school degree, a sibling who had dropped out of high school, been

held back in school, changed high school more than two times, or had a child in high school. I used the welfare question as a proxy for Swail, Cabrera, and Lee's income question—for example, growing up in a family with an income less than $15,000. I did not have data for whether the respondent was home alone for more than three hours a day or whether the respondent had a C average or lower in high school. Thus, my measurement of risk factors errs on the side of caution and may understate respondents' relative risk.

17. Public assistance was defined as the family having received benefits from welfare, reduced or free school lunch, WIC (Women, Infants, and Children), food stamps, Medicaid, subsidized housing (public housing or Section 8), and/or Social Security.
18. This was certainly the case for the nine Dominican respondents who grew up in Lawrence, Massachusetts; in 2004 Latinos made up 17.5 percent of the population in the Lawrence primary metropolitan statistical area (PMSA), and 32.2 percent of the Latino population there was living in poverty (Kala and Jones 2006a, 2006b).
19. In the ISGMNY, the median South American, Russian, and Chinese respondents lived in better-off communities compared to the Dominicans, Puerto Ricans, and native blacks but still fared worse than native whites, who tended to grow up in areas with the least disadvantage.
20. There were questions that tended to reveal documentation status unintentionally. For instance, we asked, "Have your parents naturalized?" This question—along with "How did your parents come to the United States: did relatives sponsor them?"—invited reflections on the migration journey.
21. These figures are based on data on 124 parents. We lacked information on this measure for 18 parents, virtually all of them fathers, and 10 fathers had died without having migrated to the United States.
22. Fifteen of the Colombian children we interviewed had less education than their parents did (one-third because their parents held master's degrees). Since most of these respondents were still relatively young and some were still in college, they could have more years of schooling in the future.
23. Nationally, about half of all Latino students do not complete high school, and only one in ten complete college (De Jesus and Vasquez 2005; Uriarte, Chen, and Kala 2008; Gándara and Contreras 2009).
24. The sample estimates are based on the most recent type of postsecondary institution attended or graduated from at the time of the interview, excluding postgraduate institutions. Most of the sixty-one respondents enrolled in a four-year school had started their career in a four-year college; only six had gone to a two-year college prior to enrolling in a four-year school.
25. The 2000 follow-up to the National Educational Longitudinal Study of 1988 (NELS-88) found that about 61 percent of Latinos who went on to college were enrolled in two-year institutions. More than four out of five were attending public institutions. Only 7.7 percent were enrolled in a selective or highly selective institution, with 1.6 percent found in the latter. The NELS is a nationally representative study of nearly 15,000 eighth-graders in 1988, who were subsequently followed up in 1990 (tenth grade), 1992 (twelfth grade), 1994 (two years out of high school), and 2000 (eight years out of high school; for further discussion, see Swail, Cabrera, and Lee 2004). An analysis

of the 1994 follow-up to the NELS-88 sample revealed that both foreign- and U.S.-born Hispanics had similar enrollment patterns along these lines (Hagy and Staniec 2002).

26. Such estimates were drawn from the ISGMNY respondents age twenty-four or older who had grown up in the metropolitan New York area and had ever attended college (for further details, see Kasinitz et al. 2008, 140–41).

Chapter 2

1. The concept of a dual frame of reference was coined by Marcelo Suárez-Orozco in *Central American Refugees and U.S. High Schools: A Psychosocial Study of Motivation and Achievement* (1989).
2. Social class plays a prominent role in social science research, and yet researchers often disagree on how to define and measure it and, similarly, its influence in social life. See Lareau and Conley (2008) for further discussion.
3. William Clark (2003) follows the lead of the University of Michigan Population Studies Center and defines the middle class as households whose income range is "from two to five times" the poverty line. According to this definition, about 30 percent of the American population was middle-class in 2000.
4. This downward mobility is different from the upward mobility over time among earlier waves of European immigrants. See Bodnar (1985), Morawska (1990), Dinnerstein and Reimers (1999), and Gerstle and Mollenkopf (2002).
5. "El Bogotazo" is a term for the unrest in Colombia in the wake of the assassination of Jorge Eliécer Gaitán, a presidential candidate, on April 9, 1948, in Bogotá. The unrest spread throughout the nation, sparking "La Violencia," a roughly ten-year period of civil war.
6. Public assistance is defined in this study as welfare, reduced or free school lunch, WIC, food stamps, Medicaid, subsidized housing (public housing or Section 8), and Social Security.
7. Armenia is the capital of Quindio, a department in Colombia.
8. This kind of downward occupational mobility resulting from migration can be a source of stress for immigrants. Rachel Lev-Wiesel and Roni Kaufman (2004), for instance, found high levels of stress among the highly educated, middle-aged immigrants from the former Soviet Union who arrived in Israel during the 1990s and in their new country were either not employed, underemployed, or working in jobs not commensurate with their qualifications.
9. In Colombia there are strong regional differences among urban areas (for further discussion, see Velez et al. 2002).
10. The informal sector is distinctive to the Latin American class structure and sets it apart from the United States and the European nations (Portes 1985; Portes and Hoffman 2003). This sector includes small-scale business owners and the family members or casual laborers who typically work for them but receive neither monetary compensation nor social security coverage and are not bound by contractual relations. Alejandro Portes and Kelly Hoffman (2003) estimate that in Latin America as a whole, 44.4 percent of the economically active labor force work in the informal sector.
11. In the period 1995 to 2002, two-thirds of Americans enjoyed higher family incomes than did their parents, while only one-third had approximated or

fallen short of their parents' income. However, only one-third of the children both earned more real family income (adjusted for inflation) and moved ahead in economic ranking compared to their parents. Another one-third of the children made more than their parents but either stayed in the same economic ranking or actually fell. A full third were "downwardly mobile in both income and economic rank" (Isaacs 2007, 21). This analysis was based on the Panel Study of Income Dynamics (PSID), a nationally representative sample of children age zero to eighteen in 1968 and subsequently tracked, along with their parents, for more than thirty-six years. Other studies have shown that black children in the highest income quintile were 30 percent less likely than whites to stay there and four times as likely to fall precipitously to the lowest quintile (Kearney 2006; Sawhill 2007).

12. See Kearney (2006) for a discussion of how labor market discrimination along the lines of race continues to exist.

Chapter 3

1. The counterexample rests with blurry boundaries, where there is space for ambiguity (Alba 2005).
2. Another reason cited in the literature is the typically lengthy wait list for available classes (see Bloemraad and Scholzman 2003; Colton 2006; Progressive States Network 2009; Boston Foundation 2011).
3. For instance, in their analysis of the determinants of immigrant parental economic outcomes, Portes and Rumbaut (2001, 79) find that knowing English has a strong effect on earnings, "increasing monthly earnings by $233 and annual incomes by approximately $2,480."
4. There is a robust debate about the factors influencing an individual's degree of perceived accent in speaking a second language, notably around age of immersion, learner's attitudes, and length of residence (see Munro and Mann 2005; Moyer 2007).
5. Researchers have found that greater length of residency is associated with higher English-language proficiency among the foreign-born. However, all things being equal, Spanish-speaking immigrants lag behind other non-English-speaking immigrants in this regard (for further discussion, see Bean and Stevens 2003).
6. Twenty-six of the Colombian 1.5- and second-generation respondents spoke of this situation, compared to only four of the Dominicans. The data for these findings were drawn from survey write-in questions about the respondent's race and ethnicity and follow-up interview questions such as the following: "I see that you identified your race as ______, and your ethnicity as ______. Is this how you usually identify for college applications, financial aid, or other kinds of forms?" "Do other people sometimes think you are a different race or ethnicity?" "(PROBE: What do other people think you are? How do you feel about that?)" Respondents could also bring up the topic on their own. When relevant, data from the interviewer's field notes were also incorporated.
7. Thomas Guglielmo (2003) argues that acceptance as white occurred at the European immigrants' time of arrival, while David Roediger (2005) argues that it took generations (see also Ignatiev 1995; Brodkin 1998). Joel Perlmann

(2002) and James Loewen (1971) show that Mexican and Chinese immigrants and their descendants from this time period were seen as nonwhite and classed with blacks but eventually were moved into the white category.

8. The U.S. government has two approaches to counting who is Hispanic. Jeffrey Passel and Paul Taylor (2009, 2) note that a 1976 federal law and its offshoots designed for purposes of data collection required that public agencies provide information on who is Hispanic among their constituencies; Hispanics are thus identified along the lines of language (speakers of Spanish) and region (originated or descended from "Mexico, Puerto Rico, Central and South America and other Spanish-speaking countries"). The Census Bureau provides no such guidelines, and thus anyone who chooses to self-identify as "Spanish/Hispanic/Latino" is counted as such.
9. Although four Colombian parents employed the term "Colombian American" to signal their attachment to the United States and to their home country, their responses were not appreciably different from those of the parents who used the term "Colombian."
10. For further discussion of the influence of contemporary immigrants on American conceptions of race and ethnicity, and vice versa, see Anderson and Fienberg (1999), Rodriguez (2000), and Marrow (2003).
11. Jorge's mother also expressed the idea that Latino is a race unto itself, along with white and black. To her, white, black, *and* Latino should all be mutually inclusive racial categories in the United States; thus, she should be able to categorize herself racially as *both* white and Latino.
12. Roberto Suro (2008) finds that media attention has tended to be episodic and to associate immigration with crime and controversy.
13. Mary Patillo-McCoy (1999) finds that many black middle-class neighborhoods sit in a buffer zone between white middle-class areas and black poverty areas. She argues that this geographic inscription has important implications for what middle-class African American youth are exposed to in their everyday lives.
14. The parents' accounts signal a relative absence of collective efficacy in their neighborhoods, namely, the facility of residents to develop sufficient group-level trust and strategies to manage the ill effects of social disorganization. As Robert Sampson, Stephen Raudenbush, and Felton Earls (1997, 922) found, such collective efficacy can "partially mediate" the relationship between "neighborhood social composition" and "violence."
15. This claim is based on the children's reports of how their parents fared with migration, relative to pre-migration, and the reports of the parental subsample.

Chapter 4

1. Here I build on Stephen Morgan's (1996) insight that aspirations are a hoped-for result, while expectations speak to a focused road map of concrete steps to realize the outcome.
2. For more discussion of the history of parental involvement in American schooling, with particular attention to minority and/or low-income and immigrant children, see Berger (1991), Hiatt-Michael (1994), Hoover-Dempsey and Sandler (1995, 1997), Tierney (2002), Walker et al. (2004), and Lew (2006).

3. I rely on the self-designation of the relevant geographic region to define "urban" and "suburban."
4. The New England Association of Schools and Colleges removed the accreditation based on the school's low attendance, high dropout rates, poor physical facilities, and declining test scores (*Boston Globe* 2004).
5. A pseudonym.
6. The Murphys also helped Sara's father—who had only completed grade school in Colombia—get a plum job with the New York City Housing Authority through their political and social connections. Sara's father was eventually promoted to a managerial position, and the job paid more and provided better working conditions and benefits than the factory had. Sara's parents were eventually able to buy a house in Woodside, Queens.
7. According to Kathleen Hoover-Dempsey and Howard Sandler (1995, 1997), there are five levels of parental involvement: (1) how parents decide to become involved; (2) how parents choose to be involved; (3) how parental involvement influences children's outcomes; (4) the mediating variables therein; and (5) the children's outcomes, whether measured in skills and knowledge or efficacy. In this chapter, I focus largely on the first three levels.
8. By comparison, only eight of the Dominicans and five of the Colombians said that their parents were not involved at all in their schooling.
9. For instance, students participating in sports could learn how to control their emotions, set goals, and take the initiative; students participating in the arts could learn how to be engaged, be motivated, and have higher self-esteem (Shernoff and Vandell 2007).
10. The range of involvement among the Colombian parents we interviewed approximated the patterns in the overall Colombian sample. However, we interviewed thirteen Dominican parents whose levels of involvement and non-involvement, as reported by their children, were lower than in the overall sample and high involvement nearly double.
11. In a study of Latino parents in Los Angeles, Chicago, and New York, Louis Tornatzky, Richard Cutler, and Jongho Lee (2002) find that socioeconomic status is associated with how much knowledge parents have about college. Overall, nearly two-thirds of the parents surveyed incorrectly answered at least half of the eight college information items, and nearly one-fifth answered only one item or none correctly. However, more than one-third of the low-socioeconomic parents answered only one item or none correctly compared to only about 5 percent of their better-off counterparts.
12. The data for the earlier study drew on interviews with second-generation Chinese Americans of diverse social class origins. The respondents were enrolled at two colleges in New York City: Hunter, a public commuter college that is a member of the City University of New York (CUNY), and Columbia, an elite private university.
13. For a sampling of relevant ethnic-specific and comparative studies across different populations that, in toto, speak to this claim, see Auerbach (2006), Delgado Gaitan (1994), Gándara (1995, 1999), Kasinitz et al. (2008), Lew (2006), Li et al. (2008), Lopez (2001), Louie (2001, 2004), Portes and Rumbaut (1990, 2001), Smith (2002, 2008), Suárez-Orozco and Suárez-Orozco (2001), Suárez-Orozco, Suárez-Orozco, and Todorova (2008), and Valdes (1996).

Chapter 5

1. This percentage is based on data on eleven of the fourteen urban public schools attended by our interviewees and is available from the U.S. Department of Education, National Center for Education Statistics (NCES), Common Core of Data (CCD), http://nces.ed.gov/ccd/index.asp.
2. There also appears to be an educational gender gap among second-generation Dominicans (see Lopez 2004; Kasinitz et al. 2008; Itzigsohn 2009).
3. For a detailed discussion of what educational testing tells us, see Koretz (2008).
4. According to Rick Fry (2007), the period between 1993 and 2006 has seen a rise in majority-minority public schools. A nearly all-minority school has fewer than 5 percent white students; a nearly all-white school has fewer than 5 percent nonwhite students.
5. Portes and Fernandez-Kelly (2008) drew from the Children of Immigrants Longitudinal Study (CILS), which followed an original sample of more than 5,200 children of immigrant parents in southern California and south Florida from early adolescence to early adulthood.
6. A pseudonym.
7. There has been considerable debate, however, about the role of family characteristics in generating this effect of Catholic schools. It is unclear whether the minority families enrolling their children in Catholic schools are more economically advantaged and have higher educational aspirations for their children. If so, the academic achievement of minority youth in Catholic schools would be an artifact of self-selectivity.
8. Magnet schools are defined by their student admission methods, missions, programs, and policies having to do with racial and ethnic composition (Blank 1984; Estes 1990; Blank and Archbald 1992; Gamoran 1996; Metz 2003; Frankenberg and Siegel-Hawley 2008). The children we interviewed attended eight magnet schools employing academic admissions criteria, including an entrance examination (for example, the Boston Latin School, New York City's Stuyvesant High School, Brooklyn Technical and Bronx Science High School, and Classical High School in Providence) or a combination of an exam, standardized test scores, grades, and, in the case of arts schools, an audition or portfolio.
9. ESL programs are typically designed as pull-out instruction. Students receive ESL instruction for one or two periods a day—or in some districts a few periods a week—and otherwise they participate in the regular English-language classroom. Instructors do not have to speak the child's native language. Structured immersion, or what is typically known in the United States as "bilingual education," provides English instruction in a self-contained classroom. Here the teacher usually knows how to speak the students' native language, and the students learn the second language and subject matter content simultaneously.
10. For further discussion of peer effects, see Matute-Bianchi (1986), Crul (2002), Goyette and Conchas (2002), Crosnoe, Cavanagh, and Elder (2003), Gibson, Gándara, and Koyama (2004), Gándara, O'Hara, and Gutiérrez (2004), Stanton-Salazar (2004), Conchas (2006), Yoshikawa and Way (2008), and Ryabov (2009).

11. Similarly, the second-generation respondents came from families with more resources than Puerto Ricans and native blacks in the study, and the justice system had more leniency for the children of immigrants.
12. Adam Gamoran (1996, 14) found a "modest" impact of attending magnet schools, but as he noted, this "probably means some have substantial effects whereas others have zero or even opposite effects." Owing to limitations with the National Educational Longitudinal Survey (NELS:88) data set, Gamoran could not ascertain the nature of the magnet school effect in more detail—for example, the impact of math/science schools versus the impact of fine arts schools. The issues of quality and equality have been important to the magnet school debates. As Scott Gelber (2008) has found in Boston, between 1968 and 1989, magnet schools were viewed either as high-performing (and elitist) or as more racially integrated (but academically inferior).

Chapter 6

1. Nor does it appear that this picture is entirely driven by students' prior preparation. Robert Haveman and Timothy Smeeding (2006) have found that the inclusion of more low-income and moderate students would not compromise the admissions standards of top institutions.
2. See Rothstein (2004) for a discussion of the relevance of social class to understanding the black-white achievement gap and a set of possible reforms. He notes, for instance, that "lower class children achieve less if the share of low income children in their schools is higher" (130).
3. The Colombians and Dominicans described the medium phenotypic category somewhat differently, although both mentioned that being tanned increased the possibility of belonging to it. By "medium" Colombians typically meant Middle Eastern/Arabic or Indian; although the Dominicans shared this view, they also mentioned being mistaken for being Mexican or Guatemalan or looking more indigenous.
4. Jason Fletcher and Marta Tienda (2010) show that high school quality matters in the minority-nonminority college achievement gap. Drawing on data from four Texas public universities and using fixed-effects models, the authors find that "differences in college preparedness associated with high school quality carry over to college careers" but find that the selectivity of the college mediates the effect (155). Their focus was on black-white and Hispanic-white achievement gaps in college.
5. Julia's point was well taken, although her timeline was not accurate—the Microsoft Office software package, which includes Word and Excel, was first introduced in the early 1990s.
6. Regardless of social class, blacks tend to be isolated from whites in some measure (O'Connor, Tilly, and Bobo 2003). Studies have found that qualified job candidates with first names more commonly found among blacks are bypassed (Bertrand and Mullainathan 2004; Fryer and Levitt 2004) and that many black professionals are confined to sectors with little promotion potential, such as community relations (Jenkins 2009; Neckerman, Carter, and Lee 1999). Highly successful black men also grapple with the pervasive characterization of black men as criminals (Lawrence-Lightfoot 1994; Patillo-McCoy 1999; Wilson 2009).

7. I use pseudonyms here.
8. I conducted research on the Chinese in 1998 and 1999 after recruiting participants in New York City at Hunter, a public commuter college, and Columbia, the Ivy League university.
9. Min Zhou and her collaborators (Zhou et al. 2008) report a similarly divergent finding with second-generation Asians and Mexicans in metropolitan Los Angeles. The Chinese and Vietnamese were less likely to feel successful, regardless of how well they had done in school or income, because so many of their coethnics and panethnics had done better. Those who had not completed college or did not go to a top university felt like failures. This research was conducted by Jennifer Lee and Min Zhou and drew on in-depth interviews with 1.5- and second-generation Chinese, Vietnamese, and Mexicans, along with smaller numbers of native-born whites and blacks. All of the targeted 140 respondents were drawn from the larger sample of the Immigrant Intergenerational Mobility in Metropolitan Los Angeles (IIMMLA) study (for further discussion of the IIMMLA, see Rumbaut et al. 2003).

Chapter 7

1. Audrey was more of a 2.5-generation Colombian. Her mother arrived in the United States at the age of five, and her father came when he was nine.
2. See Smith (forthcoming[b]) for further discussion of Latino immigrants' positive view, in some contexts, of being black.
3. The other school was the former Math/Science Institute run by New York City's board of education and designed to prepare students for the entrance examination for the city's specialized high schools. It is now called the Specialized High Schools Institute.
4. Smith (forthcoming[a]) uses the term "black" as "both a racial descriptor and a broader social category, describing a set of habits associated with blackness" that make up what is popularly understood to be "cool, urban culture."
5. Of the twenty-four Dominicans who had dated outside the panethnic group, five dated both blacks and whites, and they were thus counted in each category. The one who dated a black/white person was counted as a separate category.

Chapter 8

1. There have been two major schools of thought about the ways in which the immigrants viewed their lives in the United States. One posits that the immigrants were "innocent peasants overwhelmed by the forces of modernization" in the New World, and consequently suffering from "loneliness, isolation and sadness" and never finding "in America the comfort and security they had known in the Old World," as Oscar Handlin (1951) famously argued (Gerstle 1997, 535, 532). Another line of thought, propagated by Herbert Gutman and Rudolph Vecoli, maintains that the immigrants had agency and formed strong collectivities to preserve ethnic cultural practices and in-

stitutions because they were under attack from strong nativist movements in the form of anti-Catholicism, anti-Semitism, and Anglo cultural conformity as well as to fight against systemic exploitation by employers; in the end they were either "indifferent or hostile to America" (Gerstle 1997, 539). As Gary Gerstle (1997) notes, the two schools of thought nonetheless share the perspective that immigrants believed American society to be exploitative and felt themselves to be alienated from it—the key difference was in how they framed and responded to their exploitation and alienation.

2. According to John Bodnar (1985, 193), as late as 1910 fewer than "10 percent of Italians, Polish, and Slovak children were attending beyond the sixth grade in Chicago and Cleveland. Jews admittedly were doing better, although two-thirds of all students regardless of their backgrounds were not in school at the time." Bodnar further argues that American Jews, who have become the quintessential immigrant group of this era to be associated with academic motivation, considered additional schooling for children an option only in cases where the family had already experienced some upward social mobility.
3. The minimum threshold should be (1) information on country of birth for the child and the child's parents (Perlmann 2002); (2) for a foreign-born child, information on the year of arrival for the child and the child's parents and, if they migrated, citizenship status and levels of schooling completed in the home country; and (3) for all children, their home language and abilities in spoken English. To allow for multigenerational analyses, it would be helpful to know the country of birth for the child's grandparents. Policy examples from other nations document the utility of such information (Organisation for Economic Co-Operation and Development 2010).
4. Cross-state comparisons of the gap between ELLs and whites cannot be done because of variation among states in the tests they use and the threshold to show proficiency (Fry 2008).
5. A look at Canada's system might be helpful: its federal and provincial governments share responsibility for direct services to immigrants with municipalities and community-based organizations (Bloemraad 2006).
6. As Maria Martinez-Cosio and Rosario Iannacone (2007, 350) find, the parent liaison strives to balance dual, sometimes conflicting, goals: teaching parents how to successfully sponsor their children's schooling and bringing to light the parents' concerns about school-based inequalities.
7. Scott Seider and James Hugeley (2009) offer several curriculum suggestions drawing on human development research, including teaching teachers about "diverse perspectives on the American Dream" (301), self-efficacy, Robert Kegan's (1982) constructive-development theory, and Erik Erikson's (1968) emerging adult theory.

Appendix

1. It is worth noting that the retrospective nature of interviews like these does tend to generate an ordering to the narrative, more so than if the respondents had been interviewed when the situations were occurring (for example,

when the parents first arrived in the United States or when the children first started high school).

2. The exceptions were two respondents who had both moved to northern California and were interviewed by phone.
3. Included among these six was a young Boston woman who was not affiliated with the CUNY DSI but was also referred to me by Dr. Hernandez.
4. I defined this broadly as children who had ever lived in a single-parent family while growing up, whether owing to divorce, separation, or the death of one parent, as this has been shown to have a "negative effect" on the child's socioeconomic outcomes as per household production theory; for example, a single-parent family would have fewer resources to support a child than a dual-parent family. Research has shown the importance of the length of time spent in a single-parent family and the period in the life stage when it occurred (the effect is greatest during the preschool years), but I did not have enough data to tap into such dimensions. See Krein (1986) for further discussion. I did not include children who were separated from one or more parents during the migration journey and were later reunited with them in an intact family structure.
5. The percentages for my sample are based on the number of mothers and fathers working in the United States at the time the children were interviewed. Based on this criterion, in the case of Colombian mothers the total was thirty-one, and thirty for the fathers. In the case of the Dominican mothers, the total was twenty-nine, and twenty-two for the fathers.
6. It is estimated that 21 percent of second-generation Hispanic children are not fluent in English, compared to 43 percent of the first generation (Fry and Passel 2009).

References

Abrego, Leisy J., and Roberto G. Gonzales. 2010. "Blocked Paths, Uncertain Futures: The Postsecondary Education and Labor Market Prospects of Undocumented Latino Youth." *Journal of Education for Students Placed at Risk* 15(1): 144–57.

Adalbjarnardottir, Sigrun, and Robert L. Selman. 1997. "'I Feel I Have Received a New Vision': An Analysis of Teachers' Professional Development as They Work with Students on Interpersonal Issues." *Teaching and Teacher Education* 13(4): 409–28.

Akresh, Ilana Redstone. 2006. "Occupational Mobility Among Legal Immigrants to the United States." *International Migration Review* 40(4): 854–84.

Alba, Richard. 1990. *Ethnicity in America: The Transformation of White America.* New Haven, Conn.: Yale University Press.

———. 2005. "Bright vs. Blurred Boundaries: Second-Generation Assimilation and Exclusion in France, Germany, and the United States." *Ethnic and Racial Studies* 28(1): 20–49.

———. 2009. *Blurring the Color Line: The New Chance for a More Integrated America.* Cambridge, Mass.: Harvard University Press.

Alba, Richard, Philip Kasinitz, and Mary C. Waters. 2011. "The Kids Are (Mostly) Alright: Second-Generation Assimilation: Comments on Haller, Portes, and Lynch." *Social Forces* 89(3): 763–73.

Alba, Richard, and Victor Nee. 2003. *Remaking the American Mainstream: Assimilation and Contemporary Immigration.* Cambridge, Mass.: Harvard University Press.

Alon, Sigal, and Marta Tienda. 2007. "Diversity, Opportunity, and the Shifting Meritocracy in Higher Education." *American Sociological Review* 72(4): 487–511.

Anderson, Margo J., and Stephen E. Fienberg. 1999. *Who Counts? The Politics of Census-Taking in Contemporary America.* New York: Russell Sage Foundation.

Angus, David L., and Jeffrey E. Mirel. 1999. *The Failed Promise of the American High School, 1890–1995.* New York: Teachers College Press.

Anyon, Jean. 1995. "Race, Social Class, and Educational Reform in Any Inner-City School." *Teachers College Record* 97(1): 69–94.

Appiah, Kwame Anthony. 2001. "Liberalism, Individuality, and Identity." *Critical Inquiry* 27(2): 305–32.

Astin, Alexander W., and Leticia Oseguera. 2004. "The Declining 'Equity' of American Higher Education." *Review of Higher Education* 27(3): 321–41.

Atkinson, Robert. 2001. "The Life Story Interview." In *Handbook of Interview Research*, edited by Jaber F. Gubrium and James A. Holstein. Thousand Oaks, Calif.: Sage Publications.

Attewell, Paul. 2001. "The Winner-Take-All High School." *Sociology of Education* 74(4, October): 267–95.

Attewell, Paul, and David Lavin. 2007. *Passing the Torch: Does Higher Education for the Disadvantaged Pay Off Across the Generations?* New York: Russell Sage Foundation.

Auerbach, Susan. 2006. "'If the Student Is Good, Let Him Fly': Moral Support for College Among Latino Immigrant Parents." *Journal of Latinos and Education* 5(4): 275–92.

———. 2007. "From Moral Supporters to Struggling Advocates: Reconceptualizing Parent Roles in Education Through the Experience of Working-Class Families of Color." *Urban Education* 42(3): 250–83.

Bailey, Benjamin. 2002. *Language, Race, and Negotiation of Identity: A Study of Dominican Americans*. New York: LFB Scholarly Publishing.

Balfanz, Robert, and Nettie Legters. 2004. "Locating the Dropout Crisis." Report 70. Baltimore: Johns Hopkins University, Center for Research on the Education of Students Placed at Risk (CRESPAR) (September).

Banks, James A. 1994. *An Introduction to Multicultural Education*. Boston: Pearson, Allyn & Bacon.

———. 2007. *Educating Citizens in a Multicultural Society*. New York: Teachers College Press.

Barrow, Lisa, and Cecilia Elena Rouse. 2005. "Do Returns to Schooling Differ by Race and Ethnicity?" *American Economic Review* 95(2): 83–87.

Bataloval, Jeanne, and Margie McHugh. 2010. "Number and Growth of Students in U.S. Schools in Need of English Instruction." Fact Sheet Series 1. Washington, D.C.: Migration Policy Institute, ELL Information Center.

Bean, Frank, and Gillian Stevens. 2003. *America's Newcomers and the Dynamics of Diversity*. New York: Russell Sage Foundation.

Berger, Eugenia Hepworth. 1991. "Parent Involvement: Yesterday and Today." *The Elementary School Journal* 91(3): 209–19.

Berger, Joseph B., and John M. Braxton. 1998. "Revising Tinto's Interactionalist Theory of Student Departure Through Theory Elaboration: Examining the Role of Organizational Attributes in the Persistence Process." *Research in Higher Education* 39(2): 103–19.

Bertrand, Marianne, and Sendhil Mullainathan. 2004. "Are Emily and Greg More Employable Than Lakisha and Jamal? A Field Experiment on Labor Market Discrimination."*American Economic Review* 94(4): 991–1013.

Blank, Rolf. 1984. "The Effects of Magnet Schools on the Quality of Education in Urban School Districts." *Phi Delta Kappan* 66(4): 270–72.

Blank, Rolf, and Douglas A. Archbald. 1992. "Magnet Schools and Issues of Educational Quality." *Clearing House* 66(2): 81–87.

Bloemraad, Irene. 2006. *Becoming a Citizen: Incorporating Immigrants and Refugees in the United States and Canada*. Berkeley: University of California Press.

Bloemraad, Irene, with Daniel Scholzman. 2003. "The New Face of Greater Boston: Meeting the Needs of Immigrants." In *Governing Greater Boston*, edited by Charles C. Euchner. Cambridge, Mass.: Rappaport Institute for Greater Boston.

Bodnar, John. 1976. "Immigration and Modernization: The Case of Slavic Peasants in Industrial America." *Journal of Social History* 10(1): 44–71.

———. 1985. *The Transplanted: A History of Immigrants in Urban America*. Bloomington: Indiana University Press.

Boston Foundation. 2011. *Breaking the Language Barrier: A Report on English Language Services in Greater Boston*. Boston: Boston Foundation.

Boston Globe. 2004. "Ready to Regain Symbol of Academic Pride." *Boston Globe*, Northwest edition, October 21, 2004, p. 1.

Bowen, William, and Derek Bok. 1996. *The Shape of the River: Long-Term Consequences of Considering Race in College and University Admissions*. Princeton, N.J.: Princeton University Press.

Brodkin, Karen. 1998. *How Jews Became Whites and What That Says About Race in America*. New Brunswick, N.J.: Rutgers University Press.

Brooks, David. 2008. "Who Will He Choose?" *New York Times*, December 5, 2008, p. A39.

Brooks-Gunn, Jeanne, Greg J. Duncan, Pamela Kato Klebanov, and Naomi Sealand. 1993. "Do Neighborhoods Influence Child and Adolescent Development?" *American Journal of Sociology* 99(2): 353–95.

Bruner, Jerome. 1991. "The Narrative Construction of Reality." *Critical Inquiry* 18(1): 1–21.

Bryk, Anthony S., Valerie E. Lee, and Peter B. Holland. 1993. *Catholic Schools and the Common Good*. Cambridge, Mass.: Harvard University Press.

Buriel, Raymond, William Perez, Terri L. de Ment, David V. Chavez, and Virginia R. Moran. 1998. "The Relationship of Language Brokering to Academic Performance, Biculturalism, and Self-Efficacy Among Latino Adolescents." *Hispanic Journal of Behavioral Sciences* 20(3): 283–97.

Bushnell, David. 1993. *The Making of Modern Colombia: A Nation in Spite of Itself*. Berkeley: University of California Press.

Cabrera, Alberto F., Kurt Burkum, and Steven M. La Nasa. 2003. "Pathways to a Four-Year Degree: Determinants of Degree Completion Among Socioeconomically Disadvantaged Students." Paper presented to the meeting of the Association for the Study of Higher Education, Portland, Ore.

California Tomorrow. 1990. "Then and Now: A Comparative Perspective on Immigration and School Reform During Two Periods in American History." In *California Perspectives: An Anthology from the Immigrant Students Project*, vol. 1, project director, Laurie Olsen. San Francisco: California Tomorrow.

Camayd-Freixas, Yoel, Gerald Karush, and Nelly Lejter. 2006. "Latinos in New Hampshire: Enclaves, Diasporas, and an Emerging Middle Class." In *Latinos in New England*, edited by Andres Torres. Philadelphia: Temple University Press.

Candelario, Ginette. 2007. *Black Behind the Ears: Dominican Racial Identity from Museums to Beauty Shops*. Durham, N.C.: Duke University Press.

Carnevale, Anthony P., and Stephen J. Rose. 2004. "Socioeconomic Status, Race/Ethnicity, and Selective College Admissions." In *America's Untapped Resource: Low-Income Students in Higher Education*, edited by Richard D. Kahlenberg. New York: Century Foundation Press.

Carreón, Gustavo Peréz, Corey Drake, and Angela Calabrese Barton. 2005. "The Importance of Presence: Immigrant Parents' School Engagement Experiences." *American Educational Research Journal* 42(3): 465–98.

Carter, Prudence. 2005. *Keepin' It Real: School Success Beyond Black and White.* Oxford: Oxford University Press.

Castano, Gabriel Murillo. 1984. "Effects of Emigration and Return on Sending Countries: The Case of Colombia." *International Social Science* 36(3): 453–67.

Cazden, Courtney B., and Catherine E. Snow. 1990. "English Plus: Issues in Bilingual Education." *Annals of the American Academy of Political and Social Science* 508(March).

Chan, Lorraine. 2006. "Race Not a Black and White Issue, Says Sociologist." *UBC Reports* 52(7, July 6). Available at: http://www.publicaffairs.ubc.ca/ubcreports/2006/06jul06/race.html (accessed October 12, 2009).

Chavez, Leo R. 2008. *The Latino Threat: Constructing Immigrants, Citizens, and the Nation*. Stanford, Calif.: Stanford University Press.

Chen, Jie-Qi, Seana Moran, and Howard Gardner, eds. 2009. *Multiple Intelligences Around the World*. San Francisco: Jossey-Bass.

Chiswick, Barry R. 1991. "Speaking, Reading, and Earnings Among Low-Skilled Immigrants." *Journal of Labor Economics* 9(2): 149–70.

Clark, William. 2003. *Immigrants and the American Dream: Remaking the Middle Class*. New York: Guilford Press.

Clarkson, Lesa M. Covington. 2008. "Demographic Data and Immigrant Student Achievement." *Theory into Practice* 47: 20–26.

Clewell, Beatriz Chu, with Clemencia Cosentino de Cohen and Julie Murray. 2007. *Promise or Peril? NCLB and the Education of ELL Students*. Washington, D.C.: Urban Institute, Program for Evaluation and Equity Research.

Coatsworth, John H. 2003. "Roots of Violence in Colombia: Armed Actors and Beyond." *Revista: Harvard Review of Latin America* 2(3): 3–7.

Cohen, Geoffrey L., Claude M. Steele, and Lee D. Ross. 1999. "The Mentor's Dilemma: Providing Critical Feedback Across the Racial Divide." *Personality and Social Psychology Bulletin* 25(10): 1302–18.

Cohen, Miriam. 1982. "Changing Education Strategies Among Immigrant Generations: New York Italians in Comparative Perspective." *Journal of Social History* 15(3): 443–66.

Coleman, James S. 1981. "Quality and Equality in American Education: Public and Catholic Schools." *Phi Delta Kappan* 62: 159–64.

———. 1988. "Social Capital in the Creation of Human Capital." *American Journal of Sociology* 94: S95–120.

Coleman, James S., and Thomas Hoffer. 1987. *Public and Private Schools*. New York: Basic Books.

Coleman, James S., Thomas Hoffer, and Sally Kilgore. 1982. *High School Achievement: Public, Catholic, and Private Schools Compared*. New York: Basic Books.

Collier, Michael, and Eduardo Gamarra. 2001. "The Colombian Diaspora in South Florida." Working paper. Miami: Florida International University, Latin American and Caribbean Center.

Colton, Tara. 2006. *Lost in Translation*. New York and Albany: Center for an Urban Future and Schuyler Center for Analysis and Advocacy.

Comer, James P. 2005a. "The Rewards of Parent Participation." *Educational Leadership* 62(6, March): 38–42.

———. 2005b. "Child and Adolescent Development: The Critical Missing Focus in School Reform." *Phi Delta Kappan* 86(10, June): 757–63.

Conchas, Gilberto. 2001. "Structuring Failure and Success: Understanding the Variability in Latino School Engagement." *Harvard Educational Review* 71: 475–504.

———. 2006. *The Color of Success: Race and High-Achieving Urban Youth*. New York: Teachers College Press.

Cookson, Peter W., and Caroline Hodges Persell. 1985. *Preparing for Power: America's Elite Boarding Schools*. New York: Basic Books.

Cornelius, Wayne A. 2002. "Ambivalent Reception: Mass Public Responses to the 'New' Latino Immigration to the United States." In *Latinos: Remaking America*, edited by Marcelo M. Suárez-Orozco and Mariela M. Páez. Berkeley and Cambridge, Mass.: University of California Press and David Rockefeller Center for Latin American Studies.

Cornell, Stephen, and Douglas Hartmann. 1998. *Ethnicity and Race: Making Identities in a Changing World*. Thousand Oaks, Calif.: Pine Forge Press.

Cremin, Lawrence A. 1951. *The American Common School: An Historic Conception*. New York: Columbia University, Bureau of Publications.

Crosnoe, Robert. 2005. "The Diverse Experiences of Hispanic Students in the American Educational System." *Sociological Forum* 20(4): 561–88.

———. 2010. *Two-Generation Strategies and Involving Immigrant Parents in Children's Education*. Washington, D.C.: Urban Institute.

Crosnoe, Robert, Shannon Cavanagh, and Glen H. Elder Jr. 2003. "Adolescent Friendships as Academic Resources: The Intersection of Friendship, Race, and School Disadvantage." *Sociological Perspectives* 46(3): 331–52.

Crul, Maurice. 2002. "Success Breeds Success: Moroccan and Turkish Student Mentors in the Netherlands." *International Journal for the Advancement of Counseling* 24(4): 275–87.

Crul, Maurice, and Jennifer Holdaway. 2009. "Children of Immigrants in Schools in New York and Amsterdam: The Factors Shaping Attainment." *Teachers College Record* 111(6): 1476–1507.

Crul, Maurice, and Jens Schneider. 2009. "Children of Turkish Immigrants in Germany and the Netherlands: The Impact of Differences in Vocational and Academic Tracking Systems." *Teachers College Record* 111(6): 1508–27.

Cushman, Kathleen. 2006. *First in the Family: Advice About College from First-Generation Students*. Providence, R.I.: Next Generation Press.

Datnow, Amanda, Daniel G. Solorzano, Tara Watford, and Vicki Park. 2010. "Mapping the Terrain: The State of Knowledge Regarding Low-Income Youth Access to Postsecondary Education." *Journal of Education for Students Placed at Risk* 15: 1–8.

Davila, Alberto, and Marie T. Mora. 2001. "Hispanic Ethnicity, English-Skill Investments, and Earnings." *Industrial Relations* 40(1): 83–88.

Davis, F. James. 1971. *Who Is Black? One Nation's Definition*. University Park: Pennsylvania State University Press.

De Jesus, Anthony, and Daniel W. Vasquez. 2005. "Exploring the Education Profile and Pipeline for Latinos in New York State." Policy brief 2(2). New York: Hunter College (CUNY), Centro de Estudios Puertorriquenos.

de los Reyes, Eileen, David Nieto, and Virginia Diez. 2008. *If Our Students Fail, We Fail, If They Succeed, We Succeed: Case Studies of Boston Schools Where Latino Students Succeed*. Boston: University of Massachusetts, Program in Public Policy and Mauricio Gaston Institute for Latino Community Development and Public Policy.

Deaux, Kay. 2000. "Surveying the Landscape of Immigration: Social Psychological Perspectives." *Journal of Community and Applied Social Psychology* 10: 421–41.

———. 2006. *To Be an Immigrant*. New York: Russell Sage Foundation.

Dee, Thomas S. 2005. "'A Teacher Like Me': Does Race, Ethnicity, or Gender Matter?" *American Economic Review* 95(2): 158–65.

Deil-Amen, Regina, and Stefanie DeLuca. 2010. "The Underserved Third: How Our Educational Structures Populate an Educational Underclass." *Journal of Education for Students Placed at Risk* 15: 27–50.

Deil-Amen, Regina, and James Rosenbaum. 2003. "The Social Prerequisites of Success: Can College Structure Reduce the Need for Social Know-How?" *Annals of the American Academy of Political and Social Science* 586(1): 120–43.

Deil-Amen, Regina, and Ruth N. Lopez Turley. 2007. "A Review of the Transition to College Literature in Sociology." *Teachers College Record* 109(10): 2324–66.

Delgado Gaitan, Concha. 1991. "Involving Parents in the Schools: A Process of Change for Involving Parents." *American Journal of Education* 100(1): 20–46.

———. 1994. "Consejos: The Power of Cultural Narrative." *Anthropology & Education Quarterly* 25(2): 137–55.

Derwing, Tracey. 2003. "What Do ESL Students Say About Their Accents?" *Canadian Modern Language Review* 59(4): 547–67.

Devos, Thierry, and Mahzarin Banaji. 2005. "American = White?" *Journal of Personality and Social Psychology* 88: 447–66.

Devos, Thierry, Kelly Gavin, and Francisco J. Quintana. 2010. "Say 'Adios' to the American Dream? The Interplay Between Ethnic and National Identity Among Latino and Caucasian Americans." *Cultural Diversity and Ethnic Minority Psychology* 16(1): 37–49.

Diamond, John B., and Kimberly Gomez. 2004. "African American Parents' Educational Orientations: The Importance of Social Class and Parents' Perceptions of Schools." *Education and Urban Society* 36(4): 383–427.

Diamond, John B., Antonia Randolph, and James P. Spillane. 2004. "Teachers' Expectations and Sense of Responsibility for Student Learning: The Importance of Race, Class, and Organizational Habitus." *Anthropology and Education Quarterly* 35(1): 75–98.

Diaz, Johnny. 2004. "Latino? Hispanic? Which Is It? Spanish Speakers Are Divided, and Others Are Confused." *Boston Globe*, January 25, 2004. Available at http://www.boston.com/news/local/articles/2004/01/25/latino_hispanic_which_is_it/?page=2 (accessed January 30, 2012).

Dicker, Susan. 2006. "Dominican Americans in Washington Heights, New York: Language and Culture in a Transnational Community." *International Journal of Bilingual Education and Bilingualism* 9(6): 713–27.

Dika, Sandra L., and Kusum Singh. 2002. "Applications of Social Capital in Educational Literature: A Critical Synthesis." *Review of Educational Research* 72: 31–60.

Dinnerstein, Leonard, and David M. Reimers. 1999. *Ethnic Americans: A History of Immigration*. New York: Columbia University Press.

Dobbie, Will, and Roland G. Fryer Jr. 2009. "Are High-Quality Schools Enough to

Close the Achievement Gap? Evidence from a Bold Social Experiment in Harlem." Working paper 15473. Cambridge, Mass.: National Bureau of Economic Research.

Dominican and Colombian Immigrant Family Study. 2009. Study by Vivian Louie.

Doucet, Fabienne, and Carola Suárez-Orozco. 2006. "Ethnic Identity and Schooling: The Experiences of Haitian Immigrant Youth." In *Ethnic Identity: Creation, Conflict, and Accommodation*, 4th ed., edited by Lola Romanucci-Ross and George DeVos. Walnut Creek, Calif.: Altamira Press.

Drago-Severson, Eleanor. 2004. *Helping Teachers Learn*. Thousand Oaks, Calif.: Corwin Press.

Dreby, Joanna. 2010. *Divided by Borders: Mexican Migrants and Their Children*. Berkeley: University of California Press.

Duany, Jorge. 1998. "Reconstructing Racial Identity: Ethnicity, Color, and Class Among Dominicans in the United States and Puerto Rico." *Latin American Perspectives* 25(3): 147–72.

Duarte, Jesús. 1998. "State Weakness and Clientelism in Colombian Education." In *Colombia: The Politics of Reforming the State*, edited by Eduardo Posada-Carbo. London and New York: Macmillan Press and St. Martin's Press.

DuBois, W. E. B. 1996. *The Philadelphia Negro*. Philadelphia: University of Pennsylvania Press. (Originally published in 1899).

Dugas, John C. 2005. "The Colombian Nightmare: Human Rights Abuses and the Contradictory Effects of U.S. Foreign Policy." In *When States Kill: Latin America, the U.S., and Technologies of Terror*, edited by Cecilia Menjívar and Néstor Rodriguez. Austin: University of Texas Press.

Duncan, Greg J., and Jeanne Brooks-Gunn. 1997. *Consequences of Growing Up Poor*. New York: Russell Sage Foundation.

Eccles, Jacquelynne, and Jennifer Appleton Goodman. 2002. *Community Programs to Promote Youth Development*. Washington, D.C.: National Academies Press.

Eckstein, Susan. 2006. "Cuban Émigrés and the American Dream." *Perspectives on Politics* 4(2, June): 297–307.

Elder, Glen H., Jr., Jacquelynne S. Eccles, Monika Ardelt, and Sarah Lord. 1995. "Inner-City Parents Under Economic Pressure: Perspectives on the Strategies of Parenting." *Journal of Marriage and Family* 57: 771–84.

Ellwood, David, and Thomas J. Kane. 2000. "Who Is Getting a College Education: Family Background and the Growing Gaps in Enrollment?" In *Securing the Future: Investing in Children from Birth to College*, edited by Sheldon Danziger and Jane Waldfogel. New York: Russell Sage Foundation.

Elmore, Richard. 2004. "Bridging the Gap Between Standards and Achievement: The Imperative for Professional Development in Education." In *School Reform from the Inside Out: Policy Practice and Performance*. Cambridge, Mass.: Harvard Education Press.

Epstein, Joyce. 1995. "School/Family/Community Partnerships: Caring for the Children We Share." *Phi Delta Kappan* 76(9): 701–12.

Erickson, Lance D., Steve McDonald, and Glen H. Elder Jr. 2009. "Informal Mentors and Education: Complementary or Compensatory Resources?" *Sociology of Education* 82(4): 344–67.

Erikson, Erik. 1968. *Identity, Youth, and Crisis.* New York: W. W. Norton.

Erlick, June Carolyn. 2010. *A Gringa in Bogotá: Living Colombia's Invisible War.* Austin: University of Texas Press.

Espenshade, Thomas J., and Maryann Belanger. 1997. "U.S. Public Perceptions and Reactions to Mexican Migration." In *At the Crossroads: Mexican Migration and U.S. Policy,* edited by Frank D. Bean, Rodolfo O. de la Garza, Bryan R. Roberts, and Sidney Weintraub. Lanham, Md.: Rowman & Littlefield.

Espinoza-Herold, Mariella. 2003. *Issues in Latino Education: Race, School Culture, and the Politics of Academic Success.* Boston: Pearson Education Group.

Estes, Nolan. 1990. "Introduction." In *Magnet Schools: Recent Developments and Perspectives,* edited by Nolan Estes, Daniel U. Levine, and Donald R. Waldrip. Austin, Tex.: Morgan Printing and Publishing.

Fairchild, Henry P. 1911. "Foreign-Americans." *The Nation* 93(2426, December 28): 626–27.

Falicov, Celia Jaes. 2002. "Ambiguous Loss: Risk and Resilience in Latino Immigrant Families." In *Latinos: Remaking America,* edited by Marcelo Suárez-Orozco, and Mariela M. Páez. Berkeley: University of California Press.

Fears, Darryl. 2003. "Latinos or Hispanics? A Debate About Identity." *Washington Post,* August 25, 2003, p. A01.

Feliciano, Cynthia. 2008. *Unequal Origins: Immigrant Selection and the Education of the Second Generation.* El Paso, Tex.: LFB Scholarly Publishing.

Ferguson, Ronald F. 2003. "Teachers' Perceptions and Expectations and the Black-White Achievement Gap." *Urban Education* 38(4): 460–507.

Fernandez, Steve. 2004. "Jim Crow: A Phoenix Rising in Boston—The Trend Towards Separate and Unequal in Boston Public Schools." In *Creating Alternative Discourses in the Education of Latinos and Latinas,* edited by Raul E. Ybarra and Nancy Lopez. New York: Peter Lang.

Fernandez-Kelly, Patricia. 2008. "The Back Pocket Map: Social Class and Cultural Capital as Transferable Assets in the Advancement of Second-Generation Immigrants." *Annals of the American Academy of Political and Social Science* 620: 116–37.

Fernandez-Kelly, Patricia, and Alejandro Portes. 2008. "Introduction." *Annals of the American Academy of Political and Social Science* 620: 12–36.

Fine, Michelle. 1993. "[Ap]parent Involvement: Reflections on Parents, Power, and Urban Public Schools." *Teachers College Record* 94: 682–710.

Fix, Michael E., and Jeffrey S. Passell. 2003. "U.S. Immigration: Trends and Implications for Schools." Washington, D.C.: Urban Institute (January 28). Available at: http://www.urban.org/publications/410654.html (accessed January 30, 2012).

Fletcher, Jason, and Marta Tienda. 2010. "Race and Ethnic Differences in College Achievement: Does High School Attended Matter?" *Annals of the American Academy of Political and Social Science* 627: 144–66.

Flores, Stella M. 2010. "State 'Dream Acts': The Effect of In-State Resident Tuition Policies on the College Enrollment of Undocumented Latino Students in the United States." *Review of Higher Education* 33: 239–83.

Foner, Nancy. 1985. "Race and Color: Jamaican Migrants in London and New York City." *International Migration Review* 19(4): 708–27.

———. 2000. *From Ellis Island to JFK: New York's Two Great Waves of Immigration.* New Haven, Conn.: Yale University Press.

———. 2006. "The Challenge and Promise of Past-Present Comparisons." *Journal of American Ethnic History* 25: 142–52.

Foner, Nancy, and Joanna Dreby. 2011. "Relations Between the Generations in Immigrant Families." *Annual Review of Sociology* 14(4): 545–64.

Foner, Nancy, and George M. Fredrickson. 2004. "Introduction: Immigration, Race, and Ethnicity in the United States: Social Constructions and Social Relations in Historical Perspective." In *Not Just Black and White: Historical and Contemporary Perspectives on Immigration, Race, and Ethnicity in the United States,* edited by Nancy Foner and George M. Fredrickson. New York: Russell Sage Foundation.

Fox, George. 1996. *Hispanic Nation.* New York: Birch Lane Press.

Frankenberg, Erica, and Genevieve Siegel-Hawley. 2008. "The Forgotten Choice: Rethinking Magnet Schools in a Changing Landscape." Los Angeles: Civil Rights Project (Proyecto Derechos Civiles) (November).

———. 2008. *The Role of Schools in the English Language Learner Achievement Gap.* Washington, D.C.: Pew Hispanic Center (June 26).

Fry, Richard, and Shirin Hakimzadeh. 2006. *Statistical Portrait of Hispanics at Mid-Decade.* Pew Hispanic Center (September 16). Available at: http://www.pewhispanic.org/2006/09/16/a-statistical-portrait-of-hispanics-at-mid-decade (accessed January 30, 2012).

Fry, Richard, and Jeffrey Passel. 2009. *Latino Children: A Majority Are U.S.-Born Offspring of Immigrants.* Washington, D.C: Pew Hispanic Center.

Fry, Rick. 2007. "The Changing Racial and Ethnic Composition of U.S. Public Schools." Report. Washington, D.C.: Pew Hispanic Center (August 30). Available at: http://pewhispanic.org/files/reports/79.pdf (accessed January 30, 2012).

Fryer, Roland G., Jr., and Steven D. Levitt. 2004. "The Causes and Consequences of Distinctively Black Names." *Quarterly Journal of Economics* 119(3): 767–805.

Fukuyama, Francis. 1994. "Immigrants and Family Values." In *Arguing Immigration: Are New Immigrants a Wealth of Diversity or a Crushing Burden?* edited by Nicholaus Mills. New York: Touchstone.

Fuligni, Andrew J. 2006. "The Academic Achievement of Adolescents from Immigrant Families: The Role of Family Background, Attitudes, and Behavior." *Child Development* 68(2, June 30): 351–63.

Fuligni, Andrew J., Vivian Tseng, and May Lam. 1999. "Attitudes Toward Family Obligations Among American Adolescents from Asian, Latin American, and European Backgrounds." *Child Development* 70: 1030–44.

Furstenberg, Frank F., Rubén G. Rumbaut, and Richard A. Settersten Jr. 2005. "On the Frontier of Adulthood: Emerging Themes and New Directions." In *On the Frontiers of Adulthood: Theory, Research, and Public Policy*, edited by Richard A. Settersten Jr., Frank Furstenberg Jr., and Rubén G. Rumbaut. Chicago: University of Chicago Press.

Galston, William, Noah Pickus, and Peter Skerry. 2009. "Breaking the Immigration Stalemate: From Deep Disagreements to Constructive Proposals: A Report from the Brookings-Duke Immigration Policy Roundtable." Washington, D.C.: Brookings Institution (October 6). Available at: http://www.brookings

.edu/~/media/Files/rc/reports/2009/1006_immigration_roundtable/1006_immigration_roundtable.pdf (accessed January 30, 2012).

Gamoran, Adam. 1996. "Student Achievement in Public Magnet, Public Comprehensive, and Private City High Schools." *Educational Evaluation and Policy Analysis* 18(1): 1–18.

Gándara, Patricia. 1995. *Over the Ivy Walls: The Educational Mobility of Low-Income Chicanos*. Albany: State University of New York Press.

———. 1999. "Telling Stories of Success: Cultural Capital and the Educational Mobility of Chicano Students." *Latino Studies Journal* 10(Winter): 38–54.

Gándara, Patricia, and Frances Contreras. 2009. *The Latino Education Crisis: The Consequences of Failed Social Policies*. Cambridge, Mass.: Harvard University Press.

Gándara, Patricia, Susan O'Hara, and Dianna Gutiérrez. 2004. "The Changing Shape of Aspirations: Peer Influence on Achievement Behavior." In *School Connections: U.S.-Mexican Youth, Peers, and School Achievement*, edited by Margaret Gibson, Patricia Gándara, and Jill P. Koyama. New York: Teachers College Press.

Gándara, Patricia, Russell Rumberger, Julie Maxwell-Jolly, and Rebecca Callahan. 2003. "English Learners in California Schools: Unequal Resources, Unequal Outcomes." *Educational Policy Analysis Archives* 11(36): 1–54.

Gans, Herbert. 1992. "Second-Generation Decline: Scenarios for the Economic and Ethnic Futures of the Post-1965 American Immigrants." *Ethnic and Racial Studies* 15(2): 173–93.

———. 2007. "Acculturation, Assimilation, and Mobility." *Ethnic and Racial Studies* 30(1): 152–64.

———. 2009. "First-Generation Decline: Downward Mobility Among Refugees and Immigrants." *Ethnic and Racial Studies* 32(9): 1658–70.

Garcia Coll, Cynthia, Daisuke Akiba, Natalia Palacios, Benjamin Bailey, Rebecca Silver, Lisa DiMartino, and Cindy Chin. 2002. "Parental Involvement in Children's Education: Lessons from Three Immigrant Groups." *Parenting: Science and Practice* 2(3): 300–324.

Gardner, Howard.1983. *Frames of Mind: The Theory of Multiple Intelligences*. New York: Basic Books.

———. 1993. *Multiple Intelligences: The Theory in Practice*. New York: Basic Books.

———. 2006. *Multiple Intelligences: New Horizons*. New York: Basic Books.

Gaus, John Merriman. 1918. "A Municipal Program for Educating Immigrants in Citizenship." *National Municipal Review* 7(3): 237–44.

Gaztambide-Fernández, Rubén A. 2009. *The Best of the Best: Becoming Elite at an American Boarding School*. Cambridge, Mass.: Harvard University Press.

Gelber, Scott. 2007. "Pathways in the Past: Historical Perspectives on Access to Higher Education." *Teachers College Record* 109(10): 2252–86.

———. 2008. "'The Crux and the Magic': The Political History of Boston Magnet Schools, 1968-1989." *Equity and Excellence in Education* 41(4): 453–66.

Gerstle, Gary. 1997. "Liberty, Coercion, and the Making of Americans." *Journal of American History* 84(2): 524–58.

———. 2000. "American Freedom, American Coercion: Immigrant Journeys in the Promised Land." *Social Compass* 47(1): 63–76.

Gerstle, Gary, and John Mollenkopf. 2002. "The Political Incorporation of Immigrants: Then and Now." In *E Pluribus Unum? Contemporary and Historical Perspectives on Immigrant Political Incorporation*, edited by Gary Gerstle and John Mollenkopf. New York: Russell Sage Foundation.

Gibson, Margaret A. 2003. "Improving Graduation Outcomes for Migrant Students." EDO-RC-03-2. ERIC Clearinghouse on Rural Education and Small Schools. Available at: http://www.eric.ed.gov/PDFS/ED478061.pdf (accessed January 30, 2012).

Gibson, Margaret, Patricia Gándara, and Jill P. Koyama. 2004. "The Role of Peers in the Schooling of U.S. Mexican Youth." In *School Connections: U.S.-Mexican Youth, Peers, and School Achievement*, edited by Margaret Gibson, Patricia Gándara and Jill P. Koyama. New York: Teachers College Press.

Gold, Steven J. 2009. "Immigration Benefits America." *Society* 46: 408–11.

Gomez, Alfredo S. 2000. "Equity and Education in Colombia." In *Unequal Schools, Unequal Chances: The Challenges to Equal Opportunity in the Americas*, edited by Fernando Reimers. Cambridge, Mass.: Harvard University Press and Harvard University David Rockefeller Center for Latin American Studies.

González de Perdomo, Consuelo, and Gustavo Moncayo. 2008. "Forgotten in the Jungle: Victims of Colombia's War." Paper presented to the Harvard-MIT Colombian Colloquium. Harvard University, Cambridge, Mass. (September 25).

Goodwin, Sherry Posnick. 2005, November. "The Parent Factor: It Can Make a World of Difference for Students." *California Educator* 10(3). Available at: http://legacy.cta.org/media/publications/educator/archives/2005/200511_cal_ed_feature01.htm (accessed January 30, 2012).

Goyette, Kimberly, and Gilberto Conchas. 2002. "Family and Non-Family Roots of Social Capital Among Vietnamese and Mexican American Children." *Sociology of Education* 13: 41–72.

Graham, Patricia Alberg. 1987. "Black Teachers: A Drastically Scarce Resource." *Phi Delta Kappan* 68(8): 598–605.

———. 2005. *Schooling America: How the Public Schools Meet the Nation's Changing Needs*. Oxford: Oxford University Press.

Grant, Gerald. 2009. *Hope and Despair in the American City: Why There Are No Bad Schools in Raleigh*. Cambridge, Mass.: Harvard University Press.

Grasmuck, Sherri, and Patricia R. Pessar. 1991. *Between Two Islands: Dominican International Migration*. Berkeley: University of California Press.

Greeley, Andrew. 1982. *Catholic High Schools and Minority Students*. New Brunswick, N.J.: Transaction Books.

Green, John W. 2000. "Left Liberalism and Race in the Evolution of Colombian Popular National Identity." *The Americans* 57(1): 95–124.

Griffith, David C. 2005. "Rural Industry and Mexican Immigration and Settlement in North Carolina." In *New Destinations: Mexican Immigration in the United States*, edited by Victor Zuniga and Ruben Hernandez-Leon. New York: Russell Sage Foundation.

Grissmer, David. 2005. "Closing the Nation's Racial Achievement Gaps." Paper presented on panel, Harvard University, Graduate School of Education. Cambridge, Mass. (May 12).

Grodsky, Eric, and Erika Jackson. 2009. "Social Stratification in Higher Education." *Teachers College Record* 111(10): 2347–84.

Grossman, Jean B., and Jean E. Rhodes. 2002. "The Test of Time: Predictors and

Effects of Duration in Youth Mentoring Relationships." *American Journal of Community Psychology* 30(2): 199–219.

Guarnizo, Luis Eduardo, and Luz Marina Diaz. 1999. "Transnational Migration: A View from Colombia." *Ethnic and Racial Studies* 22(2): 397–421.

Guarnizo, Luis Eduardo, Arturo Ignacio Sanchez, and Elizabeth M. Roach. 1999. "Mistrust, Fragmented Solidarity, and Transnational Migration: Colombians in New York City and Los Angeles." *Ethnic and Racial Studies* 22(2): 267–396.

Guglielmo, Thomas A. 2003. *White on Arrival: Italians, Race, Color, and Power in Chicago, 1890–1945*. Oxford: Oxford University Press.

Guilamo-Ramos, Vincent, Patricia Dittus, James Jaccard, Margaret Johansson, Alida Bouris, and Neifi Acosta. 2007. "Parenting Practices Among Dominican and Puerto Rican Mothers." *Social Work* 52(1): 17–30.

Gupta, Monisha Das. 1997. "What Is Indian About You? A Gendered, Transnational Approach to Ethnicity." *Gender and Society* 11(5): 572–96.

Gutierrez, Rochelle. 2002. "Beyond Essentialism: The Complexity of Language in Teaching Mathematics to Latina/o Students." *American Educational Research Journal* 39(4): 1047–88.

Gutmann, Amy. 1994. "Introduction." In *Multiculturalism: Examining the Politics of Recognition*, edited by Charles Taylor and Amy Gutmann. Princeton, N.J.: Princeton University Press.

Hagy, Alison P., and J. F. O. Staniec. 2002. "Immigrant Status, Race, and Institutional Choice in Higher Education." *Economics of Education Review* 21(4): 381–92.

Haller, William, Alejandro Portes, and Scott M. Lynch. 2011a. "Dreams Fulfilled, Dreams Shattered: Determinants of Segmented Assimilation in the Second Generation." *Social Forces* 89(3): 733–62.

———. 2011b. "On the Dangers of Rosy Lenses." *Social Forces* 89(3): 775–82.

Handlin, Oscar. 1951. *The Uprooted*. Boston: Little, Brown.

Hao, Lingxin, and Suet-Ling Pong. 2008. "The Role of School in the Upward Mobility of Disadvantaged Immigrants' Children." *Annals of the American Academy of Political and Social Science* 620: 62–89.

Harding, Heather, Ned Rimer, and Camrin Fredrick. 2007. "Volunteers in Service to Youth: Citizen Schools." *Voices in Urban Education* 16: 45–51.

Harris, Angel L., Kenneth M. Jamison, and Monica H. Trujillo. 2008. "Disparities in the Educational Success of Immigrants: An Assessment of the Immigrant Effect for Asians and Latinos." *Annals of the American Academy of Political and Social Science* 620: 90–114.

Hartmann, Edward George. 1948. *The Movement to Americanize the Immigrant*. New York: Columbia University Press.

Harvard Graduate School of Education. 2002. "Tongue Tied: Bilingual Education in the Nation of Immigrants." *Ed.* magazine, April 1. Available at: http://www.gse.harvard.edu/news/features/bilingualed04012002.html (accessed January 30, 2012).

Haskins, Ron. 2007. "Immigration: Wages, Education, and Mobility." In *Getting Ahead or Losing Ground: Economic Mobility in America*, edited by Julia B. Isaacs, Isabel V. Sawhill, and Ron Haskins. Washington, D.C.: Brookings Institution.

Haveman, Robert, and Timothy Smeeding. 2006. "The Role of Higher Education in Social Mobility." *The Future of Children* 16(2): 126–50.

Hearn, James C., and Janet M. Holdsworth. 2002. "Influences of State-Level Policies and Practices on College Students' Learning." *Peabody Journal of Education* 77(3): 6–39.

Hernandez, Deborah Pacini. 2006. "Quiet Crisis: A Community History of Latinos in Cambridge, Massachusetts." In *Latinos in New England*, edited by Andres Torres. Philadelphia: Temple University Press.

Hernandez, Donald J., Nancy A. Denton, and Suzanne E. Macartney. 2008. "Children in Immigrant Families: Looking to America's Future." *Social Policy Report* 22(3): 3–23.

Hernández, Ramona. 2002. *The Mobility of Workers Under Advanced Capitalism: Dominican Migration to the United States*. New York: Columbia University Press.

Hernández, Ramona, and Glenn Jacobs. 2004. "The Drift of Latino Students Through Public Higher Education." In *Creating Alternative Discourses in the Education of Latinos and Latinas*, edited by Raul E. Ybarra and Nancy Lopez. New York: Peter Lang.

Hiatt-Michael, Diana. 1994. "Parental Involvement in American Public Schools: A Historical Perspective, 1642–2000." *School Community Journal* 4(2): 247–58.

Hill, Lori Diane. 2008. "School Strategies and the 'College Linking' Process: Reconsidering the Effects of High Schools on College Enrollment." *Sociology of Education* 81(1): 53–76.

Hill, Nancy E., and Kathryn Torres. 2010. "Negotiating the American Dream: The Paradox of Aspirations and Achievement Among Latino Students and Engagement Between Their Families and Schools." *Journal of Social Issues* 66(1): 95–112.

Hing, Bill Ong. 2004. *Defining American Through Immigration*. Philadelphia: Temple University Press.

Hochschild, Jennifer L. 1992. "The Word 'American' Ends in 'Can': The Ambiguous Promise of the American Dream." *William and Mary Law Review* 34: 139–70.

———. 1995. *Facing Up to the American Dream: Race, Class, and the Soul of the Nation*. Princeton, N.J.: Princeton University Press.

Hochschild, Jennifer, and Porsha Cropper. 2010. "Immigration Regimes and Schooling Regimes: Which Countries Promote Successful Immigrant Integration?" *Theory and Research in Social Education* 8(1): 21–61.

Hochschild, Jennifer, and Nathan Scovronick. 2003. *The American Dream and the Public Schools*. New York: Oxford University Press.

Hoffnung-Garskof, Jesse. 2008. *Tale of Two Cities: Santo Domingo and New York After 1950*. Princeton, N.J.: Princeton University Press.

Hogan, David. 1978. "Education and the Making of the Chicago Working Class, 1880–1930." *History of Education Quarterly* 18: 227–70.

Holdaway, Jennifer, and Richard Alba. 2009. "Introduction: Educating Immigrant Youth: The Role of Institutions and Agency." *Teachers College Record* 111(3): 597–615.

Holdaway, Jennifer, Maurice Crul, and Catrin Roberts. 2009. "Cross-National Comparison of Provision and Outcomes for the Education of the Second Generation." *Teachers College Record* 111(6): 1381–1403.

Hondagneu-Sotelo, Pierrette. 2001. *Domestica: Immigrant Workers' Cleaning and Caring in the Shadow of Affluence*. Berkeley: University of California Press.

Hoover-Dempsey, Kathleen V., and Howard M. Sandler. 1995. "Parental Involvement in Children's Education: Why Does It Make a Difference?" *Teachers College Record* 97(2): 310–31.

———. 1997. "Why Do Parents Become Involved in Their Children's Education?" *Review of Educational Research* 67(1): 3–42.

Horn, Laura J. 1998. "Stopouts or Stayouts: Undergraduates Who Leave College in Their First Year." Washington, D.C.: U.S. Department of Education.

Hossler, Don, and Karen Gallagher. 1987. "Studying College Choice: A Three-Phase Model and the Implication for Policy Makers." *College and University* 2: 207–21.

Huntington, Samuel P. 2004. *Who Are We? The Challenges to America's National Identity.* New York: Simon & Schuster.

Ignatiev, Noel. 1995. *How the Irish Became White*. New York: Routledge.

Inter-American Development Bank (IADB). 2000. *Development Beyond Economics: Economic and Social Progress Report 2000.* Washington, D.C. and Baltimore: IADB and Johns Hopkins University Press.

Irvine, Jacqueline J., and Michèle Foster, eds. 1996. *Growing Up African American in Catholic Schools*. New York: Teachers College Press.

Isaacs, Julia B. 2007. "Economic Mobility of Families Across Generations." In *Getting Ahead or Losing Ground: Economic Mobility in America*, edited by Julia B. Isaacs, Isabel V. Sawhill, and Ron Haskins. Washington, D.C.: Brookings Institution.

Itzigsohn, José. 2009. *Encountering American Faultlines: Race, Class, and the Dominican Experience in Providence*. New York: Russell Sage Foundation.

Itzigsohn, Jose, and Carlos Dore-Cabral. 2000. "Competing Identities? Race, Ethnicity, and Panethnicity Among Dominicans in the United States." *Sociological Forum* 15(2): 225–47.

Itzigsohn, Jose, and Silvia Giorguli-Saucedo. 2002. "Immigrant Incorporation and Sociocultural Transnationalism." *International Migration Review* 36(3): 766–98.

Jaret, Charles. 1999. "Troubled by Newcomers: Anti-Immigrant Attitudes and Action During Two Eras of Mass Immigration to the United States." *Journal of American History* 18(3): 9–39.

Jenkins, Alan. 2009. "Recovering Opportunity: Racial Barriers Continue to Hold Back Millions of Americans—and Our Economy." *The American Prospect* 20(August 16). Available at: http://prospect.org/article/recovering-opportunity-0 (accessed January 30, 2012).

Jensen, Leif, Jeffrey H. Cohen, Almeida Jacqueline Toribio, Gordon F. De Jong, and Leila Rodriguez. 2006. "Ethnic Identities, Language, and Economic Outcomes Among Dominicans in a New Destination: A Research Note." *Social Science Quarterly* 87(5): 1088–99.

Jensen, Lene Arnett. 2008. "Immigrants' Cultural Identities as Sources of Civic Engagement." *Applied Developmental Science* 12(2): 74–83.

Jia, Gisela. 2007. "Acquisition of English Grammatical Morphology by Native Mandarin-Speaking Children and Adolescents: Age-Related Differences." *Journal of Speech, Language, and Hearing Research* 50(5): 1280–99.

Jimenez, Emmanuel, Marlaine E. Lockheed, Eduardo Luna, and Vicente Paqueo. 1991. "School Effects and Costs for Private and Public Schools in the Dominican Republic." *International Journal of Educational Research* 15(5): 393–410.

Jiménez, Tomás. 2010. *Replenished Ethnicity: Mexican Americans, Immigration, and Identity.* Berkeley: University of California Press.

———. *Immigrants in the United States: How Well Are They Integrating into Society?* Washington, D.C.: Migration Policy Institute.

Johnson, Susan Moore. 1990. *Teachers at Work: Achieving Success in Our Schools.* New York: Basic Books.

Jones-Correa, Michael. 2008. "Race to the Top? The Politics of Immigrant Education in Suburbia." In *New Faces in New Places: The Changing Geography of American Immigration*, edited by Douglas S. Massey. New York: Russell Sage Foundation.

Jost, John T., and Mahzarin R. Banaji. 1994. "The Role of Stereotyping in System-Justification and the Production of False Consciousness." *British Journal of Social Psychology* 33: 1–27.

Jost, John T., Mahzarin R. Banaji, and Brian A. Nosek. 2004. "A Decade of System Justification Theory: Accumulated Evidence of Conscious and Unconscious Bolstering of the Status Quo." *Political Psychology* 25(6): 881–919.

Kahlenberg, Richard D. 2009. "Turnaround Schools That Work: Moving Beyond Separate but Equal." *The Agenda.* New York and Washington, D.C.: The Century Foundation.

Kala, Mandira, and Charles Jones. 2006a. *Boston Fact Sheet.* Boston: University of Massachusetts, Program in Public Policy and Mauricio Gaston Institute for Latino Community Development and Public Policy.

———. 2006b. *Lawrence Fact Sheet.* Boston: University of Massachusetts, Program in Public Policy and Mauricio Gaston Institute for Latino Community Development and Public Policy.

Kaminsky, Amy. 1994. "Gender, Race, Raza." *Feminist Studies* 20(1): 7–32.

Kao, Grace. 2004. "Social Capital and Its Relevance to Minority and Immigrant Populations." *Sociology of Education* 77(2): 172–75.

Kao, Grace, and Marta Tienda. 1995. "Optimism and Achievement: The Educational Performance of Immigrant Youth." *Social Science Quarterly* 76(1): 1–19.

Karabel, Jerome. 2005. *The Chosen: The Hidden History of Admission and Exclusion at Harvard, Yale, and Princeton.* Boston: Houghton Mifflin.

Kasinitz, Philip. 1992. *Caribbean New York: Black Immigrants and the Politics of Race.* Ithaca, N.Y.: Cornell University Press.

———. 2008. "Becoming American, Becoming Minority, Getting Ahead: The Role of Racial and Ethnic Status in the Upward Mobility of the Children of Immigrants." *Annals of the American Academy of Political and Social Science* 620: 253–69.

Kasinitz, Philip, John H. Mollenkopf, and Mary C. Waters. 2004. *Becoming New Yorkers: Ethnographies of the New Second Generation.* New York: Russell Sage Foundation.

Kasinitz, Philip, John H. Mollenkopf, Mary C. Waters, and Jennifer Holdaway. 2008. *Inheriting the City: The Children of Immigrants Come of Age.* Cambridge, Mass. and New York: Harvard University Press and Russell Sage Foundation.

Kearney, Melissa. 2006. "Intergenerational Mobility for Women and Minorities in the United States." *The Future of Children* 16(2): 37–53.

Kegan, Robert. 1982. *The Evolving Self: Problem and Process in Human Development.* Cambridge, Mass.: Harvard University Press.

Kerwin, Donald M., Doris Meissner, and Margie McHugh. 2011. *Executive Action on Immigration: Six Ways to Make the System Work Better.* Washington, D.C.: Migration Policy Institute.

Khan, Shamus Rahman. 2011. *Privilege: The Making of an Adolescent Elite at St. Paul's School.* Princeton, N.J.: Princeton University Press.

Kim, Claire Jean. 2000. *Bitter Fruit: The Politics of Black-Korean Conflict in New York City.* New Haven, Conn.: Yale University Press.

Kim, Doo Hwan, and Barbara Schneider. 2005. "Social Capital in Action: Alignment of Parental Support in Adolescents' Transition to Postsecondary Education." *Social Forces* 84(2): 1181–1206.

Kohut, Andrew, Roberto Suro, Scott Keeter, Carroll Doherty, and Gabriel Escobar. 2006. "America's Immigration Quandary." Report. Washington, D.C.: Pew Hispanic Center. Available at: http://www.people-press.org/files/legacy-pdf/274.pdf (accessed January 30, 2012).

Koretz, Daniel. 2008. *Measuring Up: What Educational Testing Really Tells Us.* Cambridge, Mass.: Harvard University Press.

Koyama, Jill P. 2006. "Approaching and Attending College: Anthropological and Ethnographic Accounts." *Teachers College Record* 109(10): 2301–23.

Kozol, Jonathan. 1991. *Savage Inequalities: Children in America's Schools.* New York: Crown.

Krein, Sheila F. 1986. "Growing Up in a Single-Parent Family: The Effect on Education and Earnings of Young Men." *Family Relations* 35(1): 161–68.

Kwong, Peter. 1987. *The New Chinatown.* New York: Noonday Press.

Lamont, Michèle, and Mario L. Small. 2008. "How Culture Matters: Enriching Our Understanding of Poverty." In *The Colors of Poverty: Why Racial and Ethnic Disparities Persist*, edited by David Harris and Ann Lin. New York: Russell Sage Foundation.

Lareau, Annette. 2000. *Home Advantage: Social Class and Parental Intervention in Elementary Education.* Lanham, Md.: Rowan and Littlefield. (Originally published in 1989).

———. 2003. *Unequal Childhoods: Class, Race, and Family Life.* Berkeley: University of California Press.

———. 2008. "Introduction: Taking Stock of Class." In *Social Class: How Does It Work?* edited by Annette Lareau and Dalton Conley. New York: Russell Sage Foundation.

Lareau, Annette, and Dalton Conley, eds. 2008. *Social Class: How Does It Work?* New York: Russell Sage Foundation.

Lareau, Annette, and Erin M. Horvat. 1999. "Moments of Social Inclusion and Exclusion: Race, Class, and Cultural Capital in Family-School Relationships." *Sociology of Education* 72(1): 37–53.

Lareau, Annette, and Elliot B. Weininger. 2008. "Class and the Transition to Adulthood." In *Social Class: How Does It Work?* edited by Annette Lareau and Dalton Conley. New York: Russell Sage Foundation.

Larrota, Clarena, and Ysabel Ramirez. 2009. "Literacy Benefits for Latino/a Parents Engaged in a Spanish Literacy Project." *Journal of Adolescent and Adult Literacy Volume* 52(7): 621–30.

Laserna, Catalina. 1988. "The Shovel and the Books: Embedded and Formal Education in San Juan, a Native American Rural Community in Southern Colombia." Ph.D. diss., University of Cambridge, Department of Social Anthropology.

Lavan, Nicole, and Miren Uriarte. 2008. *Status of Latino Education in Massachusetts: A Report*. Boston: University of Massachusetts, Mauricio Gastón Institute for Latino Community Development and Public Policy.

Lawrence-Lightfoot, Sara. 1978. *Worlds Apart: Relationships Between Families and Schools*. New York: Basic Books.

———. 1983. *The Good High School*. New York: Basic Books.

———. 1994. *I've Known Rivers: Lives of Loss and Liberation*. Reading, Mass.: Addison-Wesley.

———. 2003. *The Essential Conversation: What Parents and Teachers Can Learn from Each Other*. New York: Random House.

Lawrence-Lightfoot, Sara, and Jessica Hoffman Davis. 1997. *The Art and Science of Portraiture*. San Francisco: Jossey-Bass Publishers.

Lee, Jennifer, and Frank D. Bean. 2010. *The Diversity Paradox: Immigration and the Color Line in Twenty-First-Century America*. New York: Russell Sage Foundation.

Lee, John Michael, Jr., and Tafaya Ransom. 2011. "The Educational Experience of Young Men of Color: A Review of Research, Pathways, and Progress." Washington, D.C.: College Board.

Lemmel, Heidi Harris, and Robert Rothman. 2007. "Leveling the Playing Field: The Promise of Extended Learning Opportunities and Supports for Youth." *Voices in Urban Education* 16: 36–44.

Lev-Wiesel, Rachel, and Roni Kaufman. 2004. "Personal Characteristics, Unemployment and Anxiety Among Highly Educated Immigrants." *International Migration* 42(3): 58–75.

Levitt, Peggy. 2001. *The Transnational Villagers*. Berkeley: University of California Press.

Lew, Jamie. 2006. *Asian Americans in Class: Charting the Achievement Gap Among Korean American Youth*. New York: Teachers College Press.

Li, Jin, Susan D. Holloway, Janine Bempechat, and Elaine Loh. 2008. "Building and Using a Social Network: Nurture for Low-Income Chinese American Adolescents' Learning." *New Directions for Child and Adolescent Development* 121(Fall): 9–25.

Liberato, Ana S. Q., Guillermo Rebollo-Gil, John D. Foster, and Amanda Moras. 2009. "Latinidad and Masculinidad in Hollywood Scripts." *Ethnic and Racial Studies* 32(6): 948–66.

Lieberson, Stanley. 1980. *A Piece of the Piece: Black and White Immigrants Since 1880*. Berkeley: University of California Press.

Light, Richard J. 2001. *Making the Most of College: Students Speak Their Minds*. Cambridge, Mass.: Harvard University Press.

Limonic, Laura. 2008. *The Latino Population of New York City, 2007*. Report 20. New York: City University of New York, Graduate Center, Center for Latin American, Caribbean, and Latino Studies (December).

Loewen, James W. 1971. *The Mississippi Chinese: Between Black and White*. Cambridge, Mass.: Harvard University Press.

Long, Bridget Terry. 2007. "The Contributions of Economics to the Study of College Access and Success." *Teachers College Record* 109(10): 2367–2443.

———. 2010. "Beyond Admissions: Reflections and Future Considerations." *Annals of the American Academy of Political and Social Science* 627(January): 216–25.

Lopez, Gerardo. 2001. "The Value of Hard Work: Lessons on Parent Involvement from an (Im)migrant Household." *Harvard Educational Review* 71(3): 416–37.

Lopez, Nancy. 2003. *Hopeful Girls, Troubled Boys: Race and Gender Disparity in Urban Education*. New York: Routledge.

———. 2004. "Unraveling the Race-Gender Gap in Education: Second-Generation Dominican Men's High School Experiences." In *Becoming New Yorkers: Ethnographies of the New Second Generation,* edited by Philip Kasinitz, Mary C. Waters, and John H. Mollenkopf. New York: Russell Sage Foundation.

Louie, Vivian. 2001. "Parents' Aspirations and Investment: The Role of Social Class in the Educational Experiences of 1.5 and Second Generation Chinese Americans." *Harvard Educational Review* 71(3): 438–74.

———. 2003. "Becoming and Being Chinese American in College: A Look at Ethnicity, Social Class, and Neighborhood in Identity Development." In *Immigrant Life in the U.S.: Multidisciplinary Perspectives*, edited by Donna R. Gabaccia and Colin Wayne Leach. New York: Routledge.

———. 2004. *Compelled to Excel: Immigration, Education, and Opportunity Among Chinese Americans.* Stanford, Calif.: Stanford University Press.

———. 2005. "Immigrant Student Populations and the Pipeline to College: Current Considerations and Future Lines of Inquiry." *Review of Research in Education* 29: 69–105.

———. 2006a. "Second Generation Pessimism and Optimism: How Chinese and Dominicans Understand Education and Mobility Through Ethnic and Transnational Orientations." *International Migration Review* 40(3): 537–72.

———. 2006b. "Growing Up Ethnic in Transnational Worlds: Identities Among Second-Generation Chinese and Dominicans." *Identities* 13(3): 363–94.

———. 2007. "Who Makes the Transition to College? Why We Should Care, What We Know, and What We Need to Do." *Teachers College Record* 109(10): 2222–51.

———. 2008. "Moving Beyond 'Quick' Cultural Explanations." In *Everyday Anti-Racism: Getting Real About Race in School*, edited by Mica Pollock. New York: New Press.

———. 2011. "Complicating the Story of Immigrant Integration." In *Writing Immigration: Scholars and Journalists in Dialogue,* edited by Marcelo Suárez-Orozco, Vivian Louie, and Roberto Suro. Berkeley: University of California Press.

Louie, Vivian, and Jennifer Holdaway. 2009. "Catholic Schools and Immigrant Students: A New Generation." *Teachers College Record* 111(3): 783–816.

Lucas, Samuel Roundfield. 1999. *Tracking Inequality: Stratification and Mobility in American High Schools*. New York: Teachers College Press.

Lucas, Tamara. 1997. "Into, Through, and Beyond Secondary School: Critical Transitions for Immigrant Youths." Washington, D.C.: Center for Applied Linguistics.

Luttrell, Wendy. 1997. *Schoolsmart and Motherwise: Working-Class Women's Identity and Schooling*. New York: Routledge.

Mahalingam, Ramaswami. 2006. "Cultural Psychology of Immigrants: An Introduction." In *Cultural Psychology of Immigrants*, edited by Ramaswami Mahalingam. Mahwah, N.J.: Lawrence Erlbaum.

Mahler, Sarah J. 1995. *American Dreaming: Immigrant Life on the Margins*. Princeton, N.J.: Princeton University Press.

Maldonado, Marta Maria. 2009. "'It Is Their Nature to Do Menial Labor': The Racialization of 'Latino/a Workers' by Agricultural Employers." *Ethnic and Racial Studies* 32(6): 1017–36.

Mann, Horace. 1868. *Life and Works*. Boston: Walker, Fuller, & Co.

Mapp, Karen. 2003. "Having Their Say: Parents Describe Why and How They Are Engaged in Their Children's Learning." *School Community Journal* 13(1): 35–64.

Marcelli, Enrico A., and Phillip J. Granberry. 2006. "Latino New England: An Emerging Demographic and Economic Portrait." In *Latinos in New England*, edited by Andres Torres. Philadelphia: Temple University Press.

Marrow, Helen. 2003. "To Be or Not to Be (Hispanic or Latino)." *Ethnicities* 3(4): 427–64.

Martinez-Cosio, Maria, and Rosario Martinez Iannacone. 2007. "The Tenuous Role of Institutional Agents: Parent Liaisons as Cultural Brokers." *Education and Urban Society* 39: 349–69.

Massey, Douglas. 2007. *Categorically Unequal: The American Stratification System*. New York: Russell Sage Foundation.

Massey, Douglas, and Nancy Denton. 1993. *American Apartheid: Segregation and the Making of the Underclass*. Cambridge, Mass.: Harvard University Press.

Massey, Douglas S., Jorge Durand, and Nolan J. Malone. 2002. *Beyond Smoke and Mirrors: Mexican Immigration in an Era of Economic Integration*. New York: Russell Sage Foundation.

Massey, Douglas, Margarita Mooney, Kimberly C. Torres, and Camille Z. Charles. 2007. "Black Immigrants and Black Natives Attending Selective Colleges and Universities in the United States." *American Journal of Education* 113: 243–71.

Massey, Douglas, and Magaly Sanchez R. 2010. *Brokered Boundaries: Creating Immigrant Identity in Anti-Immigrant Times*. New York: Russell Sage Foundation.

Matute-Bianchi, Maria Eugenia. 1986. "Ethnic Identities and Patterns of School Success and Failure Among Mexican-Descent and Japanese-American Students in a California High School: An Ethnographic Analysis." *American Journal of Education* 95(1): 233–55.

McDermott, Monica. 2006. *Working-Class White: The Making and Unmaking of Race Relations*. Berkeley: University of California Press.

McDermott, Ray. 1987. "The Explanation of Minority Failure, Again." *Anthropology and Education Quarterly* 18(4): 361–64.

McDevitt, Jack, Anthony A. Braga, and Shea Cronin, with Edmund F. McGarrell and Tim Bynum. 2007. "Project Safe Neighborhoods: Strategic Interventions—Lowell, District of Massachusetts: Case Study 6." Washington: U.S. Department of Justice, Office of Justice Programs (February). Available at: http://www.ojp.usdoj.gov/BJA/pdf/Lowell_MA.pdf (accessed January 30, 2012).

McEwan, Patrick. 1998. "The Effectiveness of Multigrade Classrooms in Rural Colombia." *International Journal of Education Development* 18(6): 432–52.

McManus, Walter S. 1985. "Labor Market Costs of Language Disparity: An Interpretation of Hispanic Earnings Differences." *American Economic Review* 75(4): 818–27.

Mehan, Hugh, Irene Villaneuva, Lea Hubbard, and Angela Lintz. 1996. *Constructing School Success:* Cambridge: Cambridge University Press.

Mendoza, Ancell Scheker. 2007. "Comparing School Level to Private Higher Education: Using the Dominican Republic as a Pioneer." Working paper 8. Albany: State University of New York, Program for Research On Private Higher Education (PROPHE).

Menjívar, Cecilia. 2008. "Educational Hopes, Documented Dreams: Guatemalan and Salvadoran Immigrants' Legality and Educational Prospects." *Annals of the American Academy of Political and Social Science* 620: 177–93.

Menjívar, Cecilia, and Cindy Bejarano. 2004. "Latino Immigrants' Perceptions of Crime and of Police Authorities: A Case Study from the Phoenix Metropolitan Area." *Ethnic and Racial Studies* 27(1): 120–48.

Menjívar, Cecilia, and Nestor P. Rodríguez. 2005. "State Terror in the U.S.-Latin American Interstate Regime." In *When States Kill: Latin America, the U.S., and Technologies of Terror,* edited by Cecilia Menjívar and Nestor P. Rodríguez. Austin: University of Texas Press.

Metz, Mary H. 2003. *Different by Design: The Content and Character of Three Magnet Schools.* New York: Teachers College Press.

Min, Pyong Gap. 1999. "A Comparison of Post-1965 and Turn-of-the-Century Immigrants in Intergenerational Mobility and Cultural Transmission." *Journal of American Ethnic History* 18: 65–94.

Mirdal, Gretty M. 2006. "Stress and Distress in Migration: Twenty Years After." *International Migration Review* 40(2): 375–89.

Mollenkopf, John. 1999. "Assimilating Immigrants in Amsterdam: A Perspective from New York." *Netherlands Journal of Social Sciences* 36(2): 126–45.

Morawska, Eva. 1990. "The Sociology and Historiography of Immigration." In *Immigration Reconsidered: History, Sociology, and Politics,* edited by Virginia Yans-Laughlin. New York: Oxford University Press.

———. 1993. "From Myth to Reality: America in the Eyes of East European Peasant Migrant Laborers. In *Distant Magnets: Expectations and Realities in the Immigrant Experience, 1840–1930,* edited by Dirk Hoerder and Horst Rossler. New York: Holmes and Meier.

Morgan, Stephen. 1996. "Trends in Black-White Differences in Educational Expectations: 1980–1992." *Sociology of Education* 69: 308–19.

Moyer, Alene. 2007. "Do Language Attitudes Determine Accent? A Study of Bilinguals in the USA." *Journal of Multilingual and Multicultural Development* 28(6): 502–18.

Munro, Miles, and Virginia Mann. 2005. "Age of Immersion as a Predictor of Foreign Accent." *Applied Psycholinguistics* 26: 311–41.

Murnane, Richard, and Frank Levy. 1996. *Teaching the New Basic Skills: Principles for Educating Children to Thrive in a Changing Economy.* New York: Martin Kessler Books/Free Press.

Museus, Samuel D., and Stephen J. Quaye. 2009. "Toward an Intercultural Perspective on Racial and Ethnic Minority College Student Persistence." *Review of Higher Education* 33(1): 67–94.

Myers, David, Robert Olsen, Neil Seftor, Julie Young, and Christina Tuttle. 2004. *The Impacts of Regular Upward Bound: Results from the Third Follow-Up Data Collection.* Washington, D.C.: Mathematica Policy Research.

National Academy of Education (NAE). 2007. "Race-Conscious Policies for Assigning Students to Schools: Social Science Research and the Supreme Court Cases." Report. Washington, D.C.: NAE, Committee on Social Science Research Evidence on Racial Diversity in Schools. Available at: http://www.naeducation.org/Meredith_Report.pdf (accessed January 30, 2010).

National Council for Accreditation of Teacher Education (NCATE). 2010. *The Road Less Traveled: How the Developmental Sciences Can Prepare Educators to Improve Student Achievement: Policy Recommendations.* Washington, D.C.: NCATE. Available at: http://www.fcd-us.org/sites/default/files/The%20Road%20Less%20Traveled-Policy%20Recommendations.pdf (accessed January 30, 2012).

National Public Radio (NPR), Kaiser Family Foundation, and Harvard University John F. Kennedy School of Government. 2004. "Immigration Survey." October. Available at: http://www.kff.org/kaiserpolls/upload/Immigration-in-America-Toplines.pdf (accessed January 30, 2012).

Neckerman, Kathryn, Prudence Carter, and Jennifer Lee. 1999. "Segmented Assimilation and Minority Cultures of Mobility." *Ethnic and Racial Studies* 22(6): 945–65.

Newman, Katherine S. 1999. *Falling from Grace: Downward Mobility in the Age of Affluence.* Berkeley: University of California Press. (Originally published in 1988).

———. 1999. *No Shame in My Game: The Working Poor in the Inner City.* New York: Knopf.

Ngai, Mae. 2004. *Impossible Subjects: Illegal Aliens and the Making of Modern America.* Princeton, N.J.: Princeton University Press.

Nicholas, Tekla, Alex Stepick, and Carol Dutton-Stepick. 2008. "'Here's Your Diploma, Mom!' Family Obligation and Multiple Pathways to Success." *Annals of the American Academy of Political and Social Science* 620: 237–52.

Nicklett, Emily, and Sarah Burgard. 2009. "Downward Social Mobility and Major Depressive Episodes Among Latino and Asian American Immigrants to the United States." Report 09-668. Ann Arbor: University of Michigan, Population Studies Center (January).

Noddings, Nel. 2002. *Starting at Home: Caring and Social Policy.* Berkeley: University of California Press.

Noguera, Pedro. 2003. *City Schools and the American Dream: Reclaiming the Promise of Public Education.* New York: Teachers College Press.

Norton, Bonny 1997. "Language, Identity, and the Ownership of English." *TESOL Quarterly* 31(3): 409–29.

Oakes, Jeannie. 1985. *Keeping Track: How Schools Structure Inequality.* New Haven, Conn.: Yale University Press.

Ochoa, Gilda. 2004. *Becoming Neighbors in a Mexican American Community: Power, Conflict, and Solidarity.* Austin: University of Texas Press.

O'Connor, Alice, Chris Tilly, and Lawrence D. Bobo, eds. 2003. *Urban Inequality: Evidence from Four Cities.* New York: Russell Sage Foundation.

Ogbu, John U. 1995. "Cultural Problems in Minority Education: Their Interpretations and Consequences—Part Two: Case Studies." *Urban Review* 27(4): 189–205.

Olneck, Michael R. 1989. "Americanization and the Education of Immigrants, 1900–1925: An Analysis of Symbolic Action." *American Journal of Education* 97(4): 398–423.

———. 2008. "American Public Schooling and European Immigrants in the Early Twentieth Century: A Post-Revisionist Synthesis." In *Rethinking the History of American Education*, edited by William J. Reese and John L Rury. New York: Palgrave Macmillan.

Orellana, Marjorie Faulstich. 2009. *Translating Childhoods: Immigrant Youth, Language, and Culture*. New Brunswick, N.J.: Rutgers University Press.

Orfield, Gary, Erica Frankenberg, and Liliana M. Garces. 2008. "Statement of American Social Scientists of Research on School Desegregation to the U.S. Supreme Court in Parents v. Seattle School District and Meredith v. Jefferson County." *Urban Review* 40: 96–136.

Orfield, Gary, and Chung-Mei Lee. 2006. *Racial Transformation and the Changing Nature of Segregation*. Cambridge, Mass.: Harvard University, Civil Rights Project.

Organisation for Economic Co-operation and Development (OECD). 2010. "System-Level Policies for Migration Education: Policies for Policy Development." April. Available at: www.oced.org/dataoecd/17/42/46679256.pdf (accessed January 30, 2012).

Pachon, Harry, and Louis DeSipio. 1998. *America's Newest Voices: Colombians, Dominicans, Guatemalans, and Salvadorans in the United States Examine Their Public Policy Needs*. Los Angeles and Claremont, Calif.: NALEO Educational Fund and Tomas Rivera Policy Institute.

Palacios, Marco. 2006. *Between Legitimacy and Violence: A History of Colombia, 1875–2002*. Durham, N.C.: Duke University Press.

Park, Julie, and Dowell Myers. 2010. "Intergenerational Mobility in the Post-1965 Immigration Era: Estimates by an Immigration Generation Cohort Method." *Demography* 47(2): 369–92.

Passel, Jeffrey, and Paul Taylor. 2009. *Who's Hispanic?* Washington, D.C.: Pew Research Center (May 28).

Patillo-McCoy, Mary. 1999. *Black Picket Fences: Privilege and Peril Among the Black Middle Class*. Chicago: University of Chicago Press.

Peirce, Bonny Norton. 1995. "Social Identity, Investment, and Language Learning." *TESOL Quarterly* 29(1): 9–31.

Perez, William. 2009. *We ARE Americans: Untold Stories of Undocumented Students in Pursuit of the American Dream*. Sterling, Va.: Stylus Publishing.

Perlmann, Joel. 1990. "Historical Legacies: 1840–1920." *Annals of the American Academy of Political and Social Science* 508: 27–37.

———. 2002. "Polish and Italian Schooling Then, Mexican Schooling Now? U.S. Ethnic School Attainments Across the Generations of the Twentieth Century." Working paper 350. Annandale-on-Hudson, N.Y.: Bard College, Levy Institute.

———. 2005. *Italians Then, Mexicans Now*. New York: Russell Sage Foundation.

Perreira, Krista M., Mimi V. Chapman, and Gabriela L. Stein. 2006. "Becoming an American Parent: Overcoming Challenges and Finding Strength in a New Immigrant Latino Community." *Journal of Family Issues* 27(10): 1383–1414.

Pessar, Patricia R., and Pamela M. Graham. 2001. "Dominicans: Transnational Identities and Local Politics." In *New Immigrants in New York*, edited by Nancy Foner. New York: Columbia University Press.

Pew Hispanic Center. 2010a. "Hispanics of Dominican Origin in the United States, 2008." April 22. Available at: http://pewhispanic.org/files/factsheets/62.pdf (accessed January 30, 2012).

———. 2010b. "Hispanics of Colombian Origin in the United States, 2008." April 22. Available at: http://pewhispanic.org/files/factsheets/64.pdf (accessed January 30, 2012).

Pollock, Mica. 2004. *Colormute: Race Talk Dilemmas in an American School.* Princeton, N.J.: Princeton University Press.

———. 2008a. "Talking Precisely About Equal Opportunity." In *Everyday Anti-Racism: Getting Real About Race in School*, edited by Mica Pollock. New York: New Press.

———. 2008b. *Because of Race: How Americans Debate Harm and Opportunity in Our Schools.* Princeton, N.J.: Princeton University Press.

Pollock, Mica, Sherry Deckman, Meredith Mira, and Carla Shalaby. 2010. "'But What Can I Do?' Three Necessary Tensions in Teaching Teachers About Race." *Journal of Teacher Education* 61(3): 211–24.

Portes, Alejandro. 1985. "Latin American Class Structures: Their Composition and Change During the Last Decades." *Latin American Research Review* 20: 7–39.

Portes, Alejandro, and Patricia Fernandez-Kelly. 2008. "No Margin for Error: Educational and Occupational Achievement Among Disadvantaged Children of Immigrants." *Annals of the American Academy of Political and Social Science* 620: 12–36.

Portes, Alejandro, with Kelly Hoffman. 2003. "Latin American Class Structures: Their Composition and Change During the Neoliberal Era." *Latin American Research Review* 38: 41–82.

Portes, Alejandro, and Ruben Rumbaut. 1990. *Immigrant America.* Berkeley: University of California Press.

———. 2001. *Legacies.* Berkeley and New York: University of California Press and Russell Sage Foundation.

Portes, Alejandro, and Min Zhou. 1993. "The New Second Generation: Segmented Assimilation and Its Variants." *Annals of the American Academy of Political and Social Science* 520: 74–96.

Powell, Arthur. 1996. *Lessons from Privilege: The American Prep School Tradition.* Cambridge, Mass.: Harvard University Press.

Prewitt, Kenneth. 2001. "Beyond Census 2000." *Carnegie Reporter* 1(3, Fall). Available at: http://carnegie.org/publications/carnegie-reporter/single/view/article/item/29 (accessed January 30, 2012).

Progressive States Network. 2009. "State Immigration Project: Policy Options for 2009." Available at: http://www.progressivestates.org/files/reports/Immigration09.pdf (accessed January 30, 2012).

Qin, Desiree B. 2003. "Gendered Expectations and Gendered Experiences: Immigrant Students' Adaptation in Schools." *New Directions for Youth Development* 100: 91–110.

———. 2006. "'Our Child Doesn't Talk to Us Anymore': Alienation in Immigrant Chinese Families." *Anthropology and Education Quarterly* 37: 162–79.

Rab, Sara, with Deborah F. Carter and Rachelle Wagner. 2007. "What Higher Education Has to Say About the Transition to College." *Teachers College Record* 109(10): 2444–81.

Ragan, Alex, and Nonie K. Lesaux. 2006. "Federal, State, and District-Level English Language Learner Program Entry and Exit Requirements: Effects on the Education of Language Minority Learners." *Education Policy Analysis Archives* 14(20): 1–32.

Ralph, John H., and Richard Rubinson. 1980. "Immigration and the Expansion of Schooling in the United States, 1890–1970." *American Sociological Review* 45: 943–54.

Ramirez, A.Y. Fred. 1999. "Survey on Teachers' Attitudes Regarding Parents and Parental Involvement." *School Community Journal* 9(2): 21–39.

———. 2003. "Dismay and Disappointment: Parental Involvement of Latino Immigrant Parents." *Urban Review* 35(2): 93–110.

Reddick, Richard J. 2007. "Shelters Through the Storm: Faculty Mentors and Their Role in Assisting African American Undergraduate Students' Responses to Racism." Ph.D. diss., Harvard Graduate School of Education.

———. 2009. "Fostering Cross-Racial Mentoring: White Faculty and African American Students at Harvard College." In *Identity in Education*, edited by Susan Sánchez-Casal and Amie A. Macdonald. New York: Palgrave Macmillan.

Reese, William. 2005. *America's Public Schools: From the Common School to "No Child Left Behind."* Baltimore: Johns Hopkins University Press.

Reisner, Edward H. 1930. *The Evolution of the American Common School*. New York: Macmillan.

Rhodes, Jean E., Jean B. Grossman, and Nancy L. Resch. 2000. "Agents of Change: Pathways Through Which Mentoring Relationships Influence Adolescents' Academic Achievement." *Child Development* 71(6): 1662–71.

Rodriguez, Cindy. 2001. "Colombians Cheer for a Dark Beauty: Miss Colombia Mirrors the True Face of Latin Nation." *Boston Globe,* December 2, 2001, p. A11.

Rodriguez, Clara. 2000. *Changing Race: Latinos, the Census, and the History of Ethnicity in the United States*. New York: New York University Press.

———. 2008. *Heroes, Lovers, and Others: The Story of Latinos in Hollywood*. New York: Oxford University Press.

Roediger, David. 2005. *Working Towards Whiteness: How America's Immigrants Became White*. New York: Basic Books.

Roffman, Jennifer, Carola Suárez-Orozco, and Jean E. Rhodes. 2003. "Facilitating Positive Development in Immigrant Youth: The Role of Mentors and Community Organizations." In *Community Youth Development: Practice, Policy, and Research*, edited by Francisco A. Villarruel, Daniel F. Perkins, Lynne M. Borden, and Joanne G. Keith. Thousand Oaks, Calif.: Sage Publications.

Roldan, Mary. 2002. *Blood and Fire: La Violencia in Antioquia, Colombia, 1946–1953*. Durham, N.C.: Duke University Press.

Roth, Wendy. 2008. "'There Is No Discrimination Here': Understanding Latinos' Perceptions of Color Discrimination Through Sending-Receiving Society Comparison." In *Racism in the Twenty-First Century: A Question of Color*, edited by Ronald E. Hall. New York: Springer Press.

Rothstein, Richard. 2004. *Class and Schools: Using Social, Economic, and Educational*

Reform to Close the Black-White Achievement Gap. New York and Washington, D.C.: Teachers College Press and Economic Policy Institute.

Rumbaut, Rubén. 1997. "Ties That Bind: Immigration and Immigrant Families in the United States." In *Immigration and the Family: Research and Policy on U.S. Immigrants*, edited by Alan Booth, Ann C. Crouter, and Nancy Landale. Mahwah, N.J.: Lawrence Erlbaum.

———. 2002. "Severed or Sustained Attachments? Language, Identity, and Imagined Communities in the Post-Immigrant Generation." In *The Changing Face of Home: The Transnational Lives of the Second Generation*, edited by Peggy Levitt and Mary C. Waters. New York: Russell Sage Foundation.

———. 2004. "Ages, Life Stages, and Generational Cohorts: Decomposing the Immigrant First and Second Generations in the United States." *International Migration Review* 38: 1160–1205.

———. 2008. "The Coming of the Second Generation: Immigration and Ethnic Mobility in Southern California." *Annals of the American Academy of Political and Social Science* 620: 196–236.

———. 2009. "Pigments of Our Imagination: On the Racialization and Racial Identities of 'Hispanics' and 'Latinos.'" In *How the U.S. Racializes Latinos: White Hegemony and Its Consequences*, edited by Jose A. Cobas, Jorge Duany, and Joe R. Feagin. Boulder, Colo.: Paradigm Publishers.

Rumbaut, Rubén, Frank D. Bean, Leo Chavez, Jennifer Lee, Susan Brown, Louis DiSpio, and Min Zhou. 2003. "Immigration and Intergenerational Mobility in Metropolitan Los Angeles (IIMMLA)." Russell Sage Foundation research program. Available at: http://www.russellsage.org/research/Immigration/IIMMLA (accessed June 10, 2010).

Ryabov, Igor. 2009. "The Role of Peer Social Capital in Educational Assimilation of Immigrant Youths." *Sociological Inquiry* 79(4): 453–80.

Safford, Frank, and Marco Palacios. 2002. *Colombia: Fragmented Land, Divided Society*. New York: Oxford University Press.

Sampson, Robert J., Stephen W. Raudenbush, and Felton Earls. 1997. "Neighborhoods and Violent Crime: A Multilevel Study of Collective Efficacy." *Science* 277(August 15): 918–24.

Sanchez, Claudio. 2009. "At School: Lower Expectations of Dominican Kids." National Public Radio, *All Things Considered*, July 31.

Sanchez, George J. 1997. "Face the Nation: Race, Immigration, and the Rise of Nativism in Late Twentieth-Century America." *International Migration Review* 31(4): 1009–30.

Sato, Charlie J. 1991. "Sociolinguistic Variation and Language Attitudes in Hawaii." In *English Around the World: Sociolinguistic Perspectives*, edited by Jenny Cheshire. Cambridge: Cambridge University Press.

Sawhill, Isabel V. 2007. "Overview." In *Getting Ahead or Losing Ground: Economic Mobility in America*, edited by Julia B. Isaacs, Isabel V. Sawhill, and Ron Haskins. Washington, D.C.: Brookings Institution.

Schneider, Barbara, and David Stevenson. 1999. *The Ambitious Generation: America's Teenagers, Motivated but Directionless.* New Haven, Conn.: Yale University Press.

Schumacher-Matos, Edward. 2011. "Illegal Immigration in a Time of Economic

Crisis." In *Writing Immigration: Scholars and Journalists in Dialogue*, edited by Marcelo Suárez-Orozco, Vivian Louie, and Roberto Suro. Berkeley: University of California Press.

Schwartz, Amy Ellen, and Leanna Stiefel. 2005. "Public Education in the Dynamic City: Lessons from New York City." *Economic Policy Review* 11(2): 157–72.

Seider, Scott. 2009. "Overwhelmed and Immobilized: Raising the Consciousness of Privileged Young Adults About World Hunger and Poverty." *International Studies Perspectives* 10(1): 60–76.

Seider, Scott, and James P. Hugeley. 2009. "Aspiring Educators, Urban Teens, and Conflicting Perspectives on the Social Contract." *Equity and Excellence in Education* 42(3): 294–312.

Shea, Jennifer, and Charles Jones. 2006. *Latinos in Massachusetts: A Mid-Decade Status Report.* Boston: University of Massachusetts, Program in Public Policy and Mauricio Gaston Institute for Latino Community Development and Public Policy.

Shernoff, David Jordan, and Deborah Lowe Vandell. 2007. "Engagement in After-School Program Activities: Quality of Experience from the Perspective of Participants." *Journal of Youth and Adolescence* 36: 891–903.

Sidanius, James, and Felicia Pratto. 1999. "Social Dominance Theory: A New Synthesis." In *Social Dominance: An Intergroup Theory of Social Hierarchy and Oppression* by James Sidanius and Felicia Pratto. New York: Cambridge University Press.

Simon, Rita J., and James P. Lynch. 1999. "A Comparative Assessment of Public Opinion Toward Immigrants and Immigration Policies." *International Migration Review* 33(2): 455–67.

Singer, Judith D., and John B. Willett. 2003. *Applied Longitudinal Data Analysis: Methods for Studying Change and Event Occurrence.* New York: Oxford University Press.

Sizer, Theodore R. 1996. *Horace's Hope: What Works for the American High School.* Boston: Houghton Mifflin.

Sizer, Theodore R., and Nancy Faust Sizer. 1999. *The Students Are Watching: Schools and the Moral Contract.* Boston: Beacon Press.

Smalls, Mario. 2009. "'How Many Cases Do I Need?' On Science and the Logic of Case Selection in Field-Based Research." *Ethnography* 10(1): 5–38.

Smith, James. 2003. "Assimilation Across the Latino Generations." *American Economic Review* 93: 315–19.

Smith, Robert C. 1994. "Bounded Solidarity." Unpublished paper, Columbia University.

———. 2002. "Life Course, Generation, and Social Location as Factors Shaping Second-Generation Transnational Life." In *The Changing Face of Home: The Transnational Lives of the Second Generation*, edited by Peggy Levitt and Mary C. Waters. New York: Russell Sage Foundation.

———. 2006. *Mexican New York: Transnational Lives of New Immigrants.* Berkeley: University of California Press.

———. 2008. "Horatio Alger Lives in Brooklyn: Extrafamily Support, Intrafamily Dynamics, and Socially Neutral Operating Identities in Exceptional Mobility Among Children of Mexican Immigrants." *Annals of the American Academy of Political and Social Science* 620: 270–90.

———. Forthcoming (a). "Black Mexicans and Assimilation Theory: What Strivers, Thugs, and Good Girls Can Teach Us About Immigration, Race, and Upward Mobility."

———. Forthcoming (b). "Horatio Alger Lives in Brooklyn . . . But Check His Papers."

Snow, Catherine. 2010. "S460: Adolescence Unit." Doctoral proseminar, Harvard Graduate School of Education (September 22).

Snow, Catherine, and Margaret Freedson-Gonzales. 2003. "Bilingualism, Second Language Learning, and English as a Second Language." In *Encyclopedia of Education*, 2nd ed., edited by James W. Guthrie. New York: Macmillan.

Social Science Research Council (SSRC). 2005. *Questions That Matter. Setting the Research Agenda on Access and Success in Higher Education.* New York: SSRC. Available at: http://files.me.com/seanxyz/4u61wt (accessed January 30, 2012).

Somers, Mary-Andree, Patrick J. McEwan, and J. Douglas Willms. 2004. "How Effective Are Private Schools in Latin America?" *Comparative Education Review* 48(1): 48–69.

Son, Yeon-Jeong. 2010. "From High School to College: The Influence of Parents, Teachers, and Peers on Dominican Students." Ph.D. diss., Harvard Graduate School of Education.

Song, Steve. 2009. "Finding One's Place: Shifting Ethnic Identities of Recent Immigrant Children from China, Haiti, and Mexico in the United States." *Ethnic and Racial Studies* 33(6): 1006–31.

Stanton-Salazar, Ricardo D. 1997. "A Social Capital Framework for Understanding the Socialization." *Harvard Educational Review* 67(1): 1–41.

———. 2001. *Manufacturing Hope and Despair: The School and Kin Support Networks of U.S.-Mexican Youth.* New York: Teachers College Press.

———. 2004. "Social Capital Among Working-Class Minority Students." In *School Connections: U.S.-Mexican Youth, Peers, and School Achievement*, edited by Margaret Gibson, Patricia Gándara, and Jill P. Koyama. New York: Teachers College Press.

Stanton-Salazar, Ricardo D., and Stephanie Urso Spina. 2003. "Informal Mentors and Role Models in the Lives of Urban Mexican-Origin Adolescents." *Anthropology and Education Quarterly* 34(3): 231–54.

Steele, Claude M. 1999. "Thin Ice: Stereotype Threat and Black College Students." *Atlantic Monthly* (August). Available at: http://www.theatlantic.com/magazine/archive/1999/08/thin-ice-stereotype-threat-and-black-college-students/4663/ (accessed January 30, 2012).

Steele, Claude M., and Joshua Aronson. 1995. "Stereotype Threat and the Intellectual Test Performance of African Americans." *Journal of Personality and Social Psychology* 69(5): 797–811.

Stein, Sandra J. 2004. *The Culture of Education Policy*. New York: Teachers College Press.

Stepick, Alex, and Carol Dutton-Stepick. 2010. "The Complexities and Confusions of Segmented Assimilation." *Ethnic and Racial Studies* 33(7): 1149–67.

Stevens, Lisa Patel. 2009. "Maps to Interrupt a Pathology: Immigrant Populations and Education." *Critical Inquiry in Language Studies* 6(1–2): 1–14.

Stevens, Mitchell. 2007. *Creating a Class: College Admissions and the Education of Elites*. Cambridge, Mass.: Harvard University Press.

———. 2008. "Culture and Education." *Annals of the American Academy of Political and Social Science* 619: 97–113.

Stolzenberg, Ross. 1990. "Ethnicity, Geography, and Occupational Achievement of Hispanic Men in the United States." *American Sociological Review* 55: 143–54.

Streicker, Joel. 1995. "Policing Boundaries: Race, Class, and Gender in Cartagena, Colombia." *American Ethnologist* 22(1): 54–74.

Suarez, Alfredo Ranqel. 2000. "Parasites and Predators: Guerillas and the Insurrection Economy of Colombia." *Journal of International Affairs* 53(2): 577–602.

Suárez-Orozco, Carola. 2001. "Afterword: Understanding and Serving the Children of Immigrants." *Harvard Educational Review* 71(3): 579–89.

Suárez-Orozco, Carola, Francisco Gaytán, Hee Jin Bang, Juliana Pakes, Erin O'Connor, and Jean Rhodes. 2010. "Academic Trajectories of Newcomer Immigrant Youth." *Developmental Psychology* 46(3): 602–18.

Suárez-Orozco, Carola, with Maria Onaga and Cecile de Lardemelle. 2010. "Promoting Academic Engagement Among Immigrant Adolescents Through School-Family Community Collaboration." *American School Counselor Association* 14(1): 15–26.

Suárez-Orozco, Carola, and Desiree Qin. 2006. "Gendered Perspectives in Psychology: Immigrant Origin Youth." *International Migration Review* 40: 165–98.

Suárez-Orozco, Carola, and Marcelo Suárez-Orozco. 2001. *Children of Immigration*. Cambridge, Mass.: Harvard University Press.

Suárez-Orozco, Carola, Marcelo Suárez-Orozco, and Irina Todorova. 2008. *Learning a New Land*. Cambridge, Mass.: Harvard University Press.

Suárez-Orozco, Marcelo. 1989. *Central American Refugees and U.S. High Schools: A Psychosocial Study of Motivation and Achievement*. Stanford, Calif.: Stanford University Press.

Suro, Roberto. 2008. "The Triumph of No: How the Media Influence the Immigration Debate." In *A Report on the Media and the Immigration Debate*. Washington, D.C.: Brookings Institution.

———. 2011. "Introduction." In *Writing Immigration: Scholars and Journalists in Dialogue*, edited by Marcelo Suárez-Orozco, Vivian Louie, and Roberto Suro. Berkeley: University of California Press.

Swail, Watson Scott, Alberto F. Cabrera, and Chul Lee. 2004. *Latino Youth and the Pathway to College*. Washington, D.C.: Pew Hispanic Center (June 23).

Symonds, William C., Robert B. Schwartz, and Ronald Ferguson. 2011. "Pathways to Prosperity: Meeting the Challenge of Preparing Young Americans for the Twenty-First Century." Report. Cambridge, Mass.: Harvard Graduate School of Education, Pathways to Prosperity Project (February).

Tafoya, Sonya. 2004. *Shades of Belonging*. Washington, D.C.: Pew Hispanic Center.

Tajfel, Henri, and John Turner. 1985. "The Social Identity Theory of Intergroup Behavior." In *Psychology of Intergroup Relations*, edited by Stephen Worchel and William G. Austin. Chicago: Burnham.

Takanishi, Ruby. 2008. "Children in Immigrant Families: All Our Children." *Social Policy Report* 22(3): 12.

Telles, Edward E., and Vilma Ortiz. 2008. *Generations of Exclusion: Mexican Americans, Assimilation, and Race*. New York: Russell Sage Foundation.

Teranishi, Robert T. 2010. *Asians in the Ivory Tower: Dilemmas of Racial Inequality in American Higher Education*. New York: Teachers College Press.

Terenzini, Patrick T., Laura I. Rendon, M. Lee Upcraft, Susan B. Millar, Kevin W. Allison, Patricia L. Gregg, and Romero Jalomo. 1994. "The Transition to College: Diverse Students, Diverse Stories." *Research in Higher Education* 35(1): 57–73.

Thomas, William Isaac, and Florian Znaniecki. 1918. *The Polish Peasant in Europe and America*. Boston: Richard G. Badger, The Gorham Press.

Tienda, Marta. 2002. "Demography and the Social Contract." *Demography* 39(4): 587–616.

Tierney, William G. 2002. "Parents and Families in Precollege Preparation: The Lack of Connection Between Research and Practice." *Educational Policy* 16(4): 588–605.

Time. 1967. "Essay: Black Power and Black Pride." *Time*, December 1, 1967. Available at: http://www.time.com/time/magazine/article/0,9171,712007-6,00.html (accessed January 30, 2012).

Tinto, Vincent. 1987. *Leaving College: Rethinking the Causes and Cures of Student Attrition*. Chicago: University of Chicago Press.

Tornatzky, Louis G., Richard Cutler, and Jongho Lee. 2002. *College Knowledge: What Latino Parents Need to Know and Why They Don't Know It*. Claremont, Calif.: Tomas Rivera Policy Institute.

Torres-Saillant, Silvio, and Ramona Hernández. 1998. *The Dominican Americans*. Westport, Conn.: Greenwood Press.

Tran, Van C. 2010. "English Gain vs. Spanish Loss? Language Assimilation Among Second-Generation Latinos in Young Adulthood." *Social Forces* 89(1): 257–84.

Tse, Lucy. 1995. "Language Brokering Among Latino Adolescents: Prevalence, Attitudes, and School Performance." *Hispanic Journal of Behavioral Sciences* 17: 180–93.

Tucker, James T. 2006. *The ESL Logjam: Waiting Times for Adult ESL Classes and the Impact on English Learners*. Washington, D.C.: National Association of Latino Elected and Appointed Officials (NALEO) Educational Fund.

Turney, Kristen, and Grace Kao. 2009. "Barriers to School Involvement: Are Immigrant Parents Disadvantaged?" *Journal of Educational Research* 102(4): 257–71.

Tyack, David B. 1974. *The One Best System: A History of American Urban Education*. Cambridge, Mass.: Harvard University Press.

UCLA Center for Mental Health in Schools. 2011. *Immigrant Children and Youth: Enabling Their Success at School*. Los Angeles: UCLA Center for Mental Health in Schools.

Uriarte, Miren, Jie Chen, and Mandira Kala. 2008. *Where We Go to School: Latino Students and Public Schools in Boston*. Boston: University of Massachusetts, Program in Public Policy and Mauricio Gaston Institute for Latino Community Development and Public Policy.

Uriarte, Miren, and Phillip Granberry. 2005. "When They Need Help the Most: Public Services for Immigrants." *New England Journal of Public Policy* 20(1): 121–37.

U.S. Census Bureau. 2000. "Table FBP-1: Profile of Selected Demographic and Social Characteristics: 2000." Washington: U.S. Government Printing Office.

U.S. Congress. Immigration Commission (Dillingham Commission). 1911. *Abstract of Reports of the Immigration Commission.* 61st Cong., 3rd sess., document 747. Washington: U.S. Government Printing Office.

U.S. Department of Education, National Center for Education Statistics (NCES). 2002. *Private Schools: A Brief Portrait.* NCES 2002-013. Washington: U.S. Government Printing Office. Available at: http://nces.ed.gov/pubs2002/2002013.pdf (accessed January 30, 2012).

———. 2007. *The Condition of Education: Indicator 33—Characteristics of Full-Time School Teachers.* NCES 2007-064. Washington: U.S. Government Printing Office. Available at: http://nces.ed.gov/pubs2007/2007064.pdf (accessed January 30, 2012).

U.S. News & World Report. 2001. "Best College Rankings 2001." 129(10).

Uy, Phitsamay Sychitkokhong. 2011. "The Educational Experiences of Lao and Khmer High School Students: The Influence of Families, Friends, and Teachers on Academic Achievement." Ph.D. diss., Harvard Graduate School of Education.

Valdes, Guadalupe. 1996. *Con Respeto: Bridging the Distance Between Culturally Diverse Families and Schools.* New York: Teachers College Press.

Valenzuela, Angela. 1999. *Subtractive Schooling: U.S.-Mexican Youth and the Politics of Caring.* Albany: State University of New York Press.

Vallejo, Jody Aguis. 2009. "Latina Spaces: Middle-Class Ethnic Capital and Professional Associations in the Latino Community." *City and Community* 8(2): 129–54.

Vandell, Deborah Lowe, David J. Shernoff, Kim M. Pierce, Daniel M. Bolt, Kimberly Dadisman, and Bradford B. Brown. 2005. "Activities, Engagement, and Emotion in After-School Programs (and Elsewhere)." *New Directions for Youth Development* 105: 121–29.

Velez, Carlos Eduardo, Mauricio Santa Maria, Natalia Millan, and Bénédicte de la Briere. 2002. *Two Decades of Economic and Social Development in Urban Colombia: A Mixed Outcome.* Archivos de Economia 003666. Bogotá: Departamento Nacional de Planeacion.

Vickerman, Milton. 2007. "Recent Immigration and Race: Continuity and Change." *DuBois Review* 4(1): 141–65.

Wade, Peter. 1993. *Blackness and Race Mixture.* Baltimore: Johns Hopkins University Press.

Walker, Francis A. 1896. "Restriction of Immigration." *Atlantic Monthly* 77(464, June): 822–29.

Walker, Joan M. T., Kathleen V. Hoover-Dempsey, Darleen R. Whetsel, and Christa L. Green. 2004. "Parental Involvement in Homework: A Review of Current Research and Implications for Teachers, After-School Program Staff, and Parent Leaders." Cambridge, Mass.: Harvard Family Research Project (October). Available at: http://www.hfrp.org/publications-resources/browse-our-publications/parental-involvement-in-homework-a-review-of-current-research-and-its-implications-for-teachers-after-school-program-staff-and-parent-leaders (accessed October 20, 2009).

Warikoo, Natasha, and Prudence Carter. 2009. "Cultural Explanations for Racial and Ethnic Stratification in Academic Achievement: A Call for a New and Improved Theory." *Review of Educational Research* 79(1): 366–94.

Warren, Mark R. 2005. "Communities and Schools: A New View of Urban Education Reform." *Harvard Educational Review* 75(2): 133–73.

Warren, Mark R., Soo Hong, Carolyn Leung Rubin, and Phitsamay Sychitkokhong Uy. 2009. "Beyond the Bake Sale: A Community-Based Relational Approach to Parent Engagement in Schools." *Teachers College Record* 111(9): 2209–54.

Waters, Mary C. 1990. *Ethnic Options: Choosing Identities in America.* Berkeley: University of California Press.

———. 1999. *Black Identities: West Indian Immigrant Dreams and American Realities.* Cambridge, Mass.: Harvard University Press.

———. 2008. "The Challenges of Studying Political and Civic Incorporation." *Applied Development Science* 12(2): 105–7.

———. 2011. "Debating Immigration: Are We Addressing the Right Issues?" In *Writing Immigration: Scholars and Journalists in Dialogue*, edited by Marcelo Suárez-Orozco, Vivian Louie, and Roberto Suro. Berkeley: University of California Press.

Waters, Mary, John Mollenkopf, and Philip Kasinitz. 1999. "The Second Generation in New York City: A Demographic Overview." Paper presented to the annual meeting of the Population Association of America. New York (March 25).

Weisz, Howard R. 1976. *Irish American and Italian American Educational Views and Activities, 1870–1900: A Comparison*. New York: Arno Press.

Wilson, William J. 1980. *The Declining Significance of Race: Blacks and Changing American Institutions.* Chicago: University of Chicago Press.

———. 1987. *The Truly Disadvantaged: The Inner City, the Underclass, and Public Policy*. Chicago: University of Chicago Press.

———. 1997. *When Work Disappears*. New York: Vintage.

———. 1999. *The Bridge over the Racial Divide: Rising Inequality and Coalition Politics.* Berkeley and New York: University of California Press and Russell Sage Foundation.

———. 2009. *More Than Just Race: Being Black and Poor in the Inner City.* New York: W.W. Norton.

Wirth, Louis. 1928. *The Ghetto*. Chicago: University of Chicago Press.

Yoshikawa, Hirokazu. 2011. *Immigrants Raising Citizens: Undocumented Parents and Their Children*. New York: Russell Sage Foundation.

Yoshikawa, Hirokazu, Erin B. Godfrey, and Ann C. Rivera. 2008. "Access to Institutional Resources as a Measure of Social Exclusion: Relations with Family Process and Cognitive Development in the Context of Immigration." *New Directions for Child and Adolescent Development* 121: 63–86.

Yoshikawa, Hirokazu, and Niobe Way. 2008. "From Peers to Policy: How Broader Social Contexts Influence the Adaptation of Children and Youth in Immigrant Families." *New Directions for Child and Adolescent Development* 121: 1–8.

Zarate, Maria Estela. 2007. *Understanding Latino Parental Involvement in Education: Perceptions, Expectations, and Recommendations.* Los Angeles: Tomas Rivera Policy Institute.

Zhou, Min, and Jennifer Lee. 2007. "Becoming Ethnic or Becoming American?

Reflections on the Divergent Pathways to Social Mobility and Assimilation Among the New Second Generation." *Du Bois Review* 4(1): 189–205.

Zhou, Min, Jennifer Lee, Jody Aguis Vallejo, Rosaura Tafoya-Estrada, and Yang Sao Xiong. 2008. "Success Attained, Deterred, and Denied: Divergent Pathways to Social Mobility in Los Angeles's New Second Generation." *Annals of the American Academy of Political and Social Science 620:* 37–61.

Zweigenhaft, Richard L., and G. William Domhoff. 1991. *Blacks in the White Establishment? A Study of Race and Class in America.* New Haven, Conn.: Yale University Press.

Index

Boldface numbers refer to figures and tables.